THROUGH THE EYES OF A TIGER

THROUGH THE EYES OF A TIGER

An Army Flight Surgeon's Vietnam Journal

JAY HOYLAND

Through the Eyes of a Tiger
An Army Flight Surgeon's Vietnam Journal

iUniverse books may be ordered through booksellers or by contacting:

iUniverse LLC
1663 Liberty Drive
Bloomington, IN 47403
www.iuniverse.com
1-800-Authors (1-800-288-4677)

Because of the dynamic nature of the Internet, any Web addresses or links contained in this book may have changed since publication and may no longer be valid. The views expressed in this work are solely those of the author and do not necessarily reflect the views of the publisher, and the publisher hereby disclaims any responsibility for them.

ISBN: 978-1-4401-3305-3 (sc)
ISBN: 978-1-4401-3307-7 (hc)

Library of Congress Control Number: 2009925370

Printed in the United States of America

iUniverse rev. date: 08/25/2014

Also by Jay Hoyland

The Palace of Versailles: A Novel

In memory of those men of courage I knew—and those to me unknown—who did not come home from Vietnam

DRY SEASON SOC TRANG

Incessant hot winds desiccate the dry Delta of my mind.
Wind-tossed shards of shattered memories
Bite, burn, blast, scour away layers of veneer.
Unbidden images—now unleashed—form and reform on the
    surface
Of the mighty Mekong, distorting watery riffles which
Reflect back bright sun and ink-black shadows.

Unimpeded thoughts race across the timeless river,
Force through dense tree lines, over canals, along dikes,
And spill into ancient rice fields yellow-brown.
Dust-devil eddies claw wildly at the parched crust of earth,
Scorched by long days of relentless sun,
Fractured open with cracks and fissures as deep as the soul.

Stripped raw from the protection time offered,
Bleeding memories erode to expose nerve endings
Desperately longing for the monsoon.

Jay Hoyland

THE UNIT ... to which an officer is assigned consists of a closely knit group around which are entwined official duties and athletic, social, and cultural activities for the benefit of all ... An officer should be a good military citizen, sharing with other good citizens responsibility for the unofficial life and activities of the garrison.

The Officer's Guide
22nd Edition, January 1956
Page 225

PREFACE

There are as many reasons for war stories as there are soldiers. Memories from a combat zone are enduring presences—peripheral ghosts not to be believed, yet remembered because they are real—some terrifying, some among the best life offers—worthy friendships.

Memories—points of view—are ultimately determined by military duty assignment and training. This journal is an attempt to describe my experience as a young doctor in the U.S. Army Medical Corps. Rapidly trained to be a reasonably confident army flight surgeon, I was an uncertain soldier during the early years of the United States' involvement in the Vietnam War.

From late 1962 to 1963, I was assigned as the medical officer in charge of the 134th Medical Detachment. We provided medical support to the Ninety-Third Helicopter Company—located in the Mekong Delta and widely known as the Soc Trang Tigers. This would prove to be a pivotal year for Vietnam, the United States, and me.

Only now, more than four decades later, am I learning about the broader picture. It has taken me these many years to want to read the history or to organize my thoughts. Much is forgotten in forty years, but entries in my sporadically kept diary, as well as letters preserved by my family, helped prompt recall.

To place events in context, I primarily used five books: *The*

Best and Brightest by Pulitzer Prize winner David Halberstam; *A Bright Shining Lie* by Neil Sheehan, for which he won both the Pulitzer Prize and the National Book Award; *Vietnam Diary*, the George Polk Award winner by Richard Tregaskis, author of the widely admired World War II *Guadalcanal Diary*; and *Vietnam: A History* by Stanley Karnow, a companion to the PBS Television series. This historical information is in bold print and can be either read or ignored. References are attributed in the endnotes. Military terms and acronyms are unavoidable; a glossary is provided to help sort these out.

Be aware that I write with a pen name. To respect privacy, I changed the names of most of the people involved. I have combined the personalities of many colleagues, officers, and men—including seventy helicopter pilots—into only a few characters. Conversations and some personal situations are embellished reconstructions in an attempt to make the narrative coherent and readable. These liberties, in the spirit of my story, make it no less true.

I am proud to be a Soc Trang Tiger. Once a Tiger, always a Tiger.

Jay Hoyland
Laguna Beach, California

Doc Hoyland's
Vietnam Journal

LAGUNA BEACH, CALIFORNIA
JULY 26, 2001

This perfect summer day would be a turning point in my life. At noon, I walked up our steep hillside driveway to see if the postman had left any mail. At the top, a little winded, I looked out at the ocean. In the distance, a cloudless blue sky turned the depths azure; the sun shimmered silver-gold on the surface. I opened the mailbox and found the usual mix: junk mail; bills; unwanted credit card offers; an *Automobile Club* magazine; a welcome two-weeks-late copy of *The Versailles Leader-Statesman*, my local Missouri hometown weekly paper to which I still subscribed; and on the bottom, a plain white business envelope with my name and address precisely printed by hand in blue ink.

I looked at the return and saw only the last name McCloud, a street address, and a city I had never heard of with the postmark: Fresno, California, July 23, 2001. Intrigued, I opened this letter first.

> Dear Sir,
> I am trying to locate a flight surgeon with the 93rd
> Transportation Company, Soc Trang Vietnam

(1962–1963). And if you are our unit doctor, I
would like to contact you further for I need help
with Veterans Administration.

Sincerely,
Thomas (Mac) McCloud

Below the name was a telephone number and e-mail address.

I sent an e-mail to let him know he had indeed found the right
person and asked what I could do to help. I also asked how he
tracked me down after all these years.

He e-mailed back.

Hi Doc,
I found u by luck … seems my records are
incomplete and they say that I was never a door
gunner and the only proof I had was from a
book *Vietnam Diary* … was thinking you might
enlighten them as to the type of flights we did do,
for I was the gunner the night we went and picked
up the small boy with arm missing … maybe (you
remember) the time u pulled me into your clinic
and weighed me, only 114 pounds and over 6 feet
… you told me if I didn't put on weight, you would
get an IV and put 10 lbs. on me.

He indicated he got my address from someone in a veterans'
chat room online, and he admitted he had attempted to forget
about our time in Soc Trang, that he had never asked for help until
August 1996 when the company he worked for medically retired
him. He added he wouldn't even talk with the doctors for years,
although he thought, now, maybe he should have.

I responded and asked him to get back to me if there was
anything I could do to help. I wrote that I, too, had talked little
about my Vietnam experience.

When I opened Mac's letter on that fine July day in Laguna

Beach, something inside me opened as well. Some memories, suppressed for years, pushed their way into consciousness.

I had not spent a lot of time thinking about my experiences in Vietnam forty years before. I had not talked much about it to anyone; like Mac, maybe I should have. But why? What difference would it make to me or anyone else? Quite an admission coming from a psychiatrist in practice for more than thirty years. Maybe it happened because I had all this free time when I retired in July 2000.

After my return from Vietnam, I never attended any war movies or plays, no matter how well-reviewed. I never read any books about the Vietnam War, although friends suggested titles and gave me several volumes, which I promptly put on a shelf in my library. I avoided the Pentagon Papers and never talked to anyone who took the time to read them. I never marched in our town's Patriot's Day parade. Friends knew—or did not know—I had been in the Army Medical Corps in the very early years of the Vietnam conflict, but no one, thankfully, pushed me for my opinion. That was good; I had nothing to say.

After Mac's letter arrived, I took out of the storeroom my two boxes packed with memorabilia. Inside, I found musty old papers, orders, unit patches, ribbons, and many photographs. I also found and re-read my old copy of *Vietnam Diary*, remembering fondly Richard Tregaskis, the author, and the time he spent with us in Soc Trang. His book, published in 1963, proved to be a valuable chronicle of the early years of the war. I looked for Mac's name; sure enough—just as he wrote me—there in black and white, proof he was a gunner.

I studied my passport photo. Could I ever have been so young? I looked thoughtful but detached, as if I was perhaps somewhat removed and knew this was my ticket for military duty in a far-off country about which I knew so little. A place, at that point in time, few in the United States had even heard of. It was "a conflict" not yet considered "a real war."

I decided to read the books collecting dust. These contained surprising answers to some of the questions I had for forty years about what was really going on back then. Buried in one box, I found my old diary. When I now opened it and read, I felt the need to write my story.

FT SAM HOUSTON, TX
MON
27 AUG 62

"Hey, Doc Hoyland. Wait up."

I recognized the familiar voice of Scott, my friend from internship, and turned around. It was impossible to pick him out of the crowd of 126 commissioned officers dressed identically in new khaki uniforms. Young civilian medical doctors only moments before, all of us now transformed—literally in an instant by swearing to uphold an oath—into active-duty captains and medical officers in the U.S. Army Reserve.

Filing out from the brief ceremony, we walked as a group toward the huge, grassy Fort Sam Houston parade grounds to stand our first official military inspection. On my right collar and the left side of my olive-drab garrison cap, I wore shiny silver captains' bars. Pinned on the left collar was the brass caduceus—two snakes wrapped around a winged staff—signifying the U.S. Army Medical Corps.

Scott caught up, a little out of breath. "Looking good, Captain Hoyland."

"Likewise, Captain Mitchell," I said.

"We're in for it now!" Scott's eyes squinted in the Texas sun and heat, bright and humid in contrast to the cool, dark auditorium.

I remembered hearing him say those words—those exact words—six months before.

Scott Mitchell, MD and I were good friends and had been since we met on July 1, 1961—the date we started our internships at Harbor General Hospital in Torrance, California. Just out of medical school, we were both eager and excited to begin our general medical internships, the final year of training required to qualify for long-sought licenses to practice medicine.

From Syracuse, New York, he was about my height, a little under six feet, but more muscular and athletic than I ever could be. He had dark hair, olive skin, and bright, inquisitive brown eyes. The cleft in his chin, he told me, was his best feature and made him irresistible to airline stewardesses. Later, I learned this to be true.

We worked hard! All of us in our intern class suffered sleep deprivation and exhaustion from too-long days and nights delivering babies on the active OB service; dealing with trauma at all hours in the busy ER; standing up overnight to assist in lengthy emergency surgeries; innumerable ward duties; and writing with a ballpoint on paper or dictating into a Dictaphone lengthy records to document everything. Time literally passed in a blur, but it exhilarated us to finally practice medicine.

Scott and I were both twenty-six, but he was a few months my senior. The future of the world lay ahead of us. Admittedly, I would always be surprised when one of the patients I attended said something like, "Are you sure you're a doctor? You don't look as old as my son," or grandson, or some other youth.

I pointed to the MD behind Jay Hoyland on my official hospital work badge, feeling more than a little cocky. No longer a medical student, I had graduated from medical school, passed my state license boards, felt confident in my skills, and was moving on with my life as a "real doctor."

After six rewarding and exciting months of training: disastrous news.

While eating a quick lunch in the noisy hospital cafeteria, Harold Baxter, an intern from Louisiana, put his tray down and joined our crowded table. Tall and slender with straight brown hair that fell down on his forehead, he usually was a fun companion and had a great sense of humor. Like most Southerners, he embellished on experiences for hilarious effect. Today, he looked glum.

"Well, y'all, it's official," he said. "Congress has done it! They passed the Doctors' Draft." He sat down heavily and slumped in his chair. "Interns will be called up first," he continued in his slow drawl, "right away."

"We're in for it now," Scott said and exhaled noisily.

Although it was not unexpected, we felt stunned at the news. All of us vaguely knew the Vietnam problem was escalating, but with demanding schedules, consuming workloads, and only brief snatches of a social life, we had neither time nor energy to pay much attention to current events.

Max Schmitt sat across the table. "Now what?" From Galen Springs, Kansas, his heart was firmly set on going into family medicine back home. With his dry sense of humor, something had to be funny to make him laugh. No laughing today. "We're screwed," he said.

"Totally screwed," Scott echoed.

Harold looked up. "We've got to go with The Berry Plan. Right away." He added, as he often did for emphasis, "You hear?"

"Why?" Scott and I asked almost simultaneously.

"To get deferred."

"Deferred?" A teddy bear kind of guy, Max loved gadgets: sports cars, cameras, tape recorders. He had short brown hair and brown eyes that closed when he laughed. Right now, his eyes were wide open.

"If we join The Berry Plan, the Army lets us finish our internships. Rather than leaving right away, we can stay here at Harbor, finish the end of June as planned, and then start active duty in July or whenever. That's what I'm doing. For sure."

Max shook his head in disappointment. "So much for going back home to start practice."

I stared at my half-finished tuna on rye, my mind reeling. "This isn't what we signed up for."

Harold nodded. "Yep. They just changed the rules of the game, moved the goal posts two years farther down the field. It won't be too hard on you single guys, but Barbara and I are getting married in July."

"You'll have to cut the honeymoon short." Scott rolled his eyes. "I'm glad I'm not the one who's got to tell her."

That night, lying in the dark on my cot in the bleak interns' quarters, I thought about my life. I stared at the bare ceiling and bulb hanging from a cord above my bunk. First, I thought of my parents, who had provided unconditional emotional and financial support. It had taken many years of education and training and sacrifice to get this far. Now, with my goal almost in reach, this unexpected two-year delay. They would share my disappointment.

I thought of my family's army service when our country fought wars. My great-grandfather, whose name I shared, served in the Sixth Kentucky Volunteer Infantry U.S.—the boys who feared no noise—during the entire Civil War. My father had a horse shot out from under him while a cavalry officer in France during World War I. After Pearl Harbor, he tried to get back in but was turned down; at fifty, he was over the age limit. My brothers, both older, served on active duty: Russell, a bombardier in the Army Air Corps, flew in the European Theater throughout World War II; Robert, an artillery officer, served during the Korean War. My only sister, Marilyn, served as a physical therapist in the Women's Army Corps during World War II.

I remembered when I was six years old, our family visited my older brother at Camp Robinson, Arkansas, where he was stationed for training. While a sophomore in college, he was in the national guard and called up for active duty immediately after the Japanese bombed Pearl Harbor. He told us of recruits who did not follow the rules and got sick from food poisoning. They didn't take the time to wash and sanitize their mess kits properly. He told us of some slackers who, to avoid duty, would put soap up their rectums and go to sick call with a fever. I remember thinking this seemed disgusting, but a good tip if I ever needed to avoid school one day.

Tomorrow would be busy; every day at Harbor General Hospital was. I'd need my energy. I made an effort to go to sleep and finally drifted off.

The next morning, things were clear. I would get deferred to finish my internship; the rest would take care of itself.

At breakfast, our somber table—Harold, Max, Scott, and I—all agreed; we were going with The Berry Plan.

"President Kennedy and Congress are making damn decisions about us, and we don't even know about it," Max said, mostly to himself.

"Yeah," I said, "Washington, DC or Honolulu or Saigon—someone sitting somewhere right now is determining the next two years of our lives." I thought to myself: right this moment, while I eat these scrambled eggs, which don't seem as tasty as usual, some military officer is probably planning for us all.

Scott finished a last sip of coffee and stood up. "I'm due in the ER. Have a good day, soldiers."

We resumed our routine duties. The future would have to wait.

In May, we received orders to report to Fort MacArthur in San Pedro to start the paperwork process, get pre-induction physicals in Los Angeles, and prepare to report for active duty in August after we officially completed our Harbor Hospital internships on June 30, 1962.

The pre-induction paperwork at Fort MacArthur was non-demanding, but it set off the official process; the army almost had me now. After I completed filling out all the forms, I took some time to look out from this historic fort located high above the harbor. The vista was breathtaking with blue-gray ocean, wispy clouds, and massive harbor traffic. Ships from everywhere moved back and forth; this old fort faithfully guarded the entrance as it had since 1888. A bronze bas-relief plaque informed me that the fort was named after Lt. Gen. Arthur MacArthur, father of Douglas MacArthur. This famous family had certainly contributed through the years with their commitment to the U.S. military.

My next appointment, a week later, took me to the immense Los Angeles examining center. Several hundred of us, none of whom I had fortunately ever seen before, reported to this huge space, which smelled like an overheated high school gym. All groups of mankind on earth seemed to be represented—every color, size, ethnicity, and shape. America was diverse with equal opportunity; this crowd proved it. The first thing we did was strip to our underwear and socks—mostly new or clean, I noticed, but not all. Everyone seemed subdued; there was little chit chat and no locker room humor here. We secured our clothing and belongings in wire baskets, guarded by bored army personnel, and moved on, papers in hand. We went from station to station in large groups to have our systems evaluated: eyes and ears, vision, nose, and throat; chest and lungs; arms and legs.

I coughed twice for a quick hernia check; I passed. Next, I joined a large circle of men; we all faced away from the doctor in the center. Upon request, we dropped our underwear, bent over, and simultaneously mooned the examiner. He came around the circle checking for hemorrhoids, fistulae, or any lesions which might interfere with active duty. I prayed I wouldn't get stationed at an examining facility like this for my active duty assignment, and I couldn't help but briefly think of my brother's story of slackers and soap and sick call—camp myth or reality? I was still not sure.

So far, so good. I finished with a "picket-fence" profile—"ones" in every area. A "one" meant no defects. I proved fit to be inducted. Several in this large, motley group apparently were not. They were mixed about being declared unfit—some relieved, some surprised, some embarrassed, and some hiding tears of keen disappointment and distress. I put my clothes back on and quickly left this mass human-flesh inspection zone. The Los Angeles air smelled fresh and cool with only a hint of petrol.

Now—on this hot and humid late August day in Texas—Scott, Harold, and I were joining other young doctors from all over the United States at Fort Sam Houston in San Antonio, Texas. Max would not report until the next class. He elected to be deferred until October so he could help his dad with the wheat harvest in western Kansas.

Recruit medics in casual civilian clothes before, we now all had short hair and the standard look of the military—officially preparing for new and mostly unwanted careers in the armed forces.

As we headed toward the quadrangle for inspection, I watched Scott walking tall. His face tanned and dark brown hair cut short in a buzz, he was the epitome of an army officer, as comfortable in this military uniform as when I last saw him in June wearing hospital whites.

I didn't feel as comfortable as he looked and hoped it didn't show. We formed ranks on the field. I reviewed in my mind where the brass was supposed to be, and with a resigned sigh, felt sure I'd pinned my name tag and brass in the right places, sewed on my patches correctly, and given my shoes an acceptable shine. The U.S. Army was serious, and I wanted to get it right.

This basic medical course at the Medical Field Service School at Fort Sam Houston would prepare our group, in a matter of weeks, for active duty. We would study advanced emergency medical care, counterinsurgency training, military justice, communications, code of conduct, the Geneva Convention, and escape and evasion. We would learn about the political and social history of Vietnam as well as a survey of their basic language.

Later in our training, they would send us on a weekend field maneuver to Camp Bullis for battle indoctrination. After completion of the course in early October, we would be ready to provide medical care anywhere in the world the U.S. Army was deployed.

As we assembled, I looked around at historic Fort Sam's handsome, sprawling red-brick buildings, tall trees, and mowed grass. I thought of all the classes which had preceded us, parading in front of the reviewing stand to the cadences of the marching band. This looked like any large college campus quadrangle. We were called to "attention;" my reverie evaporated as I stood straight and tall, chest out as far as it would go.

After passing inspection, we returned to quarters and resumed the student life. We sorted through newly issued books and manuals we would use to study for lecture classes, laboratories, dissections, and tests; none of these tasks would be new. Military customs, organization, ranks, saluting; all of these would be new. At first, we went out of our way to avoid senior officers and the uncomfortable expectation of salutes. The evasions took too much energy, so that tactic didn't last long. With a little practice, I soon found a snappy salute a surprisingly pleasant greeting to both give and receive. I also grew to appreciate name tags and insignias. You knew immediately just who was who—a good idea.

We studied the organization of the armed forces and military history. We learned and practiced triage, advanced first aid, and how to deal with mass casualties that come from warfare, a disaster, or—heaven forbid—nuclear attack. From this training we also learned that medicine historically made more advances during wartime than during periods of peace. We practiced the grim task of proper registration of the dead: the use of toe tags, dog tags, and olive-drab body bags.

During a break, I found a quiet spot away from the others and sat on some cement steps, the hot Texas breeze offering slight cooling in the shade of the portico. I felt glad to be a medic. I wouldn't have to shoot anyone with anything worse than a needle. I wouldn't be shot at. I wondered if I would have the guts and courage to shoot another human being with a gun. I didn't think so.

My thoughts wandered in the heat and my aloneness. Why did I choose to go to medical school? Why did I want to be a physician? I thought of my hometown family practitioners. Two brothers, they were devoted to the community; they were revered and deserved to be. Valuable citizens. I knew I wanted to be a valuable citizen, to help others, to relieve pain. My mother had rheumatic fever as a child and later suffered severe deformity and arthritic pain. I couldn't help her. I wanted to. My family and community respected physicians; one of my dad's uncles had been a physician. I knew I wanted to earn respect; deep down, I guess I wanted the power to work miracles, to be like the Great Physician. I shook my head at my own naiveté. But medical education, for whatever my motivation, had been exciting up to this point. I had learned much more than I could have thought possible. I felt ready. I wanted to get out there and get to work.

That evening, Scott and I and most of the others in our class were hanging out at the cave-like Rathskeller in the basement of one of the oldest buildings on the quad. It was dark and cool and welcoming. We drank beer, ate peanuts we peeled from shells, told bad jokes, laughed, and complained; together, we awaited fate to play its hand.

FT SAM HOUSTON, TX
THUR
30 AUG 62

"Here they are, gentlemen. What you've been waiting for. Your next duty stations." The captain posted the long list.

Scott said, "You first, Jay."

I read mine and couldn't help but smile. "I'm going to Ireland Army Hospital. That should be great. I've never been to Ireland."

Harold Baxter let out a whoop. "Hey, y'all. I'm going to a hospital near Towson, Maryland. What luck. It's close to Barbara's folks in Washington, DC. Great assignment."

Scott cheered. "It's back to California for me. Fort Ord."

"You lucked out." I couldn't help but feel some envy.

"Jay, have you ever been there?" Harold asked. "To Kentucky?"

"Kentucky?"

"Sure. Fort Knox. I'm pretty certain Ireland Army Hospital is there or Fort Campbell. Somewhere around there. You know that?"

"Oh." I hesitated. "No. I've never been there." Could I really have thought there were U.S. Army troops stationed somewhere in northern Ireland? I hated to admit it even to myself, but I guess I had. Oh well, I'd never been to Fort Knox either.

"At least Scott won't need the dreaded exotic immunizations for yellow fever and dengue." Harold laughed. "Doc Hoyland, on the other hand, I'm not so sure. You may require those for Kentucky."

FT SAM HOUSTON, TX
FRI
7 SEP 62

We reported to a lab that was so well-equipped, it looked like medical school. Loaded with examining tables for teams of six and all the equipment, we practiced intensive first-aid skills. I was glad I had experience in emergency room training at Harbor General, a very busy ER due to freeway and nearby industrial accidents. I had enjoyed the fast pace of emergency medicine so much that I took a second month for an elective. Today, our training focused on mass casualties.

Triage, during internship, meant sorting out the truly emergent and urgent from patients using the ER for routine care because they didn't have a regular doctor or any insurance. Here, it meant honing skills to deal with mass casualties and backup systems. During the Korean conflict, medical evacuations were greatly expedited by designated medical helicopters. This innovation remarkably reduced mortality; wounded soldiers, stabilized on the battlefield, could be flown by med. evac. choppers to a surgery suite in a remarkably short time. The results were impressive.

After class, Frank McClaren and I were called to the personnel office. I hadn't met Frank before. He had pale blue eyes, light freckles, and even though his sandy-colored hair was cut short, it still was curly. He told me he was from Kentucky, and his speech had a pleasant twang. His summer uniform, fresh in the morning, looked rumpled. "Where are you headed?" he asked as we walked to our appointment. "For your next duty station?"

"Ireland Army Hospital."

"Damn. I wonder if we could trade assignments? I'm married. I'd love it there—close to our folks."

"How about you?"

"Fort Lewis, Washington."

"Captain Hoyland; Captain McClaren." A young lieutenant handed us a large sheaf of orders. "There are several copies here, as you may need them. But be sure and keep the originals."

"What's the deal?" Frank said.

"Your amended orders. Changes to your next duty assignments."

Now familiar with enough military jargon to read and mostly understand orders, I quickly saw that I was no longer going to Ireland but had been re-assigned to the 134th Medical Detachment, APO 143 San Francisco. I needed a passport and visa. I would be prepared to arrive in Vietnam wearing summer uniform and have work uniform and combat boots in my baggage allowance of sixty-six pounds. Additional baggage of 134 pounds could be sent later. I needed immediate immunizations for Southeast Asia and to correct all medical or dental defects.

Even Frank's freckles turned pale as he read his orders. He handed them to me. Exactly the same, but he was assigned to the 130th Medical Detachment.

That night, thoughts again crowded fitful sleep. Vietnam. Where was it? What would it be like? Up until now, I'd had it easy. I grew up in the 1940s and 50s in a small midwestern town, carefree and healthy. My father graduated from the University of Illinois and recovered from the Great Depression. He built a successful real estate and development business, a good father and provider. My mother, a "homemaker," as were all the women in the town at that time, had been an elementary school teacher and a good mother. I had been blessed. They both valued education and saw to it all four of us had college educations. What good was education without using it?

It was now time for me to give back.

CAMP BULLIS, TX
FRI
14 SEP 62

We assembled in the cool of early morning—recruit doctors dressed in full battle fatigues and new, still-shiny combat boots. We carried duffle bags stuffed with gear for a long weekend. When loaded, the five olive-green camouflaged army buses in our convoy roared off; next stop, Camp Bullis. We would spend the weekend in field-training exercises. The drowsy warriors on my bus, usually free with wise-cracks and buoyant good humor, were unusually silent.

I got a window seat and watched our speeding bus leave the neat suburbs and civilization behind. The Texas morning was clear, cloudless, and clean. The rolling hills spread to the horizon. On the interstate, I saw cars, pickups, panel trucks, and eighteen wheelers, all piloted by and filled with civilians heading somewhere. They seemed like a different species. Individuals freely driving around this country to someplace they wanted to go; in the bus, dressed in uniforms and traveling in a large herd, we were being delivered someplace we were not too keen to visit. I wondered if the civilian drivers and passengers even saw our convoy. I doubted it. After all, we were camouflaged, invisible literally and figuratively. I took a deep breath and knew in the future I would never look at a prison bus the same way again. I'd have more empathy for those out-of-luck incarcerated passengers.

After we traveled several hours from San Antonio—all the while envying the freedom of the civilian traffic we passed on the interstate—our buses finally arrived at Camp Bullis. Situated in rolling hills covered with scrub and trees, desolate country stretched uninhabited for many square miles in every direction.

We quickly unloaded and assembled, as ordered, in formation. A burly instructor, dressed in clean, starched fatigues, called, "Attention."

He looked us over. "At Ease. Gentlemen, we are getting right to work. Time is short. Your first problem is a map course. You will be in teams of four and issued maps and compasses. We'll transport each team to a different location. You will be left there with coordinates and compass headings. From those locations, you will eventually end up back in camp. Use the map-reading skills we taught you in the classroom. Questions?"

There were none.

"Good. You brought canteens in your gear. Fill them at the water point, and be sure to drink plenty of it during the exercise. It's easy to get dehydrated out here. I don't need to tell you gentlemen how important hydration is. Be careful. This is snake country. They were here first; you are guests in their home. Look where you step. Now, count to four, by the numbers, count."

We strapped on filled canteens and gathered in four-man teams. We quickly boarded trucks. Drivers took us up and down dusty service roads slashed through the barren Texas country. Dust extended behind us in huge plumes. I remembered those dust clouds from old cowboy movies I saw during Saturday matinees as a child. Those dust clouds always alerted the good guys when the bad guys were headed their way, or vice versa. This whole country looked to me like the set for an epic cowboy movie, and I felt like an actor uncertain of my lines and anxious about my role in the film.

One by one, teams were dropped off at random and remote locations. I looked carefully at the countryside—featureless unless you really looked. Hills and ravines were covered with tenacious scrub, acclimated to arid country. Our team, next to last to be unloaded, watched the truck disappear in the distant dust cloud. The four of us looked first at the desolation, then at one another.

A thin, pale man with washed-out blue eyes, who would be more at home holding a violin than a canteen, broke the silence.

"Anyone know what the hell we're doing?" He spoke with a decided New England accent.

Captain Woolery, the only black member of our team, told us he was an Eagle Scout. He smiled broadly. "No problem. Drink some water, and we'll take off. Let's hustle. We'll be back before the truck. It's only about three miles."

We hustled but didn't make it back before the truck. It was rough, sweaty going in the bright sun, already hot in midmorning. Our course, on a north-northeast heading, had several hills and impassable gullies. We were forced to make several long, painful detours. Our topographical map gave elevations, and soon, the hills did not all look alike. In the distance, we saw one or two other teams going in different directions, but we plugged on. Miraculously, with Captain Woolery's help, we found camp.

Back by noon, we devoured stacks of ham-and-cheese sandwiches the cooks had already prepared, and we rehydrated with gallons of cold iced tea. It never tasted better.

After the brief lunch break, we reassembled in formation and stood again at "attention" in the hot sun, now directly overhead.

"At ease!" our instructor yelled, standing in front of us with his fatigues still starched and neat. "Your next training area is battle indoctrination—running the daytime infiltration course."

I noticed the ironed creases in his pants. His combat boots shined like patent leather, even beneath a light coating of powdery red dust. Sweaty and grubby, I looked at my scuffed, dirty combat boots. They no longer had a shine.

The instructor continued, "This course is designed to increase your stealth and confidence under fire. You crawl from one end of the course to the other. Keep moving as someone is coming along right behind you. Do not, under any circumstance, raise up. We use live ammunition. You could be killed or seriously injured. We don't want that to happen—now you're U.S. government property. Your families probably don't either."

He asked the now familiar, "Any questions?"

We put on our steel helmets and assembled in long lines at one end of the course. I was in the middle of the line and saw that the large, treeless field had barbed wire strung across at intervals low to the ground. Barren, with no grass or weeds, it was hard scrabble dirt and rocks. Machine guns were positioned at one side, placed to fire across the field.

With the yell, "Go," deafening machine gun fire commenced. The first line crawled onto the course, then the next; wave after wave clawed and scratched across. Sweat ran down my armpits and sides. The musty dirt smelled like a chemistry lab in my nostrils. Dust caked my mouth. I was breathing rapidly. The ceaseless, deafening roar of the machine guns rang and echoed across the field and in my ears. I wanted to look to the side and to the back, but I knew better. I focused, as ordered, toward the front, desperately looking for the end.

Next, we had training in hand-to-hand combat and ran an obstacle course. This seemed like fun and a cinch after the infiltration course with the live gunfire; wouldn't get killed there. Then we had weapons familiarization. Here we learned to take apart, clean, and put a rifle back together. When my group finished, we were issued arms and ammunition to fire on the rifle range. We also fired rounds with the handheld personal .45-caliber sidearm. By the time we finished, it was late afternoon—time for chow.

I hadn't seen Scott or Harold all day, as we had been on different buses. When we assembled to eat an early dinner at long outdoor tables, I found them both at one side of the group.

"How're you holding up, comrades?" I asked.

"You're joking, right? Sit down if you can," Harold said. "This torture is killing me."

"At least we've made it through the first day," Scott said. "Wonder what shore excursions our cruise director has on the agenda for tomorrow?"

The next morning, the sound of a taped bugle blowing reveille rudely pulled me from exhausted sleep into a cool, clear Texas pre-dawn. I saw the eastern sky already faintly blushed with pink and orange from the rising sun.

At formation, our instructor appeared in fresh fatigues, all traces of dust gone from his black polished boots. He yelled a cheery, "Good morning. Trust you rested well and are ready to go. Your next problem is the gas-mask drill."

These odd-looking masks were passed out quickly, and he demonstrated how to put them on and take them off. We followed his example.

"Practice again before you go into the building. It's filled with tear gas. The real thing. You'll go through in groups wearing gas masks. Once inside, we will tell you when to take them off. After it is completely off, replace it as quickly as possible. Remain in place with your masks on until told to exit through the rear."

I saw the building. It was an old barracks in the middle of a small stand of trees, windows boarded up with plywood. It had a front and back door. We seriously practiced putting the masks on and taking them off. With the order, "Masks on," compliance was rapid. Looking like odd extra-terrestrials, small group by small group we herded through the building.

Once inside, the entrance door slammed shut with a noise so loud, I jumped. I felt anxious and sweaty. Our group huddled together in the dim greenish-yellow haze, vision severely limited by small, glass eye-holes. We breathed silently, awaiting the dreaded order in the hellish atmosphere.

"Remove masks" echoed through the small space.

I slipped mine off and immediately coughed; my eyes teared-up uncontrollably. My nose stung with what felt like the prick of a hundred needles. I tried not to breathe, but finally, I had to. Invasive acrid gas intensely irritated all openings. Tears poured from my now burning eyes. My eyelids clamped down tight, a reflexive but ineffective action.

Finally we heard the over-loud order, "Replace masks."

No need to hear that twice. I immediately fumbled, trying to rapidly replace the mask. Anxiety interfered with my motor skills. When the mask was finally secured, it helped, but the damage was done.

The order, "Exit through the rear," did not need to be repeated either.

Outside, in the beautiful fresh air, I heard the chaos of all the coughing, wheezing, and gasping for breath. Above it all I heard, "Oh, hell." I recognized Scott's voice.

My eyes and lungs begin clearing. I didn't know until now that

Scott had been in my group. Wearing those masks, everyone looked the same. I saw him, eyes red-rimmed while copious tears flowed down his cheeks toward that cleft chin.

That afternoon, we had a break to sit in bleachers and watch an expert staff unload tons of equipment from trucks and assemble a Mobile Army Surgical Hospital—MASH—in front of us. It was as exciting as it would be to watch roustabouts put up a circus tent. When they finished, we saw and toured a fully functional hospital prepared to receive patients. It was an amazing and impressive performance.

Over dinner, Harold told Scott and me, "Y'all, let's stand in line so we go through the night infiltration course together."

Scott and I nodded agreement.

With only a crescent moon, the rural darkness was lit with thousands of stars seen only away from the glare of a city. The infiltration course, bare with foreboding barbed wire, was lit with only a few spotlights. It looked ominous. No fenced prison yard could look more foreboding and sinister.

The fire-safety officer stood in front of our formation. "Proceed exactly as before, except it is night, and you will see tracers. This lets you know the line of fire. Remember not to raise up, and do not stop. Keep moving. Someone behind you is as anxious to get to the other side as you are. Good luck."

Line by line, we knelt down. For the fifth and final time, I re-checked my steel helmet strap to be sure it was secure. When the man in front of me cleared the lane, I crawled under the barbed wire and scratched my way across the course as the roar of machine gun fire filled the night sky above me. Tracers streaked reddish-orange in the darkness like small blazing comets, screeching barely overhead. In the dark, they seemed so low. I was absolutely stunned by how many rounds could be fired so quickly by machine guns. It was hard to see ahead on the dirt course, barely lit by the eerie tracers, but I kept my eyes on the soles of the boots of the guy in front of me; the course seemed interminable, much longer at night. Scott was to my left and Harold to my right. I was grateful my buddies were on either side.

We all survived. After rehydration at the water point, we again assembled in formation.

"Gentlemen," our still impeccably neat instructor said, "for this last field problem, you will again be dropped off at a remote location with your map-reading team. You will have the same equipment you had for the day course, but we will also issue one flashlight per team. We will be looking out over the ranges with binoculars. Unlike an enemy, we do not want to see any light to reveal your location or presence. Practice discipline. It's a fair night. The stars should almost provide enough light to read maps.

"Be advised: The coordinates—your final coordinates—will not be here at base camp, but on a road somewhere out there." He waved his arm in no particular direction. "As an incentive, and to celebrate your successful completion of the field exercises, a beer truck is located at the last coordinate. First come, first served. Don't be last, or the truck may run out. It only holds so much. Be careful out there. The terrain is rough. Good luck, and we hope to see you back before midnight."

Our team, dropped off in darkness, watched the red taillights of the truck disappear. We quickly assembled, stranded as before. Captain Woolery took over again, but this time, we all had more confidence after success with the day course. Looking at our compass and map with the faint light from the hand-covered flashlight, we all agreed on the first direction across a low hill. The night made it tough going, but the trade-off was cool night air. Hopefully, the snakes had retired, but I heard coyotes howling in the distance. It took us a long time to get back. We arrived at about 2300, but there was still plenty of beer to ease our pain. When you were really dry and thirsty, a cold beer tasted really good. The last group did not limp in until 0200 hours the next morning. One of the team members twisted an ankle, and that slowed them down. I fell asleep on the truck ride back to camp.

The trumpeted reveille in early Sunday dawn was welcome; we boarded buses and headed back to Fort Sam for hot showers, bed, and the rest of the day off.

The bus convoy retraced our interstate route to San Antonio.

"Camp Bullis is a Boy Scout camp gone bad." Harold accentuated *bad*.

Scott recounted the gas-mask drill in detail. "I cried like a baby," he moaned.

"God-awful, I'm telling you," Harold said. "I'm not sure we needed this much training. At least I'm ready to protect the good nurses of Maryland in case of enemy attack."

"How about the arms training? The rifle's OK, but the .45's got a wicked kick," I said. "I hope I never have to fire one of those again."

"You never know. The instructor told us docs in Vietnam are issued .45s for personal protection," Scott said.

"Scott, my man, you may get caught fooling around with those women around Fort Ord. like you did with those stewardesses in Playa del Rey. You'll want one for protection," Harold said. We all laughed.

After a long pause, I said, "We're wimps. We had it easy. Camp Bullis makes you appreciate what hell real army recruits go through in basic training."

NEW YORK
HARPER'S MAGAZINE
SEPTEMBER 6, 1962

In the article "Terror in Vietnam," Dr. Stanley Millet, a visiting American professor at Saigon University, concluded:

> **"It is very late. But perhaps there is still time for us to act. When and if we do, there will be at least a possibility of ending the civil war without a Communist victory or an American commitment to a war in the Algerian pattern. But until we stop supporting Diem there is indeed nothing for the Vietnamese people to do but wait. And hope."[1]**

FT SAM HOUSTON, TX
TUES
25 SEP 62

At morning roll call, Scott and I, along with Frank McClaren, were summoned to the personnel office. A captain handed each of us a new stack of official orders.

Scott took his first. "What's this?"

"Amendments to your last orders," the captain said. I hadn't seen Frank at Camp Bullis, but we both smiled in greeting. He and I read our orders at the same time. We looked up at one another. Now even our amended orders were changed. After we finished at Fort Sam, we were now to report on 10 Oct 62 to the U.S. Army Hospital at Fort Rucker, Alabama, for four weeks OJT at the Army School of Aviation Medicine before we went to Vietnam. Scott had similar orders to go to the same school, but he would then report to Fort Ord.

"What's the OJT?" Frank asked.

"On-the-job training," the captain explained. "You three are a test class to see if we can speed up training for aviation medical officers. With the increase in deployment of helicopter companies to Vietnam, the army needs many more flight surgeons than we have available."

"Will we be doing surgery?" Scott said.

"No. It's a title, like surgeon general; he's not a surgeon. You won't be doing surgery like in a MASH. As an aviation medical officer, you will be assigned to take care of pilots and flight crews on the front line.

"At Fort Rucker, you'll learn about flying and medical requirements unique for pilots and flight crews. For icing on the cake, you'll get flight time."

"Flight time?" I said.

"Sure. Aviation medical officers get the fundamental training non-pilot flight personnel need to qualify for flight status. After you have some real experience in the field, your designation becomes flight surgeon. There's a lot to learn in a short time. Good luck."

That evening, in the Rathskeller, Scott said, "I looked it up.

Vietnam is eleven thousand miles from New York City. Halfway around the world. I'm sure after going to aviation medical training, Fort Ord will just be my first stop on the way. Jay, you and Frank are lucky in a way. The sooner you go over there, the sooner home."

"Tough luck, y'all. Really tough luck." Harold had joined us for a night out with the boys. He said, "What are the odds that out of the over one hundred men in our class here, they'd choose two Harbor interns?"

SAIGON
MON
1 OCT 62

President Ngo Dinh Diem opened the fall session of the National Assembly of South Vietnam: "Everywhere we are taking the initiative ... sewing insecurity in the Communists' strongholds, smashing their units one after another."

When U.S. Army and Marine helicopters were first introduced in the field earlier this year, the Army of the Republic of Vietnam—ARVN—had a few quick victories. VC fighters, caught off-guard and initially fearful, ran away; no match for these iron birds. But soon, in scattered training camps around the country, they learned to stand and fight.

They discovered shooting choppers took the same skills as bringing down water fowl flying over the rice fields.[2]

FT SAM HOUSTON, TX
TUE
2 OCT 62

More orders arrived. After completion of the Fort Rucker training, Frank and I would report to the passenger service counter at Travis Air Force Base near San Francisco November 26, 1962, at 2000 hours. We would board Flight 549 with orders and immunization records, prepared for transport to the Republic of Vietnam. Scott reported the same day to Fort Ord, California.

FT SAM HOUSTON, TX
FRI
5 OCT 62

We completed our technical classes, somehow survived the marching practices in the Texas heat and humidity, stood up straight enough for repeated inspections in full winter uniforms under the blazing sun in one hundred-plus degree heat, and finally marched in a grand dress parade on the quadrangle with several units from various other schools. The official army band sounded great. Our class officially graduated from the Basic Medical Course.

We would leave San Antonio with a lot more than just new knowledge, medical skills, and a commission. We now had several sets of uniforms, many manuals, combat boots, hats, caps, duffle bags, and shoes. Our cars were packed; it was time for this class of 126 new medical officers to spread out across the globe.

"The three musketeers have come a long way from Harbor Hospital." Scott shook Harold's hand good-bye.

"Best of luck to you and Barbara," I said as we shook hands. "Good doctor, have a safe trip."

The three of us saluted good-naturedly. Harold got in his packed car to go pick up his wife. I wondered where she would sit with all the stuff he had loaded in there. He yelled as he drove off, "Come and see us up in Maryland as soon as you get back, y'all hear? I mean it."

Harold's car disappeared down the street. Scott got in his car, honked his horn, waved, and took off. I followed close behind. We planned to drive in tandem and have a brief stop in New Orleans. Frank McClaren and his wife had already left for Fort Rucker. We'd meet up there. Good-bye, Texas; hello, Alabama.

MEKONG DELTA
FRI
5 OCT 62

In the northern half of the Mekong Delta, west of the city of My

Tho, most of a forty-man Vietnamese Ranger platoon were killed or wounded in a battle near the Plain of Reeds. The American advisor saved the platoon from total annihilation. The VC shot up the American helicopters; two were forced to crash land.[3]

FT RUCKER, AL
MON
10 OCT 62

Almost mid-October, but unseasonably hot, humid weather persisted in the South. We found Fort Rucker to be a pleasant place, nestled in beautiful tree-covered, rolling Alabama hills. Without cold nights, the leaves did not yet show any effects of autumn.

As we learned from our Fort Sam officers' training, the first thing we did was sign the officers' duty roster at the post headquarters; we were now officially back on duty. Next, Scott and I located the army hospital, the site for our training. We drove by and saw it was a typical one-story barracks-style hospital built during World War II.

Mother Rucker, as the base was affectionately known by pilots in flight training, had no available bachelor officers' quarters or temporary housing. Scott and I rented a furnished house in nearby Dothan. Frank and his wife had found an apartment not far away.

Our first challenge proved to be pesky Alabama gnats. These tiny insects collected in swarms around any human head exposed outside. To newcomers, these persistent insect devils were agony as they aggressively tried to get into any facial orifice. Locals laughingly called these gnats the state bird of Alabama.

It proved easy to tell how long someone had been in the area by the way they dealt with the infestation. New arrivals, like us, got agitated and violently flapped two hands to chase them from crawling in the corners of eyes, mouths, or up noses. The experienced resident did not waste so much energy. They replaced flapping by the occasional fanning, in one or two casual passes, of one hand. Long-time citizens, with even more economy of motion and energy, dispensed with hand movements entirely. They used only strategic pursed lips to send jets of puffed air directed toward the general area affected.

On Monday morning, promptly at 0800 hours and in proper uniform, Frank, Scott, and I reported to the hospital and the office of Lt. Col. Tom Watson, Commanding Officer.

A slight, thin man with bushy white hair neatly combed, he sat behind his desk, which was covered with papers in orderly stacks. After returning our salutes, he stood to shake our hands and offered us chairs.

"Gentlemen, welcome to this new short course for aviation medical officers. You will have pretty much the same specialty training we give our regular flight surgeons, but speeded up. With things as they are, need outstrips supply. We are confident we can train you three effectively and efficiently. If it works as well as we hope, we will continue this short course in the future.

"You'll be immersed in flight medicine, flying, and the unique medical requirements for pilots and their crews on flight status. A lot of new information in a short time."

We wasted no time and started classes that morning. We quickly qualified as FAA examiners so we could perform annual flight physicals. These documented physical examinations had to be current for all pilots on flight status, no matter where they were stationed in the world.

We trained with ophthalmologists; qualified vision for pilots is vital. We learned about the critical need for ear plugs to prevent hearing loss; helicopter engines and gunfire are particularly damaging. We spent a long time learning how to participate as a medical expert in accident investigations. The FAA rules apply anywhere the military flies, and the need to investigate and document any downed aircraft is the same in peace or war, in the United States or Vietnam.

We took basic parachute training and jumped from low platforms to learn how to tuck and roll. We flew as eager passengers in several types of helicopters. With instructor pilots at our side, we performed touch-and-go landings in small fixed-wing aircraft—exhilarating and heady experiences.

"How about that contour flying?" Scott enthused. "Fantastic."

"Fast and low," I said, "barely above the trees."

"I swear the landing gear brushed some tree branches; we were only three or four feet off the ground." Frank's pale-blue eyes were still open wide.

"For sure," Scott said. "And you can see how deadly utility wires could be."

"When you're in the air, they're almost invisible." I said. "Hit them, and that's all she wrote."

"True." Frank nodded his head. "Pilots who don't want to crash don't want to run into them."

FT RUCKER, AL
WED
24 OCT 62

Soon, seasonal cold nights arrived, and the devil gnat pests disappeared. The leaves turned golden and brown, and the hazy countryside settled into comfortable Indian Summer. Today was a crisp fall morning. Scott and I rode in to the hospital together in his car. As we pulled into the parking lot, we saw Frank arriving just ahead of us.

"Where's everyone's cars?" Frank looked around the parking lot. "Is it a government holiday, and no one told us?"

We looked around. He was right. The parking lot seemed almost empty except for Col. Watson's space. Inside the hospital, corridors were eerily silent. No one was around.

"What's happening?" I asked the first corpsman we saw coming down the long hallway.

"You didn't hear? We're on red alert. Mobilized. Everybody's left for Florida."

Lt. Col. Watson was waiting and beckoned us into his office. "Gentlemen. An unexpected situation here. Our doctors and MASH units have been mobilized. Almost everyone's deployed.

"Hopefully, Khrushchev and Castro will back off, 'cause JFK isn't going to budge an inch after the Bay of Pigs last April." He sighed heavily. "We don't have time for this. We've got other fish to fry.

"The four of us are about the only physicians left. I need you to cover the hospital. Classes are on hold. Here's the on-call schedule." He handed us duty rosters; just like days back at Harbor General.

WASHINGTON, DC
WED
24 OCT 62

JFK raised U.S. military readiness to the highest level in U.S. history: DEFCON 2. The United States would face down Cuba and Russia.

FT RUCKER, AL
FRI
26 OCT 62

Cuba and Castro, Russia and Khrushchev, America and JFK caught in a triangle, the most unstable of relationships: two always in, one always out. The possible outcome was unthinkable—nuclear war. As if hit to the solar plexus, we were stunned and held our breath, along with the rest of the world. We watched news broadcasts closely and continuously. Something had to give. The U.S. military, which now included me, had to be ready for action. I was not ready, not by a long shot.

MOSCOW
SUN
28 OCT 62

Khrushchev announced the USSR installations in Cuba would be dismantled; all missiles would be returned to the Soviet Union.

FT RUCKER, AL
MON
29 OCT 62

Thankfully, we had a quick resolution of the Cuban Missile Crisis, and civilization had a long, collective sigh of relief. Physicians and troops returned to Fort Rucker as rapidly as they had left. The hospital, trained for rapid deployment, seemed remarkably normal almost by the next day. Freed from the on-call duty roster, we resumed Aviation Medicine classes.

In the evening, Scott and I were off-duty and at our leisure when the telephone rang. This was definitely an unusual event; we hadn't had a call since we rented the house. Scott answered and talked briefly. He hung up with a yell.

"Whoopee! Good news." He ran into the living room. "Mindy, one of the stewardesses from Marina del Rey I told you about, is on a car trip to Florida. She's stopping by Dothan this Saturday."

"Sounds good," I said.

"Not only good, but great. She's driving with another stew—Elizabeth. They're both knockouts."

Sure enough, two blonde, good-looking California girls arrived in Mindy's new red Chrysler on Saturday morning. They couldn't stay long, but their visit improved our morale. Feeling sorry for us, they promised to send pinup pictures before we left Fort Rucker.

"Something for you soldiers to remember us by," they said as they took off for Florida.

FT RUCKER, AL
FRI
9 NOV 62

We completed the last of our classes, and Lt. Col. Watson presented us with the coveted winged badge awarded to aviation medical officers. I felt empowered with an unexpected surge of emotion when he pinned this oxidized silver badge above the left pocket of my uniform. These wings—mine now and forever—were a source of pride.

The end of school meant hasty good-byes. Frank and his wife, Donna, left for Kentucky. She would stay with her parents. He had told us she was feeling nauseous again, and she might, or might not, be pregnant.

"See you at Travis, Jay," Frank yelled as they drove off.

Scott and I shook hands.

"It's been quite an experience, buddy. I'm sure we'll meet up again," Scott gave a half-salute from the driver's seat of his car.

"Hope so, but in the meantime, take care of that cleft chin of yours."

Scott smiled and winked an eye as he took off.

I got into my spotless six-month-old beige '62 Ford Galaxy convertible with a white interior and top and headed for my family in Missouri. As I drove leisurely from Alabama to Missouri, I saw beautiful country I had never seen before. The rolling hills and fields basked in the late autumn sun. With pleasant weather, I felt lulled by mile after mile of the peaceful scenery. This area had not always known peace. I thought of my great-grandfather during the Civil War a century before. Each generation seemed to have its war, and soon, mine would be Vietnam.

I reluctantly left my first new car and most of my civilian possessions in Missouri. I wouldn't be needing them for the next twelve months.

SAIGON
WED
28 NOV 62

The air force transport jet landed at Saigon's sprawling Tan Son Nhut airport at 1430. I was glad to stretch my legs after the flight from Clark Air Force Base in the Philippines. Frank and I stepped off the plane into bright sunlight, and I caught my breath. Cloying air, warm and humid, assaulted my nostrils. It was permeated with a complex mixture of mold, mildew, charcoal smoke, blooming and decaying vegetation mixed with many unknowable odors. An unforgettable smell—as unfamiliar and intriguing as heady, exotic incense.

Army buses took us to temporary housing, where Frank and I met Capt. Drew Lemmon, a personable young doctor from Chicago. Tan Son Nhut was his duty station, but he hadn't started yet, as the army physician he was to replace would still be on duty for a few more days. Luckily, Doc Lemmon would have some time to help us with our orientation to Vietnam.

"Over here, doctors have to look out for one another," Doc Lemmon said. He told us he was used to that, as he was from a large Catholic family. A wiry and active man, he had light brown hair and hazel eyes, bright and inquisitive. The alert and curious type, he already knew a lot about Saigon, even though he had arrived himself only a few days before. Tan Son Nhut was the plum assignment, and we all knew it. I couldn't help but like him anyway. He was genuinely a nice guy.

Frank and I would stay in Saigon for three days of briefings to get acclimated. Then we would be sent to join our units. I would go to the 134th Medical Detachment, located about one hundred miles south of Saigon in the Mekong Delta at Khanh Hung, now called Soc Trang. As the aviation medical officer and only physician, I would be the commanding officer—in fact, the only officer.

This challenge seemed intimidating and exciting at the same time. How would it be down there by myself, the only medical practitioner miles from anywhere? Would I know enough? I wished I'd had more experience, but then I thought of the busy nights in the ER when I had been an intern at Harbor General Hospital. If I made it through that, I could make it through this. But I did wish for even one other doc to share the responsibility. Down in the Delta, there would be no colleagues, no peers, no mentors—all the things important to my medical education up to this point. This challenge was the real world.

The 134th Medical Detachment was a small field unit with the mission of providing medical support to the Ninety-Third Transportation Helicopter Company. They were widely known as the Soc Trang Tigers. Frank would go up north for similar duty. His unit, the 130th Medical Detachment, supported the Eightieth Helicopter Company in Pleiku.

We had brought only basic gear with us in army duffle bags.

Our foot lockers, packed with books and civilian clothing essential for a one-year tour, were scheduled to arrive sometime next month. I mostly wanted the rest of my medical books. The ability to look things up in a medical reference could be critical. I only had my basic medical and surgical texts, Emergency First Aid reference book, and a *Physican's Desk Reference.*

"First things, first," Doc Lemmon said as he planned a trip to downtown Saigon to buy civilian clothes. He had already found a tailor from one of many and would take us there. We climbed in a cab waiting at the main Tan Son Nhut military gate. The cabbie fearlessly competed with pedicabs called cyclos, Lambretta and Vespa motor scooters, motor bikes, bicycles, loaded buses, and tiny Renault cabs. The traffic moved in chaos, churning in two-way, never-ending streams.

We drove past tall palm trees which lined the boulevard near downtown. Handsome French colonial villas stood on either side of the wide street. Peeling yellow and ochre stucco, gray in areas from mildew, gave the grand buildings a faded elegance.

Although quickly becoming desensitized to the exotic, I appreciated a new city smell; pungent gasoline fumes now combined with whiffs of the charcoal smoke from dozens or hundreds of small braziers manned by cooks, squatting on their haunches, selling street food.

Graceful women crowded the sidewalks, all dressed in the flowing *au dai*—white or colorful high-collared silk dresses with tight bodices and long overskirts split on both sides to the waist over long pajama-like pants. Young, beautiful, slender girls rode on the back of Vespas, holding on to brave, wiry young male drivers. Bars and cocktail lounges, protected by heavy anti-grenade screens in front, enticed with names: Sporting, Josephine, Phoenix, and Capitol.

"Madame Nhu clamped down on what goes on in those bars," Doc Lemmon yelled. "In May, she pressured the National Assembly to pass 'morality laws.' The taxi girls—I heard there are three thousand—aren't allowed to dance anymore. But that's not all: no beauty contests, no prostitution, no birth control, and no singing or listening to sad or sentimental songs."

"Why the songs?" Frank asked.

"Lowers morals," Doc Lemmon laughed. "They call Madame Nhu 'the Dragon Lady of Vietnam' for good reason."

Shoppers and street vendors filled Tu Do Street, which was lined with outdoor cafes, restaurants, and smart stores; a still-fashionable street, it ran down to the piers in the river.

As we drove by, Doc Lemmon pointed out the landmark Opera House, which he told us was now where the Vietnamese National Assembly convened. We passed the Majestic Hotel and the nearby riverfront park with a floating restaurant. When our cab neared the venerable Continental Palace Hotel, Doc Lemmon pointed out the new Caravelle Hotel across Le Loi Square.

"I can see why Saigon is called the Paris of the Orient," I yelled over the din of traffic. Exotic, it seemed to me a city filled with danger, mystery, and intrigue.

Doc Lemmon and Frank nodded in agreement.

The driver amazingly understood the address and dropped us off in front of a small tailor's shop that looked liked many others lining a busy commercial street. We entered the open door, and I heard a bell ring. Two men immediately came in from the back and appeared to recognize Doc Lemmon. Frank and I selected some materials. The tailors rapidly and expertly measured us. We paid for several pairs of pants each and were assured we could pick up our new clothes in two days. We also bought some loose sport shirts off a rack. We were fully outfitted in about fifteen minutes for less than forty American dollars.

"Now, let's eat. There's this great Chinese place floating on the river." Doc Lemmon hailed pedicabs. These carts with seats were pulled by bicycle-peddling drivers who could weave in and out of the confusing traffic with uncommon ease.

These pedicabs had replaced the man-pulled rickshaws in the Orient. We arrived at a broad promenade along the river, and lining the walk I saw countless charcoal grills tended by men on their haunches cooking crab for the many people who leisurely strolled in the park.

"This is the Saigon River." Doc Lemmon pointed toward the muddy water. "We're about fifty miles upstream from the South

China Sea." He pointed north. "Frank, Pleiku's in that direction." He then pointed south across the river. "It's pretty much VC territory down there.

I didn't see any life on that side of the river.

Doc Lemmon added, "I've never been south of Saigon and don't plan to. Jay, Soc Trang is down there somewhere among the strategic hamlets."

MEKONG DELTA
FALL 1962

The American and South Vietnamese governments had agreed on a plan—which started in April 1962—to set up strategic hamlets in the rural areas. The plan involved moving farmers and their families into rustic compounds surrounded by barbed wire and muddy moat-like trenches laced with rows of spiked bamboo stakes for defense. These villages were designed to deny Vietcong (VC) access to the peasants for recruitment. Over seven million peasant families had been relocated in thousands of completed hamlets. The government program, headed up by President Diem's brother and political advisor Nhu, planned to have twelve thousand hamlets by the end of 1963.

These hamlets were unpopular with the farmers forcibly removed from their old homes and villages. Critics called them "successful"—"successful" in driving the undecided into becoming VC sympathizers. Unknown to Nhu, his chief assistant for the program, Col. Pham Ngo Thao, was a VC agent who undermined the project.

President Diem liked strategic hamlets; the program did not require the Army of the Republic of Vietnam (ARVN) for defense of his government—only civilians. These uprooted farmers were issued American weapons and limited training, and they were instructed to defend both their families and these isolated outposts from the VC.

Designated the Self Defense Corps, SDC militia-farmers were paid small monthly sums. If wounded, rather than taking up space in military hospitals reserved for the ARVN, they were treated at civilian hospitals. **Often crude and understaffed, the civilian facilities were chronically short of medicines and supplies—precious commodities frequently stolen and sold on the black market or to the VC.**[4]

SAIGON
FRI
30 NOV 62

In the gray sky, dark, threatening clouds piled high and signaled a bad turn in the weather.

"Lucy's headed this way," Doc Lemmon said.

Weather Central was closely following Typhoon Lucy, still over the ocean one or two days out. Storm preparations meant closed shutters on all the buildings, choppers pushed into hangars, and fixed-wing planes tied down facing into the wind. The air force flew some planes as far away as Japan to get out of the storm's projected path.

With the forecast for such threatening weather, no one went into the city. Frank, Doc Lemmon, and I had dinner in the officers' mess; the cooks prepared a delicious chicken dinner. It was still early, so we ended up at the Than Son Nhut Officers' Club.

Doc Lemmon knew a lot about Saigon, but he did not know much about the boondocks. Lucky stiff; he didn't need to. He told me he had heard fighting was the worst right then in the Delta, but he didn't know much more.

MEKONG DELTA
FALL 1962

The Diem government, on the defensive, had pretty much forfeited most of the southern half of the Mekong Delta to the guerrillas.

Senior American commanders in Saigon were unrealistically optimistic based on reports provided by the Vietnamese government. American advisors out in the field were in conflict

with the U.S. Military Assistance Command, Vietnam (MACV) in Saigon about how the war was going. They knew the ARVN reports were inflated and dishonest. Those advisors, who spoke honestly of their concerns to American journalists, were chastised. The reporters—who tried to report the truth—were vigorously attacked by Saigon and Washington.[5]

SAIGON
SAT
1 DEC 62

My first typhoon was a bust. Lucy did not hit very hard last night—only a little rain with some moderate winds. Not as exciting as expected, but the military escaped with no damage. Now it would be back to business as usual with the return of sunny, warm weather. Doc Lemmon had to work today, so Frank and I ventured out by ourselves to pick up the civilian clothes from the tailor. We were both pleased with the perfect fit of the trousers and could not resist buying some more bargain shirts.

This would be the last evening in civilization for Frank and me. To celebrate, Doc Lemmon planned a night on the town. All three of us crowded into a cab at the now-familiar heavily guarded Tan Son Nhut front gate. Our driver, who had nerves of steel, pulled quickly out onto the main road. I watched him closely. Fearless, he did not even turn his head to look back for oncoming traffic.

"The Caravelle," Doc Lemmon said with grand nonchalance. The cabbie understood and hit the accelerator without saying a word.

The Caravelle Hotel, as opposed to the venerable Continental Palace across the square, was only four years old. Designed by the French and named for the small sailing vessel, it stood ten stories tall—a handsome mid-city Western hotel with air-conditioning.

The three of us exited the elevator on the top level with its fine dining room. We went to the outdoor terrace and ordered drinks. As we looked out over the city, the sun was setting. On the dusky street below, we observed the bustling scene of milling people, traffic, and thriving sidewalk businesses.

"Over there is a good view of the Opera House," Doc Lemmon said, like an expert tour guide, "and if you look down rue Catinat, you can just make out the front of Saigon's famous Notre Dame Cathedral."

Night descended, and lights came on in the streets and buildings, eliminating the decay in the darkness. Busy downtown Saigon, bathed in a beautiful, glowing neon patina, did not look like a city in a country at war.

We left the balmy terrace to brave evening traffic.

"We'll take a cab." Doc Lemmon hailed one easily. He certainly knew his way around, maybe because he was from Chicago and accustomed to traffic.

The Cercle Sportif, where we planned to meet three other officers for dinner, proved to be an exclusive French club frequented by foreigners and the Vietnamese upper class. The dining room had elegant high ceilings, potted palms, whitewashed interior, and slowly revolving ceiling fans. It looked like a set for the movie *Casablanca*. Feeling very much the adventurer, I envisioned myself as Harry Lime, Graham Greene's cagey international spy in *The Third Man*.

During dinner, an American captain approached our table. "I'm Captain Brewster from the Ninety-Third. I understand one of you chaps is headed to Soc Trang tomorrow?"

"Yes, sir." I stood to introduce myself. We shook hands.

"So you're the new flight surgeon who'll replace Doc Greene. Will he ever be happy to see you. He's chomping at the bit for you to get down there so he can go home."

Capt. Brewster, an officer in the regular army, motioned for me to step outside on the terrace that overlooked the gardens and brightly lit tennis courts. A strong, sturdy-appearing man with a broad face, red from the sun and wind, he looked like a man born to wear the wings of an army pilot on his uniform.

"Jay, I have a top secret message for the POL officer. For his ears only. He must get this first thing when you get there tomorrow." Capt. Brewster looked around and then whispered the information in my ear.

"Thanks," he said as we walked back to the table. "We can't send classified messages by radio. The VC have our frequencies."

"Enjoy dinner and your last night in Saigon. It may be awhile before you get back." He lightly patted my shoulder. "See you in Soc Trang day after tomorrow. I still have two days up here in the 'ville before I'm due back."

Now Harry Lime for sure, I had a secret message. Forbidden to write it down, I couldn't even tell Frank or Doc Lemmon. I did not know what a POL officer was and I did not know the meaning of the message, but I did know how to keep a secret from the enemy. If I had the bad luck to be captured by the VC tomorrow on my way down to Soc Trang—even if tortured—I would give only name, rank, and serial number. I learned that at Fort Sam.

I silently repeated Capt. Brewster's information several times to commit it to memory. It had to do with something about types and amounts, and I hoped I wouldn't be so anxious I'd be inaccurate, or worse, forget it entirely. The Ninety-Third must be preparing for a big operation; the message was for real, and the U.S. Army was depending on me with this first assignment.

SAIGON
SUN
2 DEC 62

I watched from the window of the Otter, a small dependable army transport plane, as swampy rice paddies replaced the last of the city. I looked at my watch. It was 1000. We headed south over the Mekong Delta. Tree lines and canals crisscrossed rice fields and dikes. Narrow paved highways connected thatched-roof hamlets and villages scattered along the waterways.

I had done some reading about the mighty Mekong. Below, this timeless, muddy river—beginning some 2,600 miles away in the highlands of Tibet—flowed east and cut through an immense Delta to empty from five mouths into the South China Sea. Vital to all life, including the VC, this river was the major transportation system and provided water essential for rice production. From the

Otter, about all I could see were the endless rice fields stretched out in every direction.

I sat next to an American civilian, who introduced himself as a TV correspondent from Cleveland—one of many reporters stationed in Saigon. "Flights like this are called milk runs," he said with a friendly smile over the noise of the aircraft when he learned this was my first flight in-country.

After we had flown about thirty minutes over this flat country, our plane began a descent for Can Tho, a scheduled stop to unload some supplies and the writer.

"Good luck, Doctor Hoyland. Hope I run into you again." The reporter waved as he stepped down on the tarmac.

The Otter crew unloaded cartons onto a waiting truck. An American civilian boarded, a physician from Virginia with MEDICO on some sort of medical mission. He told me he was on his way to Saigon and would be going back to the United States next week. I could only sigh.

After this quick stop, we soon were back in the air above the Delta—next stop, Soc Trang.

Again, I mentally reviewed the message for the POL officer. In the light of day, I felt more the queasy schoolboy than suave Harry Lime. I knew now I was not cut out for the espionage business.

Sooner than I felt prepared, the pilot began a descent. From my window, I saw a single airstrip parallel to an almost empty highway leading to the nearby city on the banks of two rivers—Soc Trang, I assumed. When we were closer, I could see a small control tower on the opposite side of the runway, a cluster of one-story buildings, and a large hangar with several helicopters inside. Many more helicopters lined the airstrip angled in a single, perfect row. On the landing approach, I could see loops of concertina wire stretched generously around the top of double-perimeter security fences. Except for the airstrip and helicopters, Soc Trang airfield looked to me like your average medium-security prison back in the States.

The pilot executed a perfect landing. We taxied, and I took in a deep breath, hoping for some Harry Lime courage. We stopped and the crew chief opened the plane door. The doctor from MEDICO stayed buckled in his seat but waved farewell. I waved back, deplaned, and grabbed my gear from the crew chief.

A captain dressed in fatigues wearing the insignia of the Medical Corps ran forward. "Doc Hoyland." His enthusiasm told me he was happy to see me. His eager greeting and broad smile told me he was extremely happy to see me. "I'm Doc Greene, at your service." Pulling off his fatigue cap, he waved it toward the buildings clustered nearby. "Welcome to Soc Trang."

Doc Greene's dark hair had a premature gray patch over his right forehead and was gray at the temples. He had smooth skin well-tanned by the sun and a wide, crooked smile. Replacing his cap at a jaunty angle, he extended his right hand and said, "Mighty glad you're here."

I shook his over-firm grip with a sinking feeling. No turning back now. No out. I couldn't get home from here if I had to. The only way back: serve my year.

Doc Greene scooped up my duffle bag. "We'll drop this over at your bunk in hootch number four."

"Before anything," I said and tried for a casual tone, "I have a message. For the POL officer. From Captain Brewster. I ran into him in Saigon last night. He said it's important."

"Sure. Right here in the operations shack." Doc Greene took me to the nearest building.

I quickly learned that POL stood for petroleum, oil, and lubricants. I delivered the message perfectly. The officer now knew how much aviation and truck fuel would be required for an operation in two days at an airstrip many miles to the south. He pursed his lips in a low whistle, surprised at the large requirement. Certain of the accuracy, I felt immediate relief mixed with a twinge of disappointment. This secret message was way too mundane for Harry Lime.

With the message delivered, Doc Greene and I headed for my bunk. We walked down the dusty street that ran through the middle of the compound. "That's the dispensary on our left next to the mess hall. Headquarters on the right."

We passed an officer going into the next building. He gave a friendly wave.

"That's Charley going into the Officers' Club. He makes sure the O-Club runs. You'll find yourself spending a lot of time there; there's nothing else to do."

We continued down the street. "This is like a small town; to keep it running, all the officers have appointed duties other than flying and maintaining planes. Someone has to make sure the PX, the O-Club, the EM-Club, and all the other systems work."

The one-story cement buildings clustered together looked alike; long, barracks-style only, no glass in the windows, and no air-conditioning or heating. Screens, shutters, and canvas provided some control of temperature, sun, rain, and profuse seasonal insects. Corrugated metal roofs provided generous overhangs that blocked the sun and drained monsoon rains. Doc Greene told me this airfield and most of the buildings had been built by the Japanese during their occupation of Vietnam in World War II.

"The Soc Trang Sheraton." Doc Greene opened the screen door to hootch #4, "home sweet home." A hallway ran the length of the building with a screen door at either end. Partitions between rooms provided small rooms on both sides of the hallway. We walked the length of the building and entered the last room on the right. A corner room, it had screened windows on two sides and was next to the back door nearest the tarmac and flight line.

"Lucky you. A corner suite." He put my gear on the bunk. A single light bulb dangled from a cord in the middle of the room, and another was in the small closet, which was just big enough to hang a few clothes and uniforms.

"Use this every night." He pointed to the mosquito netting hanging in folds over the bunk.

He took me to a room a few doors down the hall. "This is my room." It had a throw rug, electric fan, and a small desk and chair.

"I'll sell you this stuff at a bargain," Doc Greene said.

"Done," I said. We settled on a nominal amount.

We left by the back door near my room to continue our tour. At the next building, Doc Greene made a gesture of presentation. "Ta-da! This is the best. Hot showers. The marines built them for us just before we left Da Nang." The empty shower building was like the other buildings, except dank and dark with shower heads lining the walls, a drain in the middle of the cement floor, and water heaters outside.

"Let's sign you in. You can meet the new CO. Then we'll go to the dispensary."

At the headquarters, Doc Greene said, "Don't look for the American flag. It's not here. We're only advisors, and this is not officially an American base."

Maj. Ewald, the Ninety-Third's commanding officer, was not in his office, but Capt. Langston, the executive officer, showed me where to sign in. With mock gravity, he said, "So, Doc Greene, did you hear the bad news? You've been extended. All rotations back to the States have been cancelled. Tough luck."

I signed in the book, now officially on duty.

Doc Greene gave Langston a mock salute with his middle finger. "Tough luck, my ass, sir. I'm leaving in two days, four Dec sixty-two, Tuesday, date certain. And leaving no forwarding address."

"Captain Greene, we're going to miss you."

"That's life, buddy. But you're a short-timer. Right?"

Capt. Langston smiled brightly. "Yeah."

"On the other hand," Doc Greene said, "I give you Doc Hoyland, my replacement."

"Ah." Capt. Langston looked at me closely. He paused between each letter. "An F-N-G."

I frowned.

Doc Greene laughed. "FNG. Fucking New Guy. You'll hear that for a while, Jay. Then it's the next guy's turn. Langston here is a short-timer, meaning he'll be rotating home soon."

"Oh, so true, Doc. Two weeks."

"And now," Doc Greene said, "to the dispensary."

The 134th Medical Detachment was located across the company street from headquarters. We entered the front door into a small waiting room with two benches for patients. The clerk, a young enlisted man, was seated at the desk behind a typewriter. He stood as we came in.

"Ralph, this is Captain Jay Hoyland. Your new CO."

I could see the name Jones printed on his name tag. A thin

young man with reddish-blond hair, he smiled, and we shook hands.

"Everyone's at chow, Doc Greene," Ralph said.

"Good idea. Let's grab some, too, Jay," Doc Greene said.

We had a quick lunch of tomato soup and grilled-cheese sandwiches in the almost empty mess hall.

After lunch, we continued the dispensary tour. A short hallway led from the waiting area, and Doc Greene opened a door. "Our supplies." I looked in and saw a large supply closet lined with shelves and stocked with many items. "We'll go through all this stuff later." He closed the door, and we walked to the back room, which had a field treatment table, a surgical light, more equipment, and a desk.

"Your office." Doc Greene pointed to the desk.

He sat down in the gray office chair behind the desk and motioned for me to sit on the gray metal folding chair next to it. He put his feet up on the desk and leaned back in the chair. "You have a pretty worn-out six-man team right now. They'll be going home in the next two weeks or so. Sergeant Sherk is in charge of the enlisted men: Jones, the clerk you just met; three medics; and an ambulance driver."

I looked around the treatment room that would be my office—serviceable, but not much else. Two large backpacks with shoulder straps, covered in black waterproof material, leaned against the wall in the corner.

Doc Greene followed my gaze and got up to retrieve one of the bags. "Your most important gear." He lifted it on to the desk. "The emergency flight kit. You'll carry one of these babies on med evacs, missions, whenever you go out in a chopper. Always restock when you get back, no matter how late or tired. You never know when you'll be called out again. Be ready. Always." He put the bag back in the corner.

"Tomorrow, we'll go over every item, count every piece of equipment, including the jeep and ambulance, and then you'll sign for them. Officially yours until you sign them over to your replacement next year.

"Wish I could say you have a good sergeant in Sherk," he said and lowered his voice, "but I'm afraid he's burned out." Doc Greene paused. "We've been a pretty good crew. Now all we want is to go home. Our ambulance driver and one medic should rotate right after the first of the year. Hopefully, your new men arrive before then.

"The things we're short on, Sergeant Sherk—or your new sergeant, who should arrive in the next ten days or so—can pick up. Sergeants run the army. I've learned to tell them what you need. When it shows up, don't ask where or how they got it. Just trust them. They take pride in helping each other, and they do a damned good job.

"We also order extra for the Green Berets. Those special forces are stationed out in the boondocks in small teams. Their supply can sometimes be slow, but usually they can get stuff before we do. They're priority, but we trade favors when we can."

We walked around the rest of the compound, and the afternoon passed quickly. We ended back at the mess hall.

"Let's get some chow. That wasn't much of a lunch; I'm starving," Doc Greene said.

The mess hall served a really good roast-beef dinner. Doc Greene introduced me around. After dinner, we crossed the street to the Officers' Club. As we entered, a tanned man dressed in shorts, T-shirt, and flip-flops waved at us.

"Hey, Sput," Doc Greene said, "meet my replacement. Doc Hoyland."

Sput Clark was probably close to thirty, but his short hair gave him a more youthful appearance. Of average height, he had noticeably broad shoulders, powerful biceps and forearms, and walked with a swagger, suggesting he needed plenty of space. When he sat, legs wide apart, he gave the same impression.

"Never met a flight surgeon I didn't like," Sput said. "Welcome, Tiger." We shook hands. I felt his powerful grip. "You two care to join me in a libation?"

Before I could answer, Doc Greene said, "You're on."

Sput yelled to the bartender, "I'm buying a welcome drink for Doc Hoyland here and a farewell drink for good ol' Doc Greene."

The Officer's Club was the typical empty interior of these long, rectangular buildings with the exception of a bar along one side. Behind it, there was a back bar, which looked well stocked, and a large refrigeration unit; in front, about twenty stools lined up, occupied currently by several customers dressed in civvies. Tables with Vietnamese leatherette chairs filled in the rest of the open floor. The club was considerably more meager than the one in Saigon, but more interesting because of the things hung on the walls: several VC unit flags and exotic captured handmade weapons such as a crossbow, bows and arrows, pipe guns, and bamboo dart shooters. On the far wall, in a place of honor, was a helicopter drive shaft shot through by a bullet hole—souvenirs of war.

The bartender stood by with a welcoming smile, a slender Vietnamese man of indeterminate age. "My name Duc," he said in clear English. Dressed in a neat blue shirt without a tie and black pants, he got to work on Sput's order.

We found a table, and Sput came over with three beers.

"Thanks." Doc Greene hoisted his bottle. "Here's to our own Captain Sputter Clark, the best damned H-21 helicopter maintenance officer in this man's army."

We clinked our longneck bottles together and took a drink. Sput wiped his mouth with the back of his hand.

"Where did the name Sput come from?" I asked.

Doc Greene answered, "According to lore, at Rucker, he once yelled at a chief mechanic, 'I don't want to hear that engine sputter.' Thus, Sputter Clark."

Before I put my bottle down on the table, someone at the door shouted, "Doc Greene. You're wanted over at the dispensary."

"Oh, hell," Doc Greene muttered under his breath.

I got up to go with him, but Doc Greene motioned me back down. "I'll handle it, Jay. You'll have plenty of time to work later. Enjoy. I'll be back shortly." The screen door slammed behind him.

"Greene's a good guy; I respect him a lot." Sput paused. "So where are you from, Doc Hoyland?"

"Missouri. Small town in the Ozarks."

"God's country," Sput said. "I've been on the Lake of the Ozarks. Great boating and water skiing."

I started to add I'd been in Los Angeles for the last year doing my internship, but I decided not to. It made me sound a little too inexperienced. "How about you?"

"From Jersey. The Garden State. With any luck, I'll be back there in a couple months." He paused to look at the date on his wristwatch with its large, complex dial. "Actually, six weeks, to be exact. January eleventh. A couple other pilots and me—we're the last of the original Fort Devens crew.

"Be glad to rotate back, but it hasn't been bad here," he said and took a gulp from the bottle, "except for my job. It's been hell trying to keep these H-21s up and flying. They're workhorses, but it's time for the pasture; hard to keep enough going to cover our missions; touch-and-go even with sweat, baling wire, piss, and vinegar." Sput took another long drink. "All the H-21s in the army—100 percent— are over here now. Thank God! I won't have to fly or maintain any of those fuckers back in the good ol' U.S. of A."

A pilot who had obviously been working on a tan in his off time passed our table. He had brown eyes and hair about the same color as his skin. Dressed in a T-shirt, swimsuit, and rubber flip-flops, he overheard Sput and good-naturedly leaned over. "Now Captain Sput, sir, watch what you say."

Sput snickered. "Doc, this is CWO Billy T. Witt, better known as Billy T. or just Witty."

His hair was cut so short, he almost looked bald, and freckles defied his deep tan.

We shook hands.

Sput said, "Witty, you came in that first group after I did; when do you rotate home?"

"In nine months, back to Mama and open my shop." Witt smiled. "Pleased to meet you, Doc. I hear you've moved into our hootch. Welcome." He got a beer from the bar and sat at a table with two other men.

"Witty is a great soldier and a terrific pilot," Sput said after he took a drink of beer. "He's from Philadelphia. Went into the army right out of high school. Got married not long after that and has two teenagers back in Pennsylvania.

"He flew in Korea, got promoted to chief warrant officer, and has his twenty in; going to retire when he gets back. Open up a machine shop. He's quite a guy."

Sput took another swig. "Now where was I? Oh, yeah. The H-21s got worn-out in Korea, totally. But we have some great new choppers in the pipeline: Bell UH-1s, called Hueys. Those suckers are only fifty-seven feet long and fifteen high, but man, do they have power. Can't wait to get my hands on one of those babies. And Chinooks; twin rotors like the H-21s but way better jet engines.

"A few Hueys are over here already flying med evacs, called Dust Offs. You'll get to know them right away. Some others out of Saigon are mounted with machine guns and rocket pods. They escort us out on missions. Deliver the firepower when we go in landing zones. I call them our protecting angels."

"Always wanted to be a flyer?" I said.

"Nah. Right out of college, I taught high school industrial arts. Too routine. One day, I woke up and decided what the hell. Why not see what the army has to offer. I dunno, it just seemed like the thing to do. When I got the opportunity to go to flight school, I jumped on it."

He savored another long drink, and after a thoughtful pause, he said, "It's been good, mostly. Even this tour. I should be on the next list and get promoted to major—Vietnam duty helps—then come back over here to help finish the job. Not just this half-assed mess we're in now."

I looked up and saw a young lieutenant opening the screen door. Before he could come in, a small mixed-breed dog with short brown fur bounded in. With wagging tail, he ran straight for Sput. "Doc, you're about to meet our mascot, Tiger."

The dog wagged his tail even more, if possible, when Sput reached down to pick up his eager friend. "We're called the Tigers. This little fella came out of nowhere, so he became one too. He's flown over ten missions with me. My good luck charm." The dog eagerly licked Sput's hand and face.

Duc, the bartender, yelled loudly, "Captain Sput. You know rule. Tiger no allowed club."

"Okay." Sput gently picked up the dog and took it outside. When he returned to the table, he asked, "So, Doc, anyone special waiting for you back home?"

"No. No one special. How about you?"

"Just Mom," Sput laughed. "And maybe Francine."

"Francine?"

"My old girlfriend—maybe. I haven't seen her in awhile."

"What's the story?"

"It's a long story," Sput said and took a drink from his beer, "but what the hell, we've got nothing but time."

He took another slug and wiped his mouth with the back of his hand. "We went to high school together, but we weren't particularly friendly back then. We both ended up at Rutgers. Got together there. By our senior year, we were engaged. Planned to get married right after graduation. My mom was tickled, bless her. She always liked Francine, from the time we were kids in the neighborhood."

Sput frowned and then added, "I got cold feet. Told Francine I wanted to wait awhile. Get settled a bit and save up some money. It like to broke her heart. She gave my ring back that night. After graduation, she moved into the city and got a job. I started teaching. First thing you know, she's getting married, all right—to someone she met at work. That like to broke my heart and Mom's too.

"My only brother was killed in Korea, and since my dad passed from lung cancer, Mom's been dying for a grandbaby. She'd like a boy to carry on the Clark name, but she says a girl would do just fine."

"That could be some kind of pressure."

"You're right. A couple months ago, I got a letter from Mom. She ran into Francine in town and gave her the third degree. Found out Francine was divorced, never had any children, and she seemed really interested to hear from me. Gave Mom her address. I wrote her; she wrote back. We're planning on getting together when I get home. I really loved that girl. Still do. Who knows?"

"Let nature take its course."

Sput looked down at his beer, and his finger traced a circle on the table from the condensation. He drained the bottle. "Care for another?"

I declined. I still had plenty left.

Sput brought over another beer. "I can tell you one thing I'm going to miss most when I go back—that little dog, Tiger. A real pal. He should be up for the Air Medal if they authorized any. I bet you didn't know we don't get medals for this war. At least not yet. Young President Kennedy doesn't want to alarm the public. Even let them know we are in a war."

Doc Greene returned and sat down, smiling broadly. The routine phone call confirmed his departure: date certain, December fourth.

"Sput, you poor bastard," Doc Greene said, "I'll be sitting down to turkey for a holiday dinner in the Bronx. This short-timer," he pointed to himself, "has only two—count 'em, two—more days," he held up two fingers, "thanks to my good ol' buddy, Doc Hoyland, here." Grinning, he slapped my back.

Sput rolled his eyes.

"Remember last December, when we were aboard ship, Sput?" Doc Greene said. "What a year!"

I quickly recalled last December; I was in California, blissfully unaware I would be on the other side of the globe this Christmas.

Sput shrugged his shoulders.

Doc Greene turned toward me. "The Ninety-Third had been stationed at Fort Devens, Massachusetts, forever."

"Since 1956," Sput interrupted.

Doc Greene continued, "Anyway, we got these orders to prepare to leave CONUS—continental United States—so we had to pack up all our gear, everything: medical supplies, jeeps, ambulances, the choppers, tools, guns, equipment. A big deal. A very big deal."

Sput nodded his head in thoughtful agreement.

"We put everything and everybody aboard the Core, an old U.S. World War II carrier, and took off from Quonset Point, Rhode Island. I'll never forget: fifteen December, 1961." He paused to recollect. "I also won't forget seeing the coastline disappear as we moved out to sea. They hadn't told us for sure where we were headed. Day after day was pretty much the same. We played a lot of cards. I did tons of reading. When we passed Gibraltar, any hope for good duty faded. We passed through the Suez Canal. When we arrived in the Philippines, we knew for sure we were coming here."

Sput interrupted, "At Subic Bay, we transferred to the USS Princeton. Finally—after forty-one days in transit—we found ourselves sitting ten miles off The Republic of Vietnam."

"We didn't sit long," Doc Greene said. "It was monsoon, and bad weather threatened. Right away, the choppers ferried everything to Da Nang. We unpacked our gear. Six days later, the Ninety-Third flew its first mission."

"Da Nang?" I asked.

"Yep," Sput said. "Up north where it's mountainous. We flew our butts off, but H-21s aren't cut out for that kind of performance. These flying crates were built in 1951, for God's sake. The vertical stabilizers kept cracking, even with modifications—a huge hazard. Meanwhile, the First Marine Aircraft Wing was down here in Soc Trang flying H-34s over the flat Delta. They're far better suited to the terrain up north, so we swapped places; arrived in Soc Trang twelve September and were up and flying our first mission four days later."

Sput drained his second beer in one long drink. "Well, doctors, enough reminiscing about the good old days. I've got to tend to some government business." He waved. "Nice to meet you, Doc Hoyland. See ya around."

At the door, he turned around. "Take everything Doc Greene says with a grain of kosher salt. It's not been that bad."

"You're a great pilot, Captain Sputter," Doc Greene yelled after him, "but a hell of a liar." Doc Greene sighed. "I'll miss Sput. Sorry you won't get to know him better. An ace volleyball player and all-'round good guy."

SOC TRANG
MON
3 DEC 62

My first day at the dispensary, I decided to go early to greet the medics as they came in for duty. Jones, the clerk, was first and on time. He went right to work. The medics came a little late. Sgt. Sherk arrived much later without apologies or excuses.

Two enlisted men were waiting on the benches for sick call. Why wait for Doc Greene? I thought. I'm ready and know where everything is. Before I could call in the first patient, the front door opened and a crew chief, holding a blood-soaked shop rag over his left thumb, came in.

Back in the treatment room, I removed the bloody cloth and saw a deep laceration.

"How did this happen?" I asked. He would need several sutures.

"A sharp metal edge on the aft cargo door. I'm fixing a mount for my machine gun."

After injecting local anesthetic, I irrigated the wound with sterile saline. This stoic soldier, unfazed, continued to relate the details of the accident.

Watching my face while I sutured, he said, "H-21s' front and back cargo doors aren't designed for machine guns. With the VC firing at us like sitting ducks when we go in landing zones, we now are issued machine guns, mostly for defense.

"They're heavy mothers, hard to move in and out of place. One of the guys devised a horizontal bar for support—hinged on one side, it swings into the cabin to clear the door. As soon as the troops off-load, we swing the gun back in place. Ready to fire away."

I finished suturing and checked for bleeders. There were none. "Fortunately, no tendons or major nerves severed," I said and gave the Spec Four a tetanus booster.

"Thanks, Doc. Glad it's not my trigger finger."

The next patient was one of the cooks. He had painful hemorrhoids. I excised an angry external purple clot and gave him oral analgesics and orders to take sitz baths. He knew where he could find a tub and hot water for a soak. I wrote an off duty slip for two days.

The third enlisted man, a private, looked barely old enough to shave—not yet eighteen years old, I felt sure.

"What brings you in?" I asked.

"A strain." He shyly mentioned the euphemism for gonorrhea. "Must've picked it up in town last week. I went in for a little R & R."

"Next time you go in for a little *R*," I said as I injected penicillin, "use a condom."

The young private nodded his head in agreement and pulled up his shorts and fatigue pants. He added, "Thanks for the shot, Doc. And the advice."

By this time, Sgt. Sherk had arrived. He got a corpsman to clean the suture kit so it could be wrapped and sterilized in the next batch for the autoclave. The back door to the treatment room opened. I looked up to see a relaxed Doc Greene.

"Glad to see you taking good care of business, Jay. How'd it go? Any questions?"

"We're doing okay."

"Great." He laughed. "You've brought bad weather. Monsoon's June through September down here. This is supposed to be the dry season, but we're on storm watch again."

I glanced outside at the sky. It was a slate gray. Moderate winds were gusting, and dust blew up from the company street.

"Next, it'll be a plague of locusts. I just hope it holds off till I'm out of here tomorrow," Doc Greene said. "But it's a great day! Let's count equipment, Sgt. Sherk; let's get to work."

The three of us inventoried cartons of bandages and large bottles of aspirin and anti-diarrhetics. We counted sterile suture trays, morphine sulfate ampules in the narcotics box, boxes of needles and syringes, even the treatment table. I found a clipboard and some paper and began to take notes of questions I wanted to ask and things I needed to remember.

Doc Greene left to do some last-minute paperwork. Sgt. Sherk and I counted emergency flight bags, stacks of forms, more suture packets, and the gasoline-powered autoclave out back.

As we started to count the stack of rolled-up litters, Sgt. Sherk said, "Doc, one of the most important things: don't hand over even one wounded man on a litter for med evac until you get an empty litter first. Sometimes it gets hectic, but if you don't, you'll be shit out of luck when you need a stretcher.

"The same's true for blankets. If we run short, I can finagle those, but litters are gold—almost impossible to replace once they're gone."

We worked our way through the long list of items in the table of organization and equipment. Sgt. Sherk left for somewhere. Doc Greene returned, and the two of us inspected both the ambulance and dispensary jeep. He explained that the motor pool maintained these vehicles on a regular schedule so they were always ready to go. Our dispensary ambulance driver would be responsible as well.

"You'll be glad to have this baby." Doc Greene patted the jeep. "She'll get you to town or wherever you need to go without getting anyone's permission. That's the one and only perk I can think of for being the town doctor." He added, "Except the cooks. They always treat docs extra fine, particularly when you do the periodic public health inspection of the kitchen and mess halls."

Back in the treatment room, he picked up several forms. I pulled out the clipboard, now filled with my notes.

"You'll need this form to document cleanliness; this one for routine cooks and food handlers' hygiene health exams; this form to document temperatures of the reefers to be sure perishables are at acceptable temperatures; and these are for documenting the chlorine at the water point."

He put his forefinger to his lips as he thought for a moment. "The only other prevention thing I can think of is your job to be sure everyone takes their Chloroquin weekly. We leave them just inside the entrance to the mess halls. The guys are so well indoctrinated about malaria, compliance isn't a problem.

"Speaking of the mess hall, let's go over there and get some coffee," Doc Greene said.

He introduced me all around to the cooks, and we filled our cups. It was not mealtime, so we were alone in the officers' mess and sat down at one of the long tables. "Let me give you a quick rundown on the support the 134th Dispensary provides.

"Anytime a med evac is called for an American, MAAG, Special Forces, MACV, whatever, you go. You mostly go if our pilots are called out to evac the Vietnamese, but sometimes they take them elsewhere, and you may not need to go." Doc Greene took a sip of coffee, shuddering. "This is really just heated crank-shaft oil," he said, but took another sip.

"Whenever the Ninety-Third flies missions to transport the Vietnamese field operations, you go and stand by at the location where the choppers pick up troops, called the staging area. If a pilot or crewman gets hit going into a landing zone, they'll return to the staging area, where you have your aid station set up to stabilize any wounds. If more definitive care is needed, on your orders, Dust Off will come in and fly the injured to Saigon or Nha Trang field hospital."

"How often do we fly these missions?"

"A lot. We also fly re-supply missions to Special Forces. Green Berets are scattered all over. And we provide transport for various personnel. Rumor has it even a U.S. senator will probably be coming in next week."

"How have the missions gone? Been busy?"

"It varies. We had some bad ones in Da Nang. We're still kinda new down here in the Delta. But they say there are more VC down here than anywhere in Vietnam right now; things are heating up."

Doc Greene bussed our empty cups. "Let's go back to the dispensary. See if there's anything I've missed. When I'm gone, I'm gone." He just couldn't help but smile, and I couldn't blame him.

Back in the office, he said, "I don't want to forget this." He indicated a top drawer in the gray filing cabinet. "Here's where we keep copies of the pilots' flight physicals. Some are due right away. The guys will usually remind you, but if things get hot and heavy, it's up to you to let them know when to come in."

I recognized the forms—the same FAA paperwork we used at Fort Rucker. Whether here or in the United States, flying status depended on these physicals being up-to-date—flight pay as well. I felt a little overloaded at this point as I glanced at my clipboard. There were so many responsibilities to keep track of, some important and some not. I would need to sort this out right away; but I thought to myself, somewhat grimly, I'll have plenty of time. Nothing but time.

"And, oh yeah, I have a stash of antibiotics for the girls in town.

They're due some in the next week or so." Doc Greene looked at his watch. "Let's go downtown right now. I'll show you around, and we'll at least go by the outside of the orphanage."

He drove the jeep and I rode shotgun the short distance into town. Doc Greene explained that we often donated supplies to the Soc Trang leprosarium and to the nearby orphanage where Catholic Sisters took care of infants and small children.

"Stuff like soap, milk, and cereal. We don't have time to take anything today, but I'll drive by so you can see where they're located."

Soc Trang looked like a busy city on the banks of two rivers, branches of the Mekong. I noticed many pedestrians, old men, and young families. Shops were crowded with people dressed in black muslin pajamas. Many sat on their haunches, watching the world go by, or at small tables in front of shops, drinking cups of tea and smoking.

Doc Greene pointed out the turn-off for the leprosarium, and farther down the street, a large old villa with fading paint that housed the orphanage. We made short stops for brief introductions at a couple of restaurants where Doc Greene checked for hygiene periodically and the three brothels frequented by GIs when the city was not off-limits. A lot to take in.

We returned to the airfield and entered through the heavily guarded front gate. Doc Greene said, "The guys have been talking up a Christmas party out here for the children who live at the orphanage and leprosarium. It'd be great if you'd head that up."

We got out of the jeep, and he looked at his watch one more time.

"Well, that's about it, Jay. All I can think of. I believe I'll take the rest of the day off. The first time I've done that since I've been here. I'll be at the O-Club if you need me, preparing for tomorrow's departure. Destination: U.S. of A."

He started across the street but turned back. "I ran into Captain Brewster this morning. He's back from Saigon. There's a big mission lined up day after tomorrow. Out of Cam Mau, about as far south as you can get."

Aha! I thought of my Harry Lime secret for the POL officer; this mission was what that message was all about.

Doc Greene yelled over his shoulder, "After dinner, come over to the club. I want to buy you a drink. Or two."

I stared after him for a few moments, took a deep breath, and went back into the dispensary by the back door. The rest of the day, I settled in and reviewed procedures and the confusing notes on my clipboard. I sorted through the emergency kits to be sure I knew what first-aid equipment and supplies I would be carrying on this first mission to Ca Mau.

This had been such a full day that I had forgotten about the forecast for a storm. I saw that the dark bank of clouds had cleared out, and Jones told me the typhoon threat had been cancelled. That was about the only good news I had had all day. After a hearty meatloaf dinner in the officers' mess hall, I walked across the street to the O-Club.

Doc Greene seemed to be in a good mood until I sat down. He turned suddenly serious. "It's been quite a year. I won't say it's been easy. A perverted adventure, going from boring on the boat ride over here to flat-out scary up north. Now down here for two months. Through it all, they've been a great bunch of guys." He gestured around the club.

The noise and laughter increased. This crowd knew how to celebrate. Tomorrow, five of Soc Trang's finest would leave for good. Doc Greene leaned over to me and yelled above the noise, "Let's get some fresh air." Outside, Delta insects swarmed the security lights in the humid, warm night. I looked up, and the humming, buzzing insects made a huge halo that looked like greenish dense fog.

"Jay, there's something I need to tell you. I've been putting it off." Doc Greene cleared his throat. "In early October, a flight surgeon got killed. Up near Quang Ngai. A navy doctor in a marine chopper. They ran into heavy clouds and plowed into a mountain. Eight aboard. Three killed outright, the rest burned. Only one survived."

In the darkness, I could hear Doc Greene sigh heavily. "Take care of yourself. After I leave tomorrow morning, you're the only

American doctor south of Saigon. The guys need a physician and depend on you. Stay alive."

Back in the noisy club, I ordered a second drink; I downed it quicker than usual. I did not feel much in the mood to celebrate with this boisterous crowd. I was an FNG; an outsider. I went the short distance to my corner room in empty hootch #4, undressed, wrapped a towel around my mid-section, and went to the deserted shower room for a long, hot shower.

I got ready for bed in shorts and T-shirt. Lying on my bunk, I was engrossed in the current *Stars and Stripes* when I heard a deep voice from my doorway.

"Hi, Doc Hoyland. I'm Bruce Harrison."

I looked up to see a tall, thin, black pilot with an easy grin that gave him a confident appearance.

We shook hands.

"How's it going?" he asked.

"So far, so good," I said.

"Soc Trang's not so bad. I came over four months after the original crew: Sput, Doc Greene, and the others. I'll be here a few more months."

Originally from Chicago, Bruce told me his father was some big-time corporate lawyer downtown, and his mother taught at the University of Chicago. He grew up in Hyde Park and had wanted to fly since he was a young boy building model airplanes. His parents wanted him to go into law or medicine, but he joined the University Army ROTC and immediately got commissioned after graduation. He jumped at the chance to learn to fly helicopters.

Witty came down the hallway, a towel around his waist, on his way to the shower. Not as tall as most of the pilots, he had to look up at Bruce. "Doc, some call me and Bruce 'Mutt and Jeff,'" Witty said.

Bruce threw his head back and laughed.

Witty continued, "Bruce here is one of the best damn pilots in the Ninety-Third. We call him Trey 'cause his name is Bruce Woodford Hamilton Harrison the third. I ask you, ain't that some handle?"

"Billy T., you are full of shit, but good buddy, I'd fly with you any day." Bruce laughed again.

Witty left for the shower room, and Bruce/Trey went back down the hall toward his room. "Glad to have you for a neighbor, Doc," he called over his shoulder. "Nice talking with you."

I picked up the diary my folks gave me when I left Missouri. I couldn't think of anything to write. After long minutes staring at the first blank page, I closed it, turned out the light, and fixed the mosquito netting around the mattress with considerable care. In the distance, I heard the hard-core celebrants singing off-key Christmas carols; in the further distance, muffled explosions and gunfire.

Sleep, slow to come, proved fitful.

SAIGON
FALL 1962

The VC regularly attacked strategic hamlets. With frequent victories, the guerillas acquired a growing stockpile of modern American weapons and ammunition. Some critics called these government outposts "VC supply points."

The VC also added to their ranks. Disaffected peasants in the hamlets, predominately Buddhists, joined up with the guerillas hoping to undermine the Saigon government and ARVN. They wanted to be free of Diem—sooner or later.

To many peasants, the idea of Communism was not as important as getting free of the Vietnam Mandarin Catholics with their overly colonial attitudes and all foreigners.

The war in Vietnam was deteriorating. The ARVN was reluctant to fight, and commanders would not attack where there were known concentrations of VC. The army also misused pre-attack artillery bombardments to alert the VC so they could clear out of an area prior to a planned assault. To further an illusion of success, Diem's commanders continued to send false after-action reports and body counts to MACV, and these were dutifully sent back to Washington, DC, as factual.

The peasants in all ten provinces of the Delta were enraged at the Diem government and his military, as daytime sweeps through a village by ARVN troops often meant the theft of poultry and food or worse. The VC benefited from this anger. They mostly tried to treat ambivalent peasants with respect in an effort to split them from the Diem government. Those who disagreed, they simply liquidated on the spot.

VC tactics did not specifically target American advisors or support units, fearful that if they did, the United States might retaliate and increase its military presence.[6]

SOC TRANG
TUE
4 DEC 62

"There she is, gentlemen," Sput told the group of about thirty of us who congregated on the tarmac next to operations to see the five veteran officers and eight enlisted men off. He pointed to an army Caribou landing at the far end of the airstrip. Those who were leaving let out a loud cheer.

Doc Greene turned to me and executed a snappy salute. "It's all yours, Dr. Hoyland. Best of luck."

"Thanks. And good luck to you." I saluted back and couldn't help but add silently, you lucky bastard.

After three passengers deplaned from the Caribou, the crew chief waved the DEROS group aboard. They sprinted toward their freedom flight and boarded quickly. The plane taxied to the end of the runway, engines revved up, and once airborne, it quickly gained altitude headed north.

I watched until the plane disappeared from view. I felt abandoned, overwhelmed, and alone; now I was bound by professional duty and honor to be here for the next twelve months. I resigned myself and took in a deep breath.

"Doc Hoyland," I heard someone yell.

I turned to see Sput standing next to one of the passengers who had gotten off the just-departed Caribou. A tall, bespectacled man, at least six feet four, he wore fatigues and an Australian bush hat with the right side pinned up. I immediately noticed his boots. They were not standard issue, but custom canvas boots that called attention to his large, oversized feet.

"Doc, meet Richard Tregaskis. A writer and friend of mine."

Richard extended his hand. "Doctor Hoyland. Kinda hard to see Doc Greene leave?"

"Yeah. But at least now the clock's ticking for me."

"Richard was here for three days last month," Sput said. "Rode with me on a hairy troop drop and now back for more. A glutton for punishment and doesn't even get flight pay."

"I'm doing a book about what's going on over here." Richard smiled and nodded his head. "I plan to document the action, and the Delta's where the action is right now."

After dinner in the mess hall, I went along with all the pilots to operations for a briefing. Capt. Brewster, the rugged man with the sunburned face I met in Saigon at the Cercle Sportif, stood at the front of the room next to a large map for the tactical briefing. He held a pointer and located the airstrip where our fleet of choppers would pick up the Vietnamese regular army and ferry them to a suspected VC location. He pointed out the coordinates of the planned landing zone where the troops would be dropped off.

"We're going back to Cam Mau. A six-day mission." The pilots groaned. Ignoring them, Capt. Brewster continued, "We don't know what we'll run into, but it's reported to be a VC training camp. I don't think the landing zone should be hot."

"Begging your pardon, sir. That's what you said the last time about the LZ, and I took three hits on the first drop," a pilot drawled. "Little Lee Roy is tired of getting holes in his skin. You know, Captain Brewster, sir, he's allergic to hot metal."

The others laughed. They all knew and liked this young pilot with the decided Southern accent who called every chopper he flew Little Lee Roy and went into great detail about the trials of his life and problems with his choppers. A sandy-haired Scots-Irish with blue eyes, I immediately surmised he was probably descended from a long line of storytellers.

Sput, sitting next to me, leaned over and said, "That's our Georgia peach. First Lieutenant Cody Williams. Everyone calls him Slick."

"This is a big operation," Capt. Brewster continued. "We will be joined by the Thirty-Third and the Fifty-Seventh. We'll have Hueys for cover. The air force will supply T-28s for a pre-strike to soften up the area."

After concluding the tactical briefing, he introduced me as the new flight surgeon. Capt. Brewster finished by reminding them, if injured, to return to Cam Mau, where I would be standing by at the aid station.

A short intelligence briefing by the G-2 officer warned of some reported anti-aircraft weapons in the area. After the briefing concluded, a few pilots strolled over to the hangar for the movie *David and Goliath*. Most of them went back to their hootches to read, write letters, or to try and get some sleep. That was what I did.

Lying on my bunk in the dark, I thought about what had happened so far. I had made it through the first day on my own. I had met most of the pilots from the Ninety-Third, and they impressed me as professional flyers. Most had been in Korea and knew the ropes. I felt confident in my professional medical skills, but how would I be as a soldier? With my job, I would be flying a lot, and choppers got shot at all the time. Would I have courage enough?

I took out my diary. I had planned to make an entry every day, but so much for good intentions. A lot had happened, and I had yet to write one word. I decided to go back to the beginning and started the first page with Frank and me leaving San Francisco twelve days before. It sure seemed a lot longer than that to me.

We had departed Travis AFB at 2300 on November 26. The first leg to Hawaii was fun and filled with anticipation, much like starting a vacation flight. We flew in a military model Boeing 707 without passenger windows. Otherwise, it seemed like a commercial flight, just without stewardesses or drinks. We did have box lunches. We arrived at Hickam AFB, Hawaii, about 0100 and left at 0600. We crossed the date line, so it was the twenty-eighth when we deplaned on Guam. It was dark and we didn't see anything but the airfield. We deplaned again for a brief refueling at Clark AFB in the Philippines. We then left at 1215 for Vietnam. I would never forget getting off the plane in Tan Son Nhut and breathing in the first exotic smells of Saigon.

I wondered how Frank was doing up in Pleiku. After I wrote

my first entry, I turned out the light, carefully fixed the mosquito netting around my bed, and prepared for sleep. The mission would kick off at dawn. I felt eager to go out and get the first one out of the way. Only 344 more days to go!

SOC TRANG
WED
5 DEC 62

It was still dark and cool when my alarm went off at 0500. By the time I was awake and fully dressed, the mess hall was brightly lit and busy with eager eaters. I was not hungry and ate little; I felt anxious to be out on the flight line. I watched the pilots. They did not seem rushed. They had been on lots of these missions and knew what to expect. Maybe they were nervous their first time, too, I thought, but that didn't help. Anyway, they had their jobs, and I had mine. I bussed my dishes and went next door to the dispensary to pickup the emergency kit.

Ready to go at first light, the crew chief helped me load two litters and my bulky kit in the second chopper in the line. I looked into the cockpit. Sput sat at the controls. I felt glad he was the pilot.

I put on my flak jacket and sat on two more—if one was good, two would be even better—thankful for this small bit of physical and psychological insurance. Cleared for takeoff, chopper by chopper fired their engines, revved up, and moved forward. We gained speed, and then—always that magical moment to me—liftoff, my first mission underway.

Sput edged the chopper nose down and kicked up the tail for better lift. The back rotor engine made a lot of noise, it seemed to me, but this was my first time on a tandem rotor H-21. I thought briefly about Sput's comments and these old machines. I was doubly glad he would be at the controls; if anything mechanically went wrong, he would sense it right away.

We left Soc Trang like a flight of huge insects in a long line. I knew from the briefing the night before that we would fly at high altitude en route to Cam Mau. Above 1,500 feet, choppers are pretty safe from small-arms ground fire. I looked out the cargo door and saw miles of the hazy, watery Delta below, gray and stark—beautiful in the early morning, but threatening.

Earplugs helped reduce the ferocious noise of the engines. It was way too loud to talk without yelling, but there was no one to talk to anyway. The crew was working, and no one else was aboard. The pilots and crew chief wore flight helmets with internal headphones and microphones for intercom and radio. I immediately wished I had one to hear what they talked about, to know what was going on.

The sun burned off the morning haze to reveal a clear sky; the only clouds I could see were on the distant horizon. This made for smooth flying. In continued formation, we headed toward the southern tip of the country. After about an hour, the strip at Cam Mau came into sight. To me, the country looked pretty much as it did around Soc Trang.

We landed one by one from formation and kicked up clouds of dust. I saw hundreds of ARVN troops lining almost the entire length of the airstrip. These combat infantry units seemed well organized and wore full battle gear. The many small squads had distinctive colorful neck scarves: red, yellow, blue, green. I saw several American battalion advisors; they stood out because they were so much taller.

I unloaded my gear and put it down in the shade of some jeeps close to the command post, at one side near the mid-point of the airstrip. From here, I had a good view of the whole operation. At the far end of the dirt strip, I saw many fuel trucks loaded with aviation gasoline for refueling as the lifts progressed. I thought of my Harry Lime POL message: This would be that gas in the trucks. My last night in Saigon already seemed a long time ago.

The choppers made lift after lift. Troops loaded on and got dropped off in the landing zone about twenty minutes away. I watched and waited. There were no reports of any shots fired at the choppers or troops. None of our men had any injuries. I had nothing to do. Finally, late in the afternoon, the choppers were released to return to Soc Trang. Picking up my unused gear,

I loaded on Sput's chopper, and we took off for Soc Trang—an uneventful flight back.

"So, Doc. How'd it go?" Sput asked after we landed.

"Not much for me to do today."

"Then that's a very good day, buddy." Sput smiled.

SOC TRANG
THUR
6 DEC 62

I awoke refreshed. I had slept well after my first mission. Hungry, I enjoyed a full breakfast including scrambled eggs and sausage. With my gear, I made it to the flight line on time, ready to go. We left at 0615.

Cam Mau airstrip was again lined with ARVN troops on one side and fuel tanker trucks at the far end.

The choppers roared off for the first troop lift. I soon heard from radio communications at the command post that choppers were receiving sporadic VC gunfire in the landing zone. The Hueys fired heavy cover; the VC must be there.

After the first quick lift, they made two more. When they returned the third time, I saw one of the Huey gunships land and a crew chief drag off a muddy, black-garbed Vietnamese; I quickly realized this must be a VC captured by the ARVN and brought back to the command post for interrogation. I looked at him carefully—the first known VC I had ever seen. Similar to all the other rice farmers, he was short, wiry, with dark hair and eyes, dressed in black, but he looked stunned, angry, and scowling.

I knew he must be fearful. Only moments before, he had fired on the enemy government troops in a local rice field near his village. Suddenly captured, he had not only experienced his first flight ever, but in a noisy enemy helicopter, thrilling and terrifying for him, I felt sure. In a matter of only minutes, he had been plucked up and flown miles away from his family and friends. Now he was surrounded by the enemy military and armed Americans.

I stared closely as the guard walked the prisoner to the command center, where two Vietnamese officers took him aside for questioning. I didn't see him again. That was all right with me. I preferred not to see the face of an actual person, knowing he was an enemy. It was unsettling to know he and I—all of us—were here to kill or be killed. Even more unsettling was my awareness we were strangers, yet I was his enemy and he, mine. This stranger would be expected to shoot me, and in the same sense, I would be expected to shoot him. For sure, I preferred not to see the face of the enemy.

I felt glad to be a physician standing by at the airstrip to try and help save lives and not going into hostile countryside to take lives. I again wondered if I could ever shoot anyone. I thought back to Fort Sam and the .45 handgun training. As promised, I had one issued. It was back at Soc Trang. I hoped I'd never need it.

These thoughts quickly dissipated. I had business. One of the young crew chiefs had been hit with shrapnel. A bullet hit the fuselage near the door where he stood with his machine gun; aluminum fragments tore loose and struck him in the face. These metal particles fortunately missed his eyes and imbedded in his forehead. These wounds were superficial and would not require sutures. We both felt lucky.

SOC TRANG
FRI
7 DEC 62

A light day in Cam Mau—no action. The operation seemed somehow less organized, and we were released earlier than usual, which was a welcome relief. The evening briefing for the next mission seemed much like the one from the day before. I was feeling more confident.

Good news. My flight status orders arrived. Now official, I would see some extra pay. I noticed the date—December 7—Pearl Harbor Day. Twenty-one years later, we were still fighting.

CAM MAU
SAT
8 DEC 62

Day four of this six-day mission at Cam Mau almost seemed liked a routine job.

But today would not be routine. Our choppers had a run of bad luck.

Maj. Ewald, the new commanding officer of the Ninety-Third, who arrived only about a week before me, flew his first combat assault mission today. His co-pilot, a veteran of many missions, was flying his last before rotating home. When they were going into the landing zone for the first troop drop-off, they had a hard landing and slammed into a dike. Their crew chief was tossed around and suffered some bruising and a broken thumb. The chopper next to them also had a hard landing. Both helicopters remained flyable but too damaged for any more troop drops. A third chopper ran into the second but sustained only a little body damage.

It didn't end there. The LZ proved to be a rice field, and the mud acted like suction on the landing gear. Three choppers blew their engines trying to get enough power to get out.

That was still not all. After the morning troop drops were finally completed and the ARVN field operations were well under way, the choppers returned to the airstrip, landed, and shut down their engines one by one. The long line of helicopters was quickly re-fueled and the crews stood by, awaiting further orders to either go back and pick up the troops in the field or be released for the day.

A small fixed-wing Beaver landed on the dirt strip, and somehow, one of its wings clipped the rotors on three of the stationary H-21s.

My friend Sput, the maintenance officers from the Thirty-Third and Fifty-Seventh, and their mechanics all had their work cut out for them. And we still had two more days to finish up this never-ending operation. Capt. Brewster, at the early evening briefing, reported we would return to Cam Mau and try again. The ARVN were still looking for a VC headquarters and radio transmitter.

SOC TRANG
SUN
9 DEC 62

We flew back down to Cam Mau with a reduced number of choppers. To my knowledge, none of the choppers had been shot at while I had been aboard. If we had been fired on, I was not been aware of it. I did know for certain we hadn't been hit; nonetheless, I still sat on two flak jackets just in case.

Not much fighting reported. The ARVN aid station had no business, and neither did I. "A very good day," as Sput would say. He's right, of course. I did not hear if they found any VC headquarters or radios, but it seemed unlikely. All this troop movement and not much to show for it but busted-up choppers from yesterday.

Everyone knew the south Delta was VC country. The night belonged to them. They melted away during the day. Peasants and the VC guerrillas both wore black pajamas and looked alike. Who could tell who was who? I wondered if even the ARVN could sort them out; I knew the American advisors couldn't possibly.

During the last three days, VC snipers has occasionally fired at the choppers in the landing zones as the ARVN troops off-loaded. The VC were there. During the second troop drop today, one of our choppers was hit leaving the LZ. Luck was with the crew. The round passed within one inch of doing serious damage to the aircraft engine.

The ARVN burned down two hamlets, but even with the hundreds of troops the choppers ferried on the mission, few enemies were seen, killed, or captured. This seemed strange to me. Where were the VC? Why weren't the ARVN finding and fighting them?

In the early evening, I went to the O-Club and bought one of the new shirts with our tiger logo. The club manager had ordered white sport shirts with a jaunty tiger standing up wearing a bush hat. The local embroidery was exceptionally well done. I put mine on right away; almost everyone did.

Lt. Slick sat at the bar, and I perched on the stool next to him. I asked him to tell me about himself. Without hesitation, he obliged.

He told me he came from a family of fifth-generation land owners in Georgia. By high school, he knew he wanted to escape the South and life on the land. He and some friends got into a little mischief in high school, so his parents sent him to military school. He thrived with the structure of the new school and soon joined the Aero Club. He loved the freedom of learning to fly a Piper Cub. After graduation, he chose to attend Texas A&M to become an engineer and an officer. With the echo of the oral history of his family's struggle during the Civil War, the army seemed a natural fit. He aced flight training and loved anything that flew, even the H-21s, which were hard to love. He finished by saying he planned to retire early from the military and become a commercial pilot.

As Slick finished his story, Richard Tregaskis and Sput came in and sat at a nearby table.

"Hey Richard," Slick called out, "is it true we have a VIP coming to see the show tomorrow?"

Richard nodded. "That's affirmative. A senator from Wyoming. He's landing with the troops tomorrow."

Slick drawled, "He's in luck. We're not going back to Cam Mau tomorrow but to another garden spot, Rach Gia. On the Gulf of Siam."

"The senator is on a fact-finding mission. Wants to see firsthand where the taxpayers' money goes. He'll be flying directly to the pickup area with senior brass from Saigon."

"Care to join us, Doc?" Sput pointed to an empty chair.

"No, thanks. I'm going to turn in early." I headed back to hootch #4.

Although tired to the bone, I felt more confident as a veteran of five missions. So far, I had not had any serious injuries to deal with at the aid station. I probably felt most tired from the long hours waiting while the choppers were out dropping off troops.

Lying on my bunk, I read *Time* magazine from cover to cover, even the letters to the editor and the ads. I thought of Doc Greene for the first time in awhile. He should be home. I did not want to, but I couldn't help but envy him. I reminded myself he had already served his time, and I had been here just one week.

SOC TRANG
MON
10 DEC 62

Day six at Rach Gia proved to be long, tedious, and uneventful for us and the ARVN. I felt thankful that the long mission had finally ended. I needed to spend more time at the dispensary.

The pressure was off; the Soc Trang Tigers and the crews from the Thirty-Third and Fifty-Seventh could cut loose. The O-Club was packed. After a round of free drinks provided by our great club manager, we dug into a steak dinner. It's true, as they say: the army travels on its stomach.

This would be my opportunity to talk up the idea of a Christmas party for the kids from the orphanage and leprosarium. The guys were feeling generous, and I collected a lot of money. The party would be on, for sure.

I opened the screen door to go back to hootch #4 with my loot, when Richard Tregaskis stopped me.

"Did you see Senator Jackson today? He got out of the chopper with the troops, wet and muddy to the chest from the rice paddies."

"I missed him."

"Sorry. It was quite a sight. By the way, Doc, you going into Soc Trang for your preventive medicine rounds soon?"

"Tomorrow. Still want to come along?"

"I told you, I go where the action is." Richard smiled broadly and went into the night.

In my room, I realized I had no word on any new medics for the dispensary. Sgt. Sherk was not doing his work. He wasn't doing anything I could see. My new sergeant had been due in today. He hadn't shown up. I had not heard one word. This bad situation was getting worse.

SAIGON
TUES
11 DEC 62

President Diem did not want ARVN casualties, fearful too many might prompt dissatisfaction and lead to a military coup d'etat. To limit deaths and injury, Diem issued verbal orders to the Vietnamese field commanders and province chiefs not to launch offensive operations. He did not want to commit the ARVN forces to engage and fight the VC. He thought he needed these troops in reserve to defend his family in the event disloyal units in the army decided to overthrow his government.

This strategy had worked before. On November 11, 1960, dissident paratroopers attacked the presidential palace trying to force government reform. Diem stalled them until loyal Colonel Cao had time to bring troops up from My Tho to successfully crush the uprising.

President Diem's verbal order—kept secret from the Americans—prompted rumors. When General Harkins, MACV Commander, heard these rumors, he confronted Diem directly about a no-casualty order. Diem denied ever giving this order and described in detail the many talks he had given the ARVN and province chiefs about taking the offensive—to attack and be aggressive whenever and wherever VC were found.

Diem's performance convinced General Harkins, and he renewed support for the government. MACV continued to relay inflated body counts and spurious reports of ARVN operations back to the Pentagon. General Harkins disputed or ignored the pessimistic reports sent to him by his own U.S. advisors and journalists out in the field.

Diem's no-attack policy gave the VC confidence and provided opportunity to recruit peasants to their cause. Diem's policy meant certain defeat, but his staff dared not oppose him. They knew better.

Diem insisted on control and would not allow American advisors to give the ARVN any orders or to interfere with his tactics. Many in the ARVN leadership went along with this plan, fearful of the effective VC and their determined leadership. Sorties and operations were planned for locations where the VC would not be engaged. ARVN refused the U.S. advisors' advice for risky night operations, even though the Americans pushed for this repeatedly. In the night and darkness, the VC moved around freely.

President Diem knew JFK and the Americans were single-minded about not letting the Communists win after having lost China. As long as his family and regime were anti-Communist, Diem reasoned he could stay in power. If the VC became too threatening, he assumed the Americans would come to Vietnam's aid and fight, and the Ngo family government would persist. Eventually, he would prevail and could rule as a modern Mandarin for a new Vietnam.[7]

SOC TRANG
TUES
11 DEC 62

The airfield hummed with activity in the early morning as H-21s, Hueys, and T-28s all went back to their home bases. This Cam Mau offensive had been a big deal. No wonder the POL officer whistled when I gave him that message. We used lots of gas.

I finished work in the late mid-afternoon and drove my jeep to headquarters, where Richard waited for me. He folded his too-long legs to fit in the front passenger seat. We left the barricaded front gate and quickly made the short trip to town. Richard yelled over the noise of the wind in the open jeep, "What's Soc Trang like?"

"I've only been there a couple of times," I said. "It's pretty busy. The people seem friendly, a mixture of Vietnamese, Cambodians who came down the river, some old-timer Chinese, and lots of shopkeepers from India."

In town, the streets were crowded as usual. Small stores with open fronts stocked cameras, watches, bolts of colorful fabrics, fish, herbal medicines, and cigarettes from America, Turkey, and

Egypt. Elderly men sat smoking at small tea and noodle shops and idly watched us drive by.

"The leprosarium is just off this road." I nodded my head to the left. "And across the next river, there's an orphanage run by Catholic nuns."

We drove by busy mothers dressed in either black or white *au dai* and conical hats, followed by small children wearing loose pajama pants with the bottoms conveniently cut out. Worn without diapers or underwear, this practical design allowed young children to be ready for quick squats over the edge of the river.

The usually bustling central market was almost empty this late in the day, but next door, the movie theater was already busy.

We passed the Buddhist temple. I pointed toward the hooked cross—a large swastika—above the entrance.

"Yeah," Richard said. "An auspicious symbol for the Buddhists. That ancient sign is shared with the Celtics, Greeks, Hindus, Native Americans, even people in the Himalayas."

"Too bad the Nazis ruined it."

Richard nodded his head in agreement.

We drove to the next block, and I pointed toward a whitish-gray colonial building covered with mildew. Once elegant, it was surrounded by an untended garden. "The province chief lives in that old French villa."

On the right was a similar but less grand colonial villa. "Most U.S. military advisors live over there across the street in that house. A few live in a hotel right downtown. Other than seeing the few river barges that sell beer ... that's about it."

"And the girls?"

"At three or four bars and a couple of hotels." I turned the jeep off the road near the graveyard and stopped in front of a large, two-story Victorian house that would looked more at home in Illinois than Asia. "This one's The Bungalow. Our first stop." I picked up my little black bag.

We crossed the empty porch and entered a spacious front room with a high ceiling. Fans slowly revolved to circulate the warm, stale air. The room was furnished with a few well-worn sofas, tables, and chairs. A small bar stood in the corner.

MaMa came toward us. She bowed slightly and said the Vietnamese word for doctor, "*Bac si.*" She appeared middle-aged, but her dyed jet-black hair, secured in a tight bun at the back of her neck, gave her a youthful look. Dressed in a purple *au dai*, she moved gracefully. "A drink? You? You friend?"

That would be about all of her English vocabulary. I shook my head, "No. No thank you." I pointed to my black bag and then toward the three young girls who gathered to watch from the landing at the top of the stairs. MaMa smiled again, her teeth stained and crooked, and she bowed slightly.

Richard towered over this small, thin woman. After declining her suggestion for "boom-boom," at her invitation, he sat on a velvet couch with a soft drink in hand. I started up the long flight of stairs on the left side of the room and overheard her tell him, "He number-one *bac si.*"

I had met her briefly before when Doc Greene brought me by on our one quick trip to town together. Obviously, she was pleased and relieved I would continue this unauthorized and informal public-health duty. I had heard from a reliable source that the VC came here much later in the night after the GI's curfew. I assumed they would be pleased as well.

"I'll be right back," I called over my shoulder to Richard as I reached the top of the long, open staircase. The young women, standing there waiting, smiled. Two had fine features of the usually pretty Vietnamese, but the third had a broad face with coarser features.

We all went into the first open door on the left. The room had a bed, small chest, nightstand, and a light with a shade covered by a red scarf. One girl hopped on the bed, pulled down her pants, and exposed her right buttock. She had done this before. The other two politely backed out of the room and closed the door to give us privacy. They waited in the hall for their turns.

With the antibiotics administered, the four of us went downstairs together. Richard was still attempting to talk with the hostess. She would never master much more than the most basic English, but what she knew worked for her.

He looked up and said, "That was quick."

The girls laughed and implied the four of us had "quickie bang-bang." The girl with the coarse face asked Richard, "You? Quickie bang-bang?"

He smiled his wide grin and declined.

As we drove away, MaMa waved from the front door.

"That old Japanese rating thing still persists: good, number one, or really bad, number ten. Doc Hoyland, I'd say they think you're number one *bac si*," Richard laughed. "So much for quickie bang-bang. Where next?"

"The hotels, then The Paradise Bar. Hannah, one of our civilian employees at the O-Club, owns The Paradise. She speaks English. Maybe you've seen her."

By the time we reached The Paradise, a crescent moon rose in the velvety night. A red neon sign showed through the anti-grenade screen in front of the small stucco building. Four young boys played noisily in the street and paid no attention to us. They had tied black water bugs, six inches long or longer, on strings. The delighted boys held one end of the string while about four feet over their heads, the captive beetle-like insects flew around and around in frantic circles, buzzing wings making loud engine-like noises for these improvised toy helicopters that required no batteries.

Hannah stood behind the small bar. She had bright eyes and a pleasant almond-shaped face, but her complexion was marred by deep pox scars on her cheeks and forehead. With no fear of Americans, she smiled and called out, "Hello, *bac si*." Before I could respond, she opened two beers.

I pointed to my black bag, and she took me to the back, explaining that only one girl would be available right then for an injection.

By the time I returned, Hannah was well along in telling Richard her life story. I had already heard the first part back at the O-Club.

Born in Hanoi, she was now thirty-two years old. As a young woman, she married an older, wealthy businessman. When the Communist Viet Minh took over, they killed her husband. She took all their cash, gold, and her jewelry and escaped with their seven-year-old son in a fast powerboat, headed south. The boat broke down from mechanical failure, and they were adrift. A French vessel picked them up. She had to give her entire savings to the crew, but they put her and her son ashore in Da Nang.

She told Richard, "I get job with army. Learn English from boyfriend. He sergeant in U.S. Army. We live together four months. He good to my son."

Since no one else was in the tiny bar, Hannah continued with a distant look in her eyes, "I move Soc Trang and work airbase. Buy bar. Save money. Son sixteen now. He good boy. I send him school one day. Paris. Sergeant back in States now. He write me all time. He get divorce. One day come back for me. I marry sergeant. Go U.S. one day. He write all time."

I looked at my watch; we were way past curfew. "We'd better go, Richard." I reached for my billfold to pay for the beers, but Hannah shook her head.

"You no pay. You give shot, *bac si.* Thank you." She bowed politely. As we left, she wiped the bar and put away the empty bottles.

Driving back to the airfield, I saw the streets were still busy and noisy.

"What's next for you, Richard?" I asked.

"Tomorrow, I'm headed back up north with the marines for a few days." He paused, looking at the crowd. "Then it's about time to head home to Honolulu. I've got plenty of material for my book. Should have. I've been here since October. I think I'll go back right after the New Year."

We approached the airfield gates. I turned off the lights and rolled to a stop. Vietnamese and U.S. military police guards gave us a close look. It was dark and late. I returned the salute. We passed through, and I noticed the glint from the familiar rows of concertina wire.

"Home sweet home," I said. "Never thought I'd welcome living behind a barbed-wire fence."

"War does strange things, crazy things, to all of us," Richard sighed.

At home, we took individual freedom for granted, I thought to myself. Here, in a war, things were different—including me.

SOC TRANG
WED
12 DEC 62

I entered the mess hall for breakfast as Trey and Billy T. were just leaving, both all smiles.

"What's up?" I said.

"Doc, we're off to the 'ville for an overnight," Trey laughed. "So don't wait up for us or leave the lights on."

"Saigon, here we come," Billy T. yelled.

"Don't forget Madame Nhu's morality laws," I said. "You guys dance with a bar girl and you might end up in the brig."

"I hadn't planned on dancing much," Trey laughed. "We're only gonna be there one night."

"Be careful," I said, but they were already out of earshot.

That evening in the O-Club, Maj. Ewald announced in his official-sounding voice, "All in favor, say aye." The crowd voted, and with unanimous support, I found myself on the new building committee. With the city of Soc Trang frequently off-limits, by default, the club became the social and recreational center of our little world. The committee, which included Trey and Charley, the club manager, would collect money from the members and oversee the timely building of an addition to our club.

"Doc, don't forget, now. We need a place to watch movies. Little Lee Roy don't like that outdoor setup at the hangar at all," Slick drawled. "Only the water bugs do."

"Here, here," echoed around the room.

Slick saw Sput enter. "Hey, Sput. Short-timers are welcome."

Sput, beer in hand, joined our table.

"How much time you got left?" I asked.

"Should be spending the night up at Tan Son Nhut in exactly one month and somewhere over the Pacific the next day."

"What's the news from home?" I asked.

"Francine says she's looking forward to giving me a big welcome."

"Whoo boy," Slick said as he raised his glass toward Sput. "You're as good as caught."

WASHINGTON, DC
WED
12 DEC 62

President Kennedy said at a press conference: "We don't see the end of the tunnel, but I must say I don't think it is darker than it was a year ago, and in some ways lighter." In recognition of the growing conflict, he authorized combat decorations for military personnel stationed in Vietnam.[8]

SOC TRANG
THUR
13 DEC 62

At dinner in the mess hall, I encountered a smiling Trey. "How was the overnight?"

"Outstanding," he beamed. "Met the most beautiful girl in town but had to tell her I'd be going home soon. What a shame to deprive her of my company." He sighed. "My last Saigon run."

After chow, Slick, Sput, and I headed for the officers' club. Tiger, the brown pup, had been patiently waiting outside the mess hall and fell in behind. The little dog abruptly turned and barked at a new pilot none of us had met before.

"Sorry 'bout that, Captain." Sput quickly looked at the name tag on the flight suit—Peabody. He scooped up the dog and added, "Meet Tiger, our mascot. This pilot's best friend."

"What kind of ferocity is this?" Peabody said. Tiger's tail wagged furiously as he licked the new captain's extended hand. "I'm John. Last name's pronounced like the letters *P B D*."

John Armstrong Peabody, who looked to be in his mid-twenties, had blond hair cut short that matted to his forehead from the heat and humidity. A receding hairline framed his broad face with an *M*. His eyes, in constant motion, gave the impression he was a seeker of both information and mischief.

"You'll have to excuse Tiger, Captain PBD, sir," Slick drawled. "He's from the south of Vietnam. Not used to Yankees."

Peabody's gray-blue eyes lit up with a mischievous grin. "I'm from Connecticut." He spoke with a pure, clipped New England accent.

"I rest my case, your honor." Slick gave a slight bow of self-satisfaction.

"How do you know I'm a Yankee?" Well over six feet tall, he looked down at Cody, who measured about five feet ten inches.

"The funny way you talk." Slick said slowly. "This is Doc; this is Sput; and I'm Cody, but my friends call me Slick. We're on our way to the O-Club. I'd like to buy Captain PBD, the FNG, a drink."

"I'd be honored," PBD said. We resumed walking toward the club, Tiger still following behind. "So what have I missed so far?"

"You just missed meeting Richard Tregaskis," I said. "A well-known writer."

"That tall, skinny civilian with big feet wearing camouflage gear and an Aussie hat? He's hard to miss; boarded the Caribou when I got off here yesterday. I wondered who he was."

"Yep," Slick said. "He wrote *Guadalcanal Diary* about World War II. Now he's doing one on us."

"He flew with me on a couple of missions last week," Sput said. "Good man."

"He told me I'm going to be in his book," Slick said. "Old Lieutenant Cody Williams in a book. How 'bout that?"

"You better wait and see what he writes," PBD laughed.

Sput stopped by the door to the club and filled Tiger's water bowl. The dog drank noisily, tail in constant motion.

Slick opened the door. "Welcome to our den; you're a Tiger now."

With longneck brown bottles all around, we lifted them in a toast: "To Soc Trang and better days."

"You also just missed a big-ass assault mission." Sput took a long swig. "A six-day operation. We flew in over three hundred Vietnamese troops each day, but they only managed to get about thirty confirmed dead. The VC somehow just floated away, disappeared."

Slick shook his head. "The VC are mighty shifty. You have to hand it to them." He took another drink. "We busted our balls and spent *beaucoup* taxpayers' dollars for thirty VC." Slick shook his head again. "To say nothing about the damage to our choppers.

"We could've paid those suckers a million each to quit fighting for good, and we'd have come out ahead."

"What's our commanding officer like?" PBD said.

"Major Ewald's a fair and honest man," Sput said. "He's just had a couple spots of bad luck. On his first mission, we were flying a resupply to Father Hoa's, and a VC got a bullet through his engine. Then about a week ago, on his first assault mission down in Cam Mau, he and a pilot from the Thirty-Third cracked up. Nothing bad, but he wasn't happy."

"On a lighter note," Slick said and gave two thumbs-up, "we're soon going to have a proper club to wile away our leisure."

"Doc here," Sput turned to face me, "is on the building committee. How's it coming along?"

"Pretty well. Signed off on the plans. The contractor's done work out here before, so he and his crew are cleared for security," I said.

"What's it like?" Slick asked.

I told them the Vietnamese contractor had designed a large, screened-in addition. He planned to take out windows on the street side and make a doorway to connect the two rooms. It would be one open room with plenty of tables and chairs. Simple and inexpensive, it would more than double the size of the club. He would pour the slab in two days and then start on the framing.

"Nothing but the best for the Ninety-Third Tigers," Slick growled as he lifted his bottle again in the direction of the rest of the patrons.

"Here, here," echoed around the room.

"In the meantime, gentlemen," I addressed the room, "we still need a little more cash for the Christmas party."

The generous pilots threw wads of cash to the center of the bar.

"That should just about do the job. Thanks."

PBD looked puzzled. "Christmas party?"

"For some kids at the orphanage in town," Sput said.

"Yeah, and some children at the leprosarium. They're normal, but someone in their family had the bad luck to get leprosy. When that happens, the whole family moves in to the colony—out of sight, out of mind."

"Those kids won't have a clue about Christmas, but at least they'll get out," Sput said.

PBD said, "I like kids. I'll be Santa."

"Would you want to go with me when I make a run into the orphanage, PBD? I plan to take in some supplies Saturday," I said.

"I'd like that. I really would." PBD nodded.

SOC TRANG
SAT
15 DEC 62

PBD met me at the dispensary, and I drove the jeep over to the mess hall. The cooks helped us load milk, flour, sugar, and some cartons of Kellogg's cereals.

We pulled up in front of the Catholic orphanage housed in an ochre stucco French building. A tall, imposing older Caucasian nun in black habit with starched white wimple came out the front door in welcome. PBD and I introduced ourselves, and I thought the sister told us her name was Sister Mary Cecil; with her heavy French-Vietnamese accent, I could not be sure. The French sister was followed by a small Vietnamese nun also dressed in a black habit, her dark eyes framed by round gold spectacles. Following closely was a third nun who looked almost exactly like the second, but younger and no glasses. All three had the smiles of saints.

As this was my first trip to the orphanage, I attempted introductions. I didn't know any Vietnamese; the oldest nun spoke French. I had studied French briefly in college, and even though it had been several years in the past, I could at least understand some of her words. By no small miracle, she picked up some of mine. She spoke such fluent Vietnamese, I assumed she must have come here as a young woman.

The sisters took us into a large, oblong room with high ceilings. Cribs and small beds filled the ward, lined up in long rows; each contained an infant or young child. I guessed there to be about sixty. It was strangely quiet, as few were crying, but coming from one crib in the corner, I heard a child's pitiable, thin-pitched shriek that sounded more like a frightened animal.

When I looked into the cribs, I saw infants and babies of indeterminate ages. Most had startling bright eyes and cheeks sunken from dehydration. Sheets, in the cribs that had any, were pieces of grayish material covering bamboo crib mats. Many children had skin abscesses, and I feared all had staph infections and diarrhea.

Another Vietnamese nun went from crib to crib to tend the babies. Bothersome black common houseflies were everywhere, flying through unscreened open windows and doors, crawling over abscesses and tiny ears, eyes, and noses. Most of the children were just prone without enough energy to even move and drive off the crawling flies.

I understood enough to learn most of these children had been left at the orphanage by widows whose husbands had been killed in the war, some loyal to the government, some VC. The sisters didn't ask; it didn't matter. Many came from the strategic hamlets. All were desperate.

PBD and I unloaded the supplies, and the nuns were overjoyed. They loved everything but seemed puzzled by the brightly colored individual cereal boxes. We opened one and ate a few of the brown flakes. We gave them the box, and they each daintily sampled the cereal. These dignified nuns nearly jumped up and down with delight. They could not believe this food did not need preparation but was ready to eat. They knew their older children in another building would be thrilled as well with this new treat.

When we left, the nuns all bowed and waved good-bye.

At first, neither of us spoke on the way back to the airfield.

I finally said, "That's overwhelming."

"Thanks for taking me, but I don't ever want to go back. It's too much," PBD said softly as he looked in the distance.

"It is, but there's a plan to get some money together to buy them a washing machine. Think of what that would do."

"You can count on me for that, for sure," PBD sighed.

SOC TRANG
SUN
16 DEC 62

The December weather was warm and sunny during the day with pleasant cool nights. Christmas carols at the O-Club seemed very weird in this tropical climate. Maj. E. announced an early Christmas present: Soc Trang would no longer be off-limits after dark. Curfew was to be extended to 2200 hours. Admittedly, there was not a lot to do in town, but it helped everyone to have someplace to go other than just the clubs.

I took Duc as an interpreter, and we went to the leprosarium and orphanage. We invited their children, aged five to twelve, to a Christmas party. The men were busy buying and wrapping small gifts.

SOC TRANG
MON
17 DEC 62

"Meet Captain Davis," Maj. Ewald said as we entered the mess hall. "CO of the Eighteenth Aviation Operating Detachment."

Capt. Hartley Davis and I shook hands. A slender man about my height, he had dark olive skin, gray eyes, and gray hair. We shook hands. He had a firm grip and sly smile. I liked him immediately.

When we were seated at the table with our chow, I asked Capt. Davis, "Operating Detachment? What do you do?"

"Air traffic control, help plan flights, instrument coordination."

Maj. Ewald said, "And boy, am I glad they're here."

"We just came in from Okinawa."

"How many in your unit?"

"Forty-four men, including me and four other officers."

"He'll be hitting you all up to help with the Christmas party," Maj. Ewald said with a smile.

"We're having it out here next Tuesday for some of the children in town," I said.

"You gotta watch out for Doc Hoyland, our social chairman," laughed the major, "always collecting for something."

Capt. Davis smiled. "I have a wife and two little boys back home. It's hard not being there. A party for kids sounds like the ticket."

SAIGON
SAT
22 DEC 62

President Diem frequently restructured the ARVN command to keep his senior officers from organizing against him. Of twenty generals, only four had actual commands. With the new year approaching, he had divided the existing three corps into four. The new IV Corps included all of the Mekong Delta. With headquarters in Can Tho, Col. Cao would be in command, rewarded by Diem for loyalty and not having too many ARVN casualties in 1962. Col. Cao was promoted to brigadier general.

Cao knew his first duty was to protect President Diem, and he would be prepared at any time to use his troops to defend the Ngo family in the event of an attempted coup. He had done this in 1960 and gained the undying favor of the president and the Nhus.

Unknown to U.S. advisors, Diem removed command of the armed personnel carriers in the Dinh Tuong Province from the ARVN and had given that command to the provincial chief. APCs were greatly feared by the VC, but the decision to change control did not come from a plan to fight the VC; instead, it came from Diem's worries about a coup. He knew he could count on the support of his loyal provincial chief but not necessarily the military. Diem's control of these APCs would be critical if his regular military revolted.

To make the failing ARVN effort look better, the government continued false after-action reports with inflated "VC casualties." For lack of a better measure of progress in this borderless guerilla war, "the body count" had been adopted.

Even if honestly reported, this would be unreliable. The VC carried off their dead for burial. Therefore, many of the bodies counted were civilian men and women—collateral damage.[9]

SOC TRANG
MON
24 DEC 62

Charcoal-grilled steaks were on the menu to celebrate Christmas Eve. Good steak. Good idea.

SOC TRANG
TUES
25 DEC 62

In my mail today, I received several Christmas cards; they seemed as out of place as "Oh Holy Night" in this warm and sunny land. It was cold and often snowy where I grew up in the Ozarks. But it would still be Christmas here and all over the world.

The mess hall provided some holiday cheer and a proper feast. Several Special Forces officers and troops, in from the hamlets and villages where they lived primitive lives, joined us for dinner at noon. We had shrimp cocktail, eggnog, turkey, giblet gravy, sliced ham, both sweet and mashed potatoes, stuffing, corn, green beans, several salads, pumpkin pie, fruit cake, ice cream, mixed nuts, and candy. No one could eat another bite. An amazing feast—I was totally impressed with our cooks' efforts.

"Doc Hoyland." Two men wearing green berets came up to me as I left the mess hall, stuffed. "I'm Captain Clay from Dutah, and this is our medic, Sergeant Runnion."

I had heard of this Special Forces camp not too far out of town. We shook hands. "How are you fixed for Tetracycline?" Sgt. Runnion asked.

"We could sure use some. We're out," I said.

Sgt. Runnion reached into a canvas bag and pulled out four bottles. "Doc Greene said he was running low last time I was here. Merry Christmas."

"Great. Really appreciate this. We haven't received any supplies since before I arrived," I said. "Called Saigon, but there's some hang-up. Anything you need? If we've got it, it's yours."

"Not right now, but I'll check in when I do. In the meantime, let me know if you need something we've got."

"Come see us," Capt. Clay said. "Spend the night. We'd like to return the hospitality. Great meal."

"Spend the night? I'd like that," I lied. "Merry Christmas." I waved as they took off in a MAAG jeep for downtown.

It was time for the children's party; we had transportation all lined up.

Two large, empty army trucks and two jeeps roared out from the airfield security gates. Dust and exhaust followed us down the highway into Soc Trang's main street. I was in the first truck. We turned onto the unpaved lane to the leprosarium; the engine noise echoed loudly in the usually quiet colony isolated from, but surrounded by, the city. The residents, elders and families, stood in a clump, waiting in the shade of a palm grove. They looked uncertain but excited.

I counted ten children of various ages and sizes. They looked like little adults in their best pajama garb, but theirs were in many colors. The youngest held hands with their older trusted companions. Animated with anticipation, the children all politely bowed their heads and crossed their arms to show respect.

"We'll take good care of them," I told the elder. I knew he did not speak English, but I could tell he understood. The parents smiled with stained or absent teeth and politely bowed. I could not help but notice the many deformities from Hansen's disease, as leprosy was now called: fingers absent, nose and facial distortions, limbs crippled, all dreadful. By contrast, the children were untouched physically. They were attractive and appealing and had lots of youthful energy. I thought how difficult it must be for them to be so segregated in this colony.

I waved my arm for them to get in the truck. They squealed in delight and ran up to our military truck driver, dressed not in combat fatigues and boots but in a khaki uniform with polished shoes. He effortlessly lifted the thin, bright-eyed children. They found seats on the facing benches that normally transported soldiers and shyly exchanged grins with one another. The brave looks and shy expressions immediately changed to wide smiles when the powerful engine started up and we moved forward—their first ride ever in a big truck.

Both jeeps and the second truck went to the orphanage, where the scene would be very similar. Fifteen scrubbed children, dressed in their best, and two adult helpers got in the back of the truck. Five Sisters, dignified in their black habits but as excited as the children, climbed in the jeeps.

At the airfield, the guests quickly unloaded and talked animatedly to one another as they met more soldiers and walked over to one of the H-21s in front of the giant hangar. They stared at this huge iron bird they had seen fly over their city for the first time only three months ago. When they realized they had permission to climb on it, even the girls climbed in and out and under in front and back. This unexpected opportunity proved irresistible even to the Sisters who, with assistance, clamored inside the hold of the chopper.

Maj. Ewald came over to the group of children. Wiry and just over six feet tall, he seemed scrappy in a good way, a man who would neither provoke nor avoid a fight. He could stand up for himself, and you felt he would stand up for you as well. He was a popular officer and a good commanding officer.

He effortlessly picked up a small girl, a live Oriental doll with penetrating eyes. She contentedly stared at his Caucasian face and light brown hair. This was the first time she had ever seen white skin so close. She touched his left cheek, and a delighted laugh escaped him.

"She's just about my little girl's age, Jay," Maj. Ewald said. "God, I miss her."

"How old?"

"Five. My boys are eight and ten."

"Where are they?"

"With my wife and her folks in Iowa. I've missed the last two Christmases with them." He looked at the little girl's delighted face.

Two boys, chased by another boy, grabbed the major's legs for protection. "Times like this," he sighed heavily, "I wonder if this man's army is worth it."

"Cartoons in the mess hall," someone yelled.

Maj. Ewald hoisted the small girl up to carry her on his shoulders. I picked up one of the boys and carried him on my shoulders. The children shrieked. Military hosts, children, and Sisters all galloped to the mess hall, where a small tree had been concocted from palm fronds. Brightly colored hard candy hung from the green leaves. A mystery to our young guests, but they seemed to like the idea.

It was movie time. The generous officer who showed our films at the O-Club had set up the projector to show some short cartoons. Once settled on the benches, the children watched in delight. The movies were in English, but the humor proved universal. Children and nuns laughed and clapped.

Following the last cartoon, the screen went dark. The sound of sleigh bells brought complete silence; the children looked at one another in curiosity.

Capt. PBD, dressed in a Santa suit the Ninety-Third brought last year on the ship from Fort Devens, arrived to greet them. He handed out to each child small gifts bought and wrapped by many of the enlisted men. Beyond young comprehension, the strangeness of the custom did not deter their wonderment as they unwrapped the toys: cars, trucks, yo-yos for the boys; small dolls with moveable limbs for the girls. They clutched their first commercial toys. One GI's mother had sent over a large bolt of cloth. When Santa gave this to one of the Sisters, she was overcome, thinking of all the clothes she could make for the children.

The final gift brought clapping and more tears, this time not just from the Sisters. Maj. Ewald removed a sheet covering a brand-new washing machine for the orphanage. The men of the Ninety-Third had contributed enough money to have it ready to go. We explained our engineers would deliver and install it soon. Everyone beamed.

A cook yelled, "Ice cream!"

The cooks brought out frozen containers from the freezer and a large sheet cake from the kitchen. One cook cut the cake; another placed ample portions on paper plates. Two others scooped vanilla ice cream to go with the chocolate cake with chocolate frosting. When served, the children fell silent, first looking at this strange, white frozen ball next to the cake, and then at one another. An older venturesome boy giggled and put his index finger into the cold mass. The others watched as this young friend tasted his sample. Without hesitation, he smiled and began to eat. They all joined him with enthusiasm.

I looked at my watch. We needed to leave right away. We had to get our guests home at the time we agreed upon.

The wondrous treats were consumed and the children clutched their gifts and gabbed excitedly as the men and officers helped load them back on the trucks. Children and nuns—briefly taken from their Soc Trang lives to another world—waved farewell. They roared off back down the familiar road to resume their daily lives, while at the airfield, we would resume our routines.

We arrived back at the leprosarium, and I saw anxious families waiting for us under the same palm trees. They heard the truck first and then saw their children laughing and talking. With relief and pleasure, the parents shouted, waved their arms, and laughed in shared delight. The children quickly got down from the truck and, clutching their presents, told of amazing adventures. We all waved to one another, and the elders bowed. Our truck left only dusty clouds as we sped back down the lane.

That evening in the club, I saw PBD. "Captain Santa, sir. You did a fine job. Thank you."

"No, Jay. Thank the kids. The looks on their faces when they first saw me, when they realized those dinky little toys were theirs to keep … I'll never forget that. Ever."

WASHINGTON, DC
WED
26 DEC 62

In December 1961, there were 3,200 American military in Vietnam. In December, 1962, there were 11,300.[10]

SOC TRANG
THUR
27 DEC 62

Cardinal Spellman from New York had been traveling up and down Vietnam to celebrate Christmas Mass. When he arrived at Soc Trang airfield, we pulled up a flatbed truck in the middle of the hangar to raise the altar so everyone could see.

The province chief and his family from town attended. There were many ARVN Catholic officers and their families. I saw several civilians. There were no enlisted men, as they were mostly Buddhist. Almost all of us at the air base attended. After Mass, the Cardinal gave a short, inspirational talk. Although he didn't stay long, we appreciated the fact this elderly man came halfway around the globe to visit our outpost to try and give us added meaning for Christmas.

Our army chaplain stationed in Saigon, Father O'Brien, came along and assisted with the Mass. A favorite of ours, he looked as if he had come from central casting. A genial, smiling Irish man from Boston with ruddy skin, blue eyes, and thin, white hair, he had a great sense of humor and knew lots of jokes that began, "There was a priest, a minister, and a rabbi ..."

SOC TRANG
FRI
28 DEC 62

At breakfast, Sput, PBD, Slick, and Trey were sitting on benches at the end of a long table drinking coffee.

PBD looked up as I entered. "Doc, I need your help here. Don't you agree we need a proper mascot? We're not the Soc Trang Pups, for God's sake."

Sput said, "Watch what you say about Tiger pup."

"We're the Tigers. What we need is a real tiger. With teeth! These guys," PBD indicated the scattered crowd eating at the long tables, "are wimps."

"And there's Charlie, the monkey, don't forget," Slick said.

The monkey joined us when the air traffic controllers arrived. On the ship coming over from Okinawa, some of them traded the Japanese crew extra C-rations for it; fortunately, no bites reported so far.

"He's a pet. Not a mascot," PBD said with feigned indignation.

"Get real, man," Trey said. "Where could we get a tiger down here?"

"Little Lee Roy don't know nothin' about tigers," Slick said, "not one thing."

I sat down next to Sput with my coffee and full plate of pancakes and bacon. "We're listening, PBD."

"Captain Jones, a friend of mine from flight-school days, flew fixed-wing in Laos. While he was there, some Special Forces buddies picked up an orphaned Royal Bengal tiger cub. Jonesy took it to raise in his apartment, got him a leash so they could go on walks and everything. When the U.S. got kicked out of there, he took the cub to the embassy in Thailand. Marine embassy guards are taking care of it for now."

"So?" I took a gulp of coffee.

"So," PBD said, "Captain Jones flew through here yesterday. We had a quick visit. He felt sorry for us bastards; thought we should have Tuffy—that's his name. Think of it, a real tiger for a mascot."

"I am thinking, and I'm thinking it's a bad idea," I said.

"And our CO? What do you think the old man would say?" Sput said with a mocking tone.

"We went right over to headquarters and I asked him. Major Ewald said, 'Okay. It'll be good for morale.' He said we'd have to have some kind of cage first, though."

PBD beamed as he continued, "I went straight over to the engineers. They agreed to build a tiger hootch out of one of those metal shipping containers."

"Who'd take care of it?" I asked.

"How old is he?" Slick asked.

"We will." PBD's enthusiasm was contagious. "He's eight months old. Born in March."

Trey beamed. "Great. Wait till the VC hear we have a tiger. They'll think a long time before hitting us."

Sput yelled, "Whoo boy! Little Lee Roy's ready."

I groaned. "You're nuts. You three are just nuts."

"Too bad, spoil sport. Tuffy is as good as on his way." PBD lifted his coffee mug in a salute.

The others in the mess hall had been listening attentively to the conversation. Trey lifted his cup. "Hell, yes. We're Soc Trang Tigers. Bring him on."

"Consider it done, gentlemen." PBD smiled in victory.

Clapping filled the mess hall. I felt like a sore loser when I didn't join in.

SAIGON
FRI
28 DEC 62

During a fly-over, Vietnamese intelligence picked up signals from a guerilla VC radio in the My Tho area, about thirty-five miles south of Saigon. The ARVN joint general staff ordered the new General Cao and the Seventh Infantry to disrupt the headquarters and capture the radio at hamlet Bac.[11]

SOC TRANG
MON
31 DEC 62

Everyone planned to go to the New Year's Eve party at the club. Not much to celebrate, but it would be a good diversion. 1962 had been eventful. What would 1963 bring? Where would I be New Year's Eve next year?

SOC TRANG
TUES
1 JAN 63

In the late afternoon, we crowded in operations for a briefing. Maj. Ewalt announced that President Diem reorganized the Army of Vietnam as of the new year. He had split the old III Corps into two. Saigon and surrounding provinces would be in the new III Corps; the Mekong Delta would be in the new IV Corps. I hoped this would make the ARVN more effective and get better results.

Capt. Brewster, wearing his casual uniform of shorts, T-shirt, and flip-flops, stood in front by the large map. "Gentlemen, tomorrow we'll kick off the new year with a major combined effort. We have choppers from the Thirty-Third and Fifty-Seventh, but we run the show.

"We're going up to this old SDC training site about twenty-nine miles south of Saigon." Capt. Brewster pointed with his index finger on the map.

I listened to the briefing and couldn't help but think those airstrips and names were starting to run together. As usual, I would set up an aid station in case any of our crew or advisors in the field got injured. Dust Off, the Huey med evac choppers from Saigon, would stand by if I needed to evacuate any Americans to the field hospital.

"Northwest of My Tho," Capt. Brewster used the pointer, "are two adjacent hamlets, Bac and Tan Thoi, population of about six hundred each. Intelligence tells us Bac," he moved his pointer a little south, "is a VC headquarters and has a radio transmitter. It's estimated 120 regular VC, if that many, are at this location. Our staging area is nearby at the Tan Hiep airstrip. Our mission will be to drop the whole ARVN battalion in quickly. We could use thirty but will have only ten choppers—all we can muster.

"Two battalions of civil guards are going to march up from the south. There will be thirteen armored personnel carriers, including a flame thrower, here." He pointed to the map. "Paratroopers in Saigon will be on standby and can be called in for a drop, if needed. The ARVN will provide artillery support. U.S. and VN Air Force will be on alert with T-28s and a B-26."

I hoped this big mission would get the new year off to a good start. It was officially 1963! I would be going home "this year." That was much better than "next year." No longer an FNG, I knew lots of guys who would be here next November when I left for Home Sweet CONUS.

BAC/TAN THOI
TUES
1 JAN 63
2200

In the quiet and darkness of the hamlet Bac, the VC commander of the 261st Main Force Battalion finished his planning for the night. Earlier in the afternoon, VC agents in My Tho had sent him word that they saw truckloads of ammo arriving from Saigon. Certain the ARVN would attack on January 2, 1963, the commander had about 320 Main Force and Regional Guerrillas in and around Tan Thoi and Bac. He knew he could also count on at least thirty men, women, and older boys of the villages to help out as medics, ammo bearers, and scouts.

This was going to be an important battle. He and his Communist provincial leaders, all seasoned Viet Minh fighters, fought the Japanese in World War II and successfully resisted the French. They were confident. But the local peasants in the villages feared the Americans were much stronger than either the Japanese or the French.

With the introduction of U.S. helicopters, it had been more difficult for the VC. The ARVN threatened the Communist hold in many areas they had previously secured. For the last several months, VC morale suffered. Some regular VC troops were requesting to be discharged so they could return to their homes. The commander knew he must have a VC victory. He knew he must show the peasants his Communists could protect them from the ARVN and their American choppers.

He was as prepared as he could be. Rather than using homemade and makeshift guerilla weapons, his forces were well-armed with modern U.S. weapons and ammunition seized from local outposts and strategic hamlets. His men had rehearsed with the villagers. The farmers knew where to go and what to do. This Delta area was their home. They knew the dikes, rice fields, tree lines, and canals.

The tree lines were naturally thick with bamboo, water palms, banana and coconut palms. Canals and dikes crossed and flooded the rice fields. Ditches behind the dikes provided safe passage to re-supply foxholes with soldiers and ammo as needed. They were just across the canal from the Plain of Reeds, a known VC stronghold. Their wounded and dead could be removed unobserved and replaced by reserves.

His troops were dug in. The VC commander had learned hard lessons from fighting the French. The men now dug foxholes so deep they could stand in them. The excavated dirt had been carried away, and the fighters were careful not to disturb the surrounding thick foliage. They had even cut extra underbrush so defects could not be seen from the air.

These meticulous preparations were successful. The foxholes would be invisible to the keen-eyed U.S. and ARVN spotters in the small, low-flying L-19 observer planes. The VC commander's intelligence indicated the attack on Bac would come from the south or west. It didn't matter. He was ready for either.

BAC/TAN THOI
WED
2 JAN 63
0400

VC scouts in My Tho heard the unmistakable roar of many ARVN truck engines starting up in the dark morning. They sent runners to alert the VC commander in Bac that an attack was imminent. The commander roused his guerrillas in the pre-dawn. Picking up their weapons, they ran to their foxholes along the raised dikes. Many of the villagers stayed, as planned, to help the VC; the rest—mainly old men, women, and young children—fled to outlying swamps for safety.

TAN HIEP AIRSTRIP
2 JAN 63
0635

Dawn painted the sky in the east a bright red as I de-planed Chopper One, the lead chopper, with my emergency gear and some litters.

I waved thanks to Trey and Billy T. in the cockpit. The morning Delta was cool, and dense ground fog dusted distant rice paddies. I didn't remember Tan Hiep and felt sure we had never been here before. I looked around. It was the typical isolated landing strip of dirt and gravel raised above surrounding rice paddies and tree lines. Shortly after we arrived, five H-21s from the Thirty-Third and Fifty-Seventh kicked up dust as they maneuvered to join our choppers in the flight line.

From Capt. Brewster's briefing yesterday, I remembered they wanted to drop 300 troops quickly to surprise the VC. Thirty helicopters would be required to transport all the troops needed in one drop. Saigon headquarters had assigned all other air-worthy choppers to a mission with a higher priority north of Tan Son Nhut, so we would make do. Each of our ten available H-21s could transport one battle-ready squad of ten soldiers, so our choppers would need to make three runs to the LZ.

The troops with full battle gear gathered in long lines on one side of the airstrip. Across the strip, a canvas roof covered an open-sided shelter for the ARVN command post, where several officers were grouped around a field radio. Nearby, a similar shelter housed the Vietnamese medical-aid station. This was more preparation than I had seen on previous missions. The aid station was manned by several ARVN medics wearing Red Cross armbands and stocked with American-provided medical supplies. I saw two ARVN ambulances and drivers close by. I stowed our litters and emergency bags near them.

"I sure could use another cup of coffee," I muttered to myself.

0650

The rotors started their thumping noises, turning at first slowly, and then speeding up until the long flight line erupted in a roaring crescendo. Dust clouds swirled in a frenzy. The troops and advisors, eyes almost closed against dust and wind, climbed into the bellies of the choppers. When loaded, they quickly departed one by one. After the helicopters were out of sight, early morning silence again descended heavily on the airstrip and surrounding rice fields.

The first troop-lift quickly delivered the ARVN squads to a landing zone north of Tan Thoi as planned. They took no fire and reported no contact with VC—a routine drop. The ten choppers, insect-like, returned in formation for the second troop load.

Before the second lift of troops could board, thick ground fog, which had been threatening all morning, closed in. Suddenly, it was impossible to even see across the airstrip. The choppers were grounded. The remaining two troop drops would have to wait until the fog cleared. Orders were shouted down the flight line, and one by one, the engines shut down. Silence again pervaded the fog-bound and now eerie Tan Hiep.

0745

The VC knew exactly where the helicopters would drop off the ARVN troops; they had been listening to all the un-coded Vietnamese radio transmissions with newly captured American radios tuned to the ARVN frequencies.

From the south, two Vietnamese Civil Guard battalions approached Bac in long columns. They had hoped to surprise the VC, but instead, the VC would surprise the civil guards and their American advisors. The VC commander, aware of the exact location of the civil guards from their broadcast coordinates, ordered the dug-in guerrillas in the front to prepare for an attack. He alerted those dug-in on the right to prepare to attack on the flank.

The American advisor halted the first civil guard battalion 150 yards south of Bac. He sent scouts forward toward the hamlet. The VC, following strict discipline, waited until the scouts were only thirty yards away before opening fire; the battle of obscure hamlet Bac was under way.

The civil guard battalion under attack tried to retreat to the dikes behind them for protection. Their CO and XO were killed immediately in the withering fire. ARVN artillery was called in, but their rounds landed well behind the VC.

0930

The sun finally burned off the fog. Orders to crank up came down the line. The ARVN squads formed up. With their tall American advisors, they loaded aboard the choppers. Lifts two and three were efficiently completed—mission accomplished.

Waiting around could be lonely and tough, but I wasn't complaining; cushy duty compared to my pilot buddies and the advisors in harm's way. I stretched out on the dirt next to the strip and used the emergency bag for a pillow.

My mind wandered. I tried to imagine what I would be doing if I was still back in the states. I wondered about my buddies from internship. Where were they? What were they doing? The beginning of a new year was always a good time to reflect about the past and future. I now knew I wanted to take a residency for some specialty training, but what? During my internship, I'd liked OB/GYN, Ophthalmology, and Internal Medicine. I couldn't seem to narrow that choice down. I also knew I had plenty of time to decide; I would not be discharged until August 1964. A decision was still a long time off.

0930

Caught off guard by the VC attack, the surprised province chief in charge of the civil guards did not notify the ARVN commander and American advisors in the command post at Tan Hiep of the onset of battle. He did not order his second battalion to go to the aid of the besieged first. He did not order any adjustments to the artillery, and throughout the ensuing battle, all the artillery rounds fell far behind the VC—useless.

Instead, he requested deployment of the reserve infantry companies waiting at the Tan Hiep airstrip. He requested they off-load in the open fields in front of the tree lines. Unknown to the province chief, these tree lines hid the VC standing in their foxholes in-wait.

An ARVN L-19, a small Cessna observation plane dubbed Bird Dog, flew back and forth over the tree lines so low it

clipped palm fronds. The American observer and Vietnamese pilot looked out of both sides of the plane. They looked carefully for any evidence of foxholes in the dikes or VC troops hidden in the tree lines. They did not see anything suspicious. After repeated passes over the site, the landing zone was approved as requested by the province chief.

The VC exercised discipline and hid silently in their foxholes. They did not fire at the plane as it swooped low over their heads. It would make an easy target, but they had learned from previous battles—shooting at this easy target would give away their position.

0940

A sudden roar of choppers firing up on the flight line interrupted my daydreams.

"What's up?" I asked a crew chief as he sprinted toward his chopper.

"Big firefight south of Ap Bac. They called for the reserves."

I watched the H-21s load up yet again with armed ARVN troops. As usual, the H-21s strained to get aloft with the heavy cargo. By contrast, the five agile and sleek Huey gunships had already left; they always seemed to just jump into the air. They had power.

1038

The ten choppers carrying the first reserve company, escorted by the Huey gunships, arrived at the LZ. The H-21s landed in the rice paddy two hundred yards from the tree line as ordered. Immediately after the ARVN reserve troops jumped off of the choppers into the rice field, shots rang out.

1040

A sergeant from the command post yelled, "Doc, there's trouble. Chopper down in the LZ."

I scrambled. The tent that served as command post felt electric with energy, filled with agitated voices of Vietnamese officers and American advisors. I heard static and strained transmissions on the field radio but could not make out what was said.

I asked the closest advisor, "What's up?"

"It's bad. Chopper one got hit as it was unloading in the LZ. He got it in the transmission and lost fore and aft controls. Chopper two is going in for the rescue."

Chopper one—that was the H-21 I had come in on that morning with Trey and Billy T. I felt physically sick.

The officers crowded around the receiver. We all strained to listen.

"Chopper two is going in to pick up the crew." An advisor said loudly so we could all hear, "Now they're down. Crew chief's shot up. Dammit!"

As a group, we all inhaled in surprise.

Chopper two; that was Slick's Little Lee Roy, I thought. I could hardly breathe.

"Huey's going for the pick up now," someone near the radio said. "They're going in! They'll pick 'em up." After a long silence, he said, "Now the Huey's down. Rolled over."

Groans filled the tent.

"Chopper three's shot up. Barely made it out." There was sudden silence, only intense listening.

That was PBD's aircraft.

"Chopper three's nursed along enough to get about three-quarter mile out before it crash landed. No injuries. But chopper's useless. Crew's okay. Picked up by chopper four."

I listened so hard my ears were ringing; my chest hurt.

The advisor's voice, now hoarse, yelled, "Huey crew chief dead. Chopper two's crew chief wounded bad. He's still aboard. Can't get him out. Pinned down. Hellish VC fire."

Time stopped. Helpless, I strained to listen to the radio while I searched the sky for any returning choppers.

Finally, I saw six H-21s and four Hueys. Shortly after they landed, the seventh and last flyable helicopter, Chopper four, reached the airstrip. When it landed, passengers PBD and crew jumped out, flight suits and boots wet and black from water and mud. They looked dazed, pale, and grim.

I saw the multiple bullet holes that punctured the choppers, their olive green fuselages ripped open by gaping black holes rimmed with jagged gray aluminum edges.

1130

Gen. Cao arrived at Tan Hiep from his headquarters in Can Tho. After a quick briefing, he reluctantly agreed to call in the paratroopers from Saigon. The American advisors pleaded for quick action, but Gen. Cao ordered the drop for 1800 hours. He also would not budge from his decision about the drop zone. Rather than to the east, as requested by the Americans to box-in the VC, he ordered the paratroopers to drop to the west. This plan made the advisors even more disgruntled; it allowed the VC an open escape route.

The thirteen ARVN armed personnel carriers traveling toward Bac encountered severe difficulties. The steep dikes and muddy rice fields made for painfully slow progress. They were much too far away to provide any support for the decimated ARVN reserves or to pick up the stranded Americans.

1145

The L-19 Bird Dog observer plane landed for the second or third time to re-fuel. The gasoline tanker truck sped over to get the job done quickly. The American colonel, flying in the observer's seat behind the Vietnamese pilot, ran to the command post. With his up-to-the-minute input, the advisors and senior Vietnamese officers devised a plan to again try and rescue the six American pilots and five crewmen pinned down in the rice field.

"We're going to send in another H-21. We'll have a second circle aloft in case anything happens. One of the Hueys is too shot-up to fly, but the three left will provide cover."

The crews for the two H-21s and three Hueys ran to their shot-up choppers and fired up the engines; rotors turned, and they were off.

"Chopper 5's going in to attempt a pickup." A voice repeated the radio message. After a leaden silence, he said, "They've landed. Wait. Their controls are hit. Can't make the pickup."

Another long pause. "They barely got out. They're down, but thank God they got out of there. They see the APCs. We'll let them do the rescue. Chopper 6, don't go in. Head back."

Shortly after, I saw the lone Chopper 6 limp back into Tan Hiep.

1300

The VC watched the APC's slow struggle toward the disabled choppers. When the APCs were about five hundred feet from the downed Americans, the VC battalion commander ordered the use of his limited store of captured 60mm mortar shells.[12]

1400

Time dragged. The radio crackled with messages. The ARVN APCs picked up three pilots, but they could not yet retrieve the bodies of the two crew confirmed dead. One APC had a flamethrower. It moved into position but would not shoot flame. The ARVN crew had mixed a faulty batch of gasoline and jelling agent.

1740

Finally, the radio message we had been waiting for: All downed American personnel were accounted for and aboard the ARVN APCs. They would be taken to a safe area and transferred to waiting trucks for transport back to Tan Hiep.

The command post ordered B-26s to bomb the tree lines at Tan Thoi and Ap Bac.

The afternoon sun was low in the west by the time truckloads of wounded and dead ARVN began arriving at the aid station. We triaged the treatable to trucks directed to a hospital in Can Tho.

We placed the dead to the side. We started IV Dextran and tried to stabilize and bandage and splint the injured.

At last, trucks arrived with the rescued American pilots and crews.

I treated our wounded. Slick and his co-pilot in Chopper Two had arm wounds and lacerations from shrapnel. Both were agitated about the death of their young crew chief. Trey, Billy T., and crew had miraculously not been wounded. The Huey pilots were both injured and in shock. After stabilization, Dust Off flew out the American wounded to the Eighth Field Hospital in Nha Trang.

As soon as they were off, I returned to the overwhelmed Vietnamese aid station. Wounded and dead were everywhere; we sorted unending casualties. In one group, I found two wounded, frightened VCs in black pajamas. One had an arm wound; the other had been shot in the jaw. I put pressure dressings on to stabilize the bleeding. To save precious time, I gave a morphine injection through their clothing to help with the pain, and they were cleared to be loaded on a truck.

In the midst of this chaos, a Vietnamese officer brought in an unconscious American advisor. A captain, he had been in the first troop drop of the morning. Shot in the neck, he remained with his troops while bleeding internally. His airway was compromised; he was pale, cold, and unresponsive. I secured his airway, breathed into his mouth, and put pressure on his chest to try and get his heart going. I started a Dextran push into both arms.

Too late. The captain wasn't able to rally. We carefully placed him in a body bag. Dust Off flew the bodies of the three dead Americans to the morgue in Saigon, the first leg of their long, final flight home.

1800

Planes carrying the paratroopers arrived from Saigon. Due to an error, the paratroopers jumped at the end rather than the beginning of the designated drop zone. They landed a half-mile from the scheduled drop zone—in front of the dug-in VC. Nineteen of the

ARVN Airborne were killed, and thirty more were wounded or injured, including two American advisors.

1900

The setting sun looked like a bloody gash in the western clouds by the time we were ready to leave Tan Hiep. The Soc Trang crew climbed aboard the only two flyable H-21s and headed south for home. I looked across the dark hold of the noisy, vibrating chopper. Sput, Trey, Billy T., and PBD—their muddy flight suits now dry—exhausted and blank, sat with their backs against the inside of the fuselage, eyes closed but I knew not in sleep.

I looked at my emergency bag; it was now as empty and exhausted as I felt. I counted my litters. Still the same number I started with in the morning, which now seemed long ago.

Ap Bac! A disaster—a mission from hell. We lost two crewmen. The crew chief from the Ninety-Third was only twenty-one years old and just married. And at the end of the day, we lost a U.S. advisor. This young captain, I would find out later, was a West Point graduate and a favorite officer of the brass in Can Tho. Everyone who knew him had been convinced he would make general one day.

I felt a part of my soul leave with those three body bags—leaving, never to return. My immature, miracle-working physician complex, confronted by truth and loss on this dense, humid, dusty Tan Hiep airstrip, was gone for good. Our brave captain and crewmen lost their lives; I only lost my naïve self-image. They lost everything forever, and so did their families back home. I still had a future.

I thought of the ARVN and VC wounded or killed, which were more than I could count. How would their families feel tonight? I was overcome with helplessness. Five choppers down. I had done what I could, and it wasn't enough. Ap Bac! Ap Bac! Forever etched in my memory. I would never forget Ap Bac!

AP BAC/TAN THOI
WED
2 JAN 63
2200

The peasant fighters from the hamlets went off into the swamps to join up with their families, who had fled early that morning. Sampans assembled; thirty-nine VC wounded were placed aboard and taken to a remote base camp for medical care. The regular VC troops, taking their eighteen dead, moved out in orderly columns. They forded a canal, unobserved in the dark. They marched all night to reach their camp in the Plain of Reeds. The legendary Battle of Ap Bac— known by the VC as the Battle of My Tho—would go down in their history as a victorious battle that helped turn the tide of the war in their favor.[13]

SOC TRANG
THUR
3 JAN 63

No one came to sick call. The airfield was quiet. I had little appetite for breakfast but forced myself to go to the mess hall at noon. It was almost empty. PBD sat at a long bench, eating alone. I got a sandwich and joined him.

"What a catastrophe," PBD said.

I could only nod my head in agreement.

"They didn't get the last load of dead ARVN trucked out until 1930 last night." PBD had a look I had never seen before; his eyes were dull and expressionless. He continued in a monotone, "Sput and his crew went out early this morning. By some miracle, he patched up Chopper Three, the one I was flying. Had it back here by 1130."

Trey joined us with a lunch tray. "I was over at headquarters; Sput and crew are being sniped at, but it looks like the main VC force left during the night. Back to the Plain of Reeds."

PBD continued, "I heard the ARVN found only three VC bodies when they finally got into Bac this morning."

"You got to hand it to them. Their intelligence was better than ours," Trey said. "The VC were ready. Stood their ground, used discipline, and now they know for sure how to shoot choppers down."

PBD said in a resigned voice, "It was like Andrew Jackson at the Battle of New Orleans; our ragtag army defeated the British with simple weapons and sound tactics. The VC turned the tables on us."

"It's going to be a tougher war from now on," Trey mumbled.

I went back to the dispensary. I sat alone at my desk and wondered why the ARVN, with so much help from the United States with weapons, firepower, and advisors, seemed so ineffective. Surely the peasants in the countryside wanted freedom and a democratic government like Diem's. What did the Communists offer that motivated the citizen farmers in places like Ap Bac? The VC certainly seemed more motivated to win this war than the government. Something was wrong.

I knew one thing for certain: Tonight, the VC, somewhere in the Plain of Reeds, would celebrate their victory at Ap Bac.

SAIGON
FRI
4 JAN 63

Gen. Harkins, angry with reporters who described Ap Bac as a defeat, was even angrier at the American advisors who talked to the newspaper correspondents. The U.S. advisors told the journalists the truth about the Vietnamese commanders and how their refusal to perform had cemented the disaster. Young American advisors were puzzled as to why their allies did not seem to want to fight the VC more aggressively.[14]

SOC TRANG
SUN
6 JAN 63

I entered the mess hall for breakfast just as Sput walked out, heading back for his fifth day to work on the choppers still down near Ap Bac.

"When will you finish up out there?" I asked.

Sput wiped the sweat from his forehead. "Just about got the last chopper out. My men are working like crazy. We should finish up today." He shouted over his shoulder, "It's been almost impossible. See ya around, Doc."

Eighty ARVN casualties and an unknown number of VC dead. I flashed back on the beleaguered Ap Bac aid station and the carnage. What could be worth this price? Only freedom. Freedom had always required such sacrifice. When political ideologues or religious zealots create power for themselves and then try to maintain their positions only by servitude, the struggle for reform and democratic freedoms erupts like a volcano; lava flows destroying all in its path.

I found PBD still at a table. He had finished breakfast and was drinking coffee.

"Any news?" I asked.

"Final official tally is eighty ARVN killed," PBD said.

"And VC? How many of them got zapped?"

"May never find out, but we paid a steep price. The Hueys fired over one hundred rockets and a hell of a lot of machine-gun rounds," PBD said. "God knows how many rounds the ARVN fired."

Slick, just back from the hospital, entered and joined us.

"How's the arm, Slick?" I asked.

"Aw, it's good as new." He pulled up his right sleeve to reveal the red, healing wounds from the shrapnel. "Doc, why don't you have some of those female-type nurses like they do in the hospital in Nha Trang? They'd do us a world of good."

"Dream on. I'm just glad you guys are back," I said. "Looks like you're ready for flight status before the choppers."

"Well, Little Lee Roy's all patched up," Slick drawled, "ready to go."

PBD looked glum. "But not to Ap Bac. When the ARVN went in the next day, they only found nine bodies of suspected VCs."

"They played us like a fiddle." Slick shook his head. "On a happier note, our hard-working ol' buddy Sput leaves for home in five days. He deserves a proper send-off."

AP BAC RECORD

ARVN: Two thousand men committed to the operation with thousands of rounds of rifle and machine-gun ammunition fired; the artillery expended six hundred shells. Hueys fired 8,400 rounds from machine guns and expended one hundred rockets. The operation included all the equipment, firepower, helicopters, and planes the U.S. could provide. The battle at Ap Bac involved ARVN ground troops, civil guards, paratroopers, APCs, and artillery. Eighty ARVN were reported killed and one hundred wounded. Three Americans were killed and eight wounded. Five helicopters were downed.

VC: Three hundred fifty men fired five thousand rounds of rifle and machine-gun ammunition and six rounds of 60mm mortars. Eighteen VC were killed, and thirty-nine were wounded.[15]

SOC TRANG
WED
9 JAN 63

It was 0730. I entered the dispensary treatment room right on time to start sick call. Our driver and one of the medics had rotated home, and no new replacements had arrived. That reduced us now to two medics and Jones, the clerk. Sgt. Sherk was present but lethargic. He did only what he was told to do, nothing more.

I worked my way through the assorted general medical problems of a typical sick call: one headache, two back strains, a pesky rash common in heat and humidity, and a painful ingrown toenail. The last patient, a headquarters clerk, had diarrhea. I went to the supply closet to get an anti-diarrhea medication.

In the far corner of the supply room, caught off-guard by my sudden entry, stood a surprised Sgt. Sherk, preparing to take a drink from an open bottle of whiskey. He tried to hide the bottle behind some cartons of bandages on a lower shelf.

"Let me smell your breath," I demanded. The heavy odor of alcohol confirmed he had already had a drink or two.

"It's not the way it looks," he said.

I picked up the medicine for the clerk in the next room. In an instant, my course of action was clear. "Stay where you are, Sergeant. I'll be right back."

I gave the clerk his medicine and told Jones to give him an off-duty slip for the rest of the day.

I returned to the storeroom. "Sergeant Sherk, you are relieved of duty at this dispensary. Report to your quarters. I will do all I can to have you sent home immediately. You are unfit for duty. You need help, and we aren't prepared to offer it."

With a garrulous smile, he took a drink, put the lid on the bottle, and stashed it in his back pocket. Without a word, he walked out of the supply closet and the dispensary.

"Staff meeting," I called out in a loud voice.

The two medics sat on the benches in the waiting room, and the clerk remained seated behind his desk.

"Sergeant Sherk is no longer the NCO in charge. As of now, he is not working here. I know we are short-staffed, but your replacements and a new sergeant NCOIC should arrive any day."

The men glanced at one another.

"This cuts us really short. I'm sorry. I know you've been extended and are anxious to get home. I don't blame you. You deserve to go. But as long as you're here, we've got jobs to do. Any questions?"

"No, sir," they all said almost in unison.

"Good. Let's get back to work."

"Sir," one of the medics said as he came back to the treatment room and stood by my desk.

"Yes?" I said.

"Sergeant Sherk's been drinking heavily most of the last month. Thought you'd want to know."

"Thanks," I managed to say. I felt a mixture of relief and anger: relief at not having the burden of this man and his problems, but anger for his letting us down. We would now be even more short-handed.

At headquarters, the clerk helped me begin the processing for Sgt. Sherk to be sent home for treatment ASAP. Things were never so bad they couldn't get worse.

SOC TRANG
THUR
10 JAN 63

Good news: my foot locker arrived with my civilian clothes, which I really could use, and best of all, my medical textbooks. At this stage of my training, I needed the security of at least knowing I had a small library for reference. I had been fortunate so far, but out here, anything could and probably would happen.

The bad news: still no sign of replacement medics. We also had not received the medical supplies we requested for January, much less those ordered back in December. To get by, I had borrowed more antibiotics from the Special Forces at outpost Dutah. They were great about sharing and knew I would pay them back as soon as ours arrived, but I didn't understand the problem. I had called Saigon many times. They hadn't understood the problem either, and so nothing happened.

The crowd at the O-Club assembled to tell three great pilots and friends good-bye. By the time I arrived, the party was geared up. I found Sput, and over the din of the celebration, asked, "Who's going to look after Tiger pup after you've gone?"

He looked serious at the mention of the dog. "One of the cooks over in the mess hall. He's been feeding Tiger right along." Sput swigged from his bottle. "Doc, be a pal and watch out for the little guy. He's been my good-luck charm."

"I will."

"Promise?"

"Promise."

The screen door flew open with a bang loud enough to make us all look up. Warrant Officer Pappy Walsh, the chopper pilot who looked like actor Broderick Crawford in a rumpled flight suit, came rushing into the club with a handful of papers.

"Hey, guys, I've got something. It's a song me and some of the Fifty-Seventh pilots wrote about Ap Bac." He handed out several copies with the words.

"You sing it to 'On Top of Old Smoky.'"

We sang tentatively the first time:

> WE WERE CALLED INTO TAN HIEP
>   ON JANUARY TWO
> WE WOULD NEVER HAVE GONE THERE
>   IF WE'D ONLY KNEW
>
> WE WERE SUPPORTING THE ARVANS
>   A GROUP WITHOUT GUTS
> ATTACKING A VILLAGE
>   OF STRAW-COVERED HUTS
>
> A TEN-'COPTER MISSION
>   A HUNDRED TROOP LOAD
> THREE LIFTS ARE NOW OVER
>   A FOURTH ON THE ROAD
>
> THE VC'S START SHOOTING
>   THEY FIRE A BIG BLAST
> WE OFF LOAD THE ARVANS
>   THEY SIT ON THEIR ASS
>
> ONE 'COPTER IS CRIPPLED
>   ANOTHER SITS DOWN
> ATTEMPTING A RESCUE
>   NOW THERE IS TWO ON THE GROUND

A HUEY RETURNS NOW
    TO GIVE THEM SOME AID
THE VC'S ARE SO ACCURATE
    THEY SHOOT OFF A BLADE

FOUR PILOTS ARE WOUNDED
    TWO CREWMEN ARE DEAD
WHEN IT'S ALL OVER
    A GOOD DAY FOR THE RED

THEY LAY IN THE PADDY
    ALL COVERED WITH SLIME
A HELL OF A SUN BATH
    EIGHT HOURS AT A TIME

AN ARMORED BATTALION
    JUST STAYED IN A TRANCE
ONE CAPTAIN DIED TRYING
    TO MAKE THEM ADVANCE

THE PARATROOPERS LANDED
    A MAGNIFICENT SIGHT
THERE WAS HAND-TO-HAND COMBAT
    BUT NO VC'S IN SIGHT

WHEN THE NEWS WAS REPORTED
    THE ARVANS HAD WON
THE VC'S ARE LAUGHING
    OVER THEIR CAPTURED GUNS

ALL PILOTS TAKE WARNING
    WHEN TREE LINES APPEAR
LET'S LAND THOSE DAMN 'COPTERS
    ONE MILE TO THE REAR

Over and over, we sang all the verses in order. Round after round of drinks, we sang louder and louder. The club reverberated with cacophony and attempted harmonies. By the end of the festivities, hoarse from the singing, I reluctantly clambered down from my perch atop the eight-foot beer cooler—I must have wanted to be closer to heaven—my lungs sung out. The words had long been swallowed up in the black Delta night, but I felt better. We all did.

TAN SON NHUT
FRI
11 JAN 63
1050

Richard Tregaskis boarded a Pan Am Boeing 707 flight that would take him home to Honolulu, eager to write his book. He had been in Vietnam since October 10, 1962, and it had been a long, hard three months. He looked forward to meeting Sput, scheduled to leave on a later plane, for drinks and war stories in Honolulu.[16]

SOC TRANG
1700

"Sput, old buddy of mine, I can't say it's been great, 'cause it hasn't. But I'll sure miss seeing you around. Who am I going to hang out with?" I said. "And Tiger pup, he's going to be mighty lonely."

"I'd take that dog with me if I could." He paused. "You're doing a good job, Doc. Keep it up. We'll get together down the road. Old chopper pilots hang together. Not to change the subject, but I'm planning on meeting up with Richard Tregaskis on my way home."

"I look forward to reading his book. Tell him hello for me. And the girls from the Bungalow."

"Will do," Sput laughed. He looked at his watch. "It's 1700. Looks like it's that time. When you get state-side, Doc, look me up. Anytime."

Maj. Ewald and the crowd that had gathered to see them off

shook hands all around. The departing pilots had broad grins. Why wouldn't they? I thought.

Sput looked up at the H-21 that would fly them to Saigon. It was from the Fifty-Seventh stationed at Tan San Nhut. "Too bad it's not one of ours, but any old ship in the storm."

The crew chief waved the three pilots aboard.

Sput gave the thumbs-up sign and yelled from the chopper door, "Good-bye, Soc Trang. Hello, New Jersey. Get your daughters off the streets; we're coming home!"

The dual rotary wings roared their familiar thump, thump, thump. Once airborne, the nose pointed down, and the chopper gained air speed. Headed north, they would be in Saigon in about an hour. Tomorrow at this time, they would be on a Pan Am contract plane somewhere over the Pacific Ocean.

"Time for supper, Doc," Maj. Ewald said. "Join me?"

When we entered the mess hall, I noticed the bowl of anti-malaria pills by the front door. "Had your dose this week, Major?"

"Those damn things. Yes. I'm up-to-date. Thanks to them, we've not had one case."

The dinner looked good: meatloaf, mashed potatoes and gravy, and peas with carrots. We filled our glasses with iced tea and sat down on benches facing one another across the table.

"Ap Bac. That was tough," I said.

"Yeah. A real disaster. It's going to take us a long time to recover." After a pause, Maj. Ewald continued, "As of today, the last of the Ninety-Third pilots who came over by ship have rotated home."

"When did you take over from the original CO?"

"He left early, before I got here, on medical; Captain Brewster was acting CO when I arrived mid-November, one or two weeks before you arrived."

"It's great not being an FNG anymore." I took a swallow of tea. "I'm impressed, though; you chopper pilots are mighty professional."

"Just doing the job we trained for. Most of us flew in Korea. This war is nothing like that. Take my word for it: The weather's better here. By a lot."

Maj. Ewald looked around the mess hall. "I'm proud of these guys. Outstanding group. It's an honor to be their CO."

"We're going to miss Sput and company," I said.

"They aren't the only ones we'll miss. Captain Brewster should get promoted to major any day. When he does, we'll lose him to Saigon. Hate to see him leave."

We were interrupted by a young lieutenant who rushed up to the table. "Major Ewald. You're needed in operations, sir. Chopper down."

"One of ours?"

"No. From the Fifty-Seventh." He paused. "It took off from here twenty minutes ago."

For a split second, the major and I locked eyes.

We jumped up and sprinted the short distance to operations. A frantic Hartley Davis was looking at the map.

"What the hell happened? Shot down?"

"No. They were up about 2,500 feet. Something mechanical. Fucking mechanical failure."

"Survivors?"

"It can't be good."

"They were about twenty-five minutes south of Tan Son Nhut. Near an outpost, here." Capt. Davis pointed to the map. "The initial radio report from an advisor said peasants witnessed the crash. Saw it just turn over and fall from the sky."

"Dammit to hell!" Maj. Ewald smashed his right fist into his left palm.

Capt. Davis continued, "The civil guard, with an American advisor, are on the way to secure the area before it gets any darker. It's VC country, and you know they saw the crash, too. We can't get in there until tomorrow."

By the time we left operations, stars filled the sky. Alone, I stood outside hootch #4 and looked across the airfield at the white half-moon low in the black sky. I thought of all the traumas in my life. There had not been that many up to this point: witnessing our high school superintendent dying in a terrible auto accident; surviving tornadoes in the Midwest that had fatalities; friends dying of drownings, mastoiditis, and peritonitis; the polio epidemic; a neighbor boy killed when he ran across a street without looking. All bad. Then Ap Bac. Now this. Three fine pilots who had done their duty above and beyond—finally on their way home to their families—now gone.

As I looked at the sky, I knew this Vietnam moon was the same moon over America last night. It would return there tomorrow night. Right now, the sun belonged to Missouri as much as it had to the Mekong Delta at noon today. Heavenly bodies did not alter their treks no matter human struggles; heavenly orbits, precise and endless, followed some other plan.

Many good men—theirs and ours—had seen this moon for the last time. Tomorrow's sun would not warm grieving families here or half the world away. I understood now: War is measured more in loss and pain than victory.

SOC TRANG
SAT
12 JAN 63

In the early light of dawn, our two choppers headed toward the crash site. I felt overwhelmed and sad. I didn't fool with sitting on any flak jackets. Who cared anyway?

About twenty-five minutes out from Soc Trang, the crew chief pointed from the open door. I looked out and could see a scarred clearing half-hidden in an otherwise undisturbed water-palm grove. I could also see the civil guards, who made a thin perimeter.

We landed at some distance from the crash site in a rice paddy. Close by, two H-21s from Tan Son Nhut had arrived and were shutting down their engines. Together, we all walked in silence to the palm grove. Exhausted civil guards looked up in relief. They had spent long hours on guard in last night's darkness, fearful the VC would attack—strip the guns, ammunition, and anything else of value, perhaps even carry away the Americans—before we could arrive.

The torn hulk of trashed metal looked more like some bizarre sculpture than the once-mighty iron bird. Scattered across the crash clearing, I saw the bodies of the ill-fated pilots and crew, amazingly intact in the soft cushion of deep mud, but twisted in grotesque un-anatomical positions.

I found my friend Sput lying face up with lifeless eyes open toward the cloudless sky. His intact features were smudged with mud. Both legs turned sideways from his torso; his combat boots, still polished, remained laced on his feet.

Annoying Delta insects hovered everywhere.

I made some notes for the report we would write later as part of the official crash investigation. When each of us had concluded this phase of our grim work, we collected personal effects. I lifted Sput's cold torso only enough to remove his billfold out of the back pocket. This was the hardest thing of all for me: removing this most private object—his billfold—the final proof of his having been here, his identity, his very essence.

Dutifully, we attached identification tags and put the broken remains in body bags—the only sounds were the zippers as each one closed. The bodies of the fallen soldiers, now all together in identical olive-drab body bags, were loaded on the choppers from the Fifty-Seventh to resume their interrupted flight to Saigon.

I sensed a measure of relief. These men were no longer lying in the mud in a God-forsaken, unnamed Mekong Delta rice field. The battered hulk of a downed chopper in this foreign land no longer contained Sput or the rest of this doomed crew. With an ache in my throat and soul, I watched the two H-21s take off for Saigon. Now out of the rice paddy and in the air, these men flew again; they resumed their journey.

The remains of seven men would soon be somewhere over the Pacific, but each one would be still alive in someone's memory. In New Jersey, Sput's mom would slowly die from the pain of grief. Wives, girlfriends, children, parents, friends—all would grieve a lifetime.

Sput wouldn't meet Richard Tregaskis for that drink in Honolulu. He would never make the rank of major. He'd never fly a Huey. He and Francine would never get together. His mom would never have grandchildren.

I did not feel tough enough for this. Not by a lot. It felt odd, but I didn't care if I got back home or not: If I did, I did; if I didn't, I didn't. It was that simple. What was so wonderful about life anyway?

VC HEADQUARTERS SOMEWHERE IN THE DELTA
TUES
15 JAN 63

Night after night, the VC overran strategic hamlets, obtaining more and more American weapons. Many of the peasants were not in sympathy with the Communists and not in favor of the VC but kept silent out of fear of reprisal. Many were glad to turn their weapons over to fellow Vietnamese. They took some pleasure knowing they were helping overthrow the unpopular Diem government and supported the VC goal of a united Vietnam, even if it would be Communistic.

The Americans had distributed 1,300 firearms, along with ammunition, radios, and grenades, to the Self Defense Corps and the Civil Guard. The firearms included carbines, shotguns, submachine guns, automatic rifles, machine guns, mortars, and recoilless rifles. The amount of these U.S. arms captured by the VC would be enough to fully arm all VC combatants in the field.[17]

SOC TRANG
TUES
15 JAN 63

"You three have been through a lot. You deserve to go home." I shook the hands of Jones, the clerk, and the two last of my medics. Sgt. Sherk was long gone, of course. The three boarded the Caribou that would take them to Saigon on the first leg of their journey back to the United States.

No new replacements had arrived, but these three men had already been here too long. Their tours of duty could not be extended again. I didn't blame them, but something was wrong with the system.

The MPs agreed to loan me a temporary driver for the ambulance, but the departure of the last medics meant, as of now, I alone would be the entire staff of the 134th Dispensary. Our mission included not only emergency and regular sick call for our airfield community, but also public health, preventive medicine, keeping records and submitting them in a timely fashion. The men working at the dispensary took call for routines, made sure supplies were ordered in a timely manner, sterilized our suture kits out back in our gas-powered autoclave, and had many other duties. I felt apprehensive. I could not do it all.

At this low point, Col. Montjoy arrived to pay the dispensary an official visit. A full-bird colonel in the U.S. Army Medical Corps, he had arrived in-country only three weeks before. With responsibility for all medical services in South Vietnam, he was inspecting every medical facility.

Col. Montjoy looked like a colonel. Tall and fit, he had broad shoulders, and his battle fatigues were neat and his brass polished. I didn't know anything about him or his background, but he certainly looked like he meant business and would know all about how military medicine worked.

He looked around at my empty building with a certain dismay.

I tried hard not to be a whiner, but I explained my first-class mess. The dispensary should be staffed by eight men, but as of today, I had none. Medications and supplies, ordered in November and December, had never arrived, and I was struggling along by borrowing supplies from the Special Forces. I concluded by telling him I had called everyone I knew, short of my congressman. And I was considering contacting him.

He thoughtfully took in all of this information and told me he regretted the failures of the medical corps and army to provide support. He assured me I would not need congressional action, and he would personally see that the problems were promptly corrected immediately.

I had an impulse to hug him out of gratitude and relief, but that wouldn't be the army way. Instead, I restrained myself, shook his hand, thanked him, and told him I would appreciate anything he could do. Col. Montjoy boarded his plane, and it took off.

I closed the door to the empty dispensary, alone again—feeling more than a little sorry for myself—but at the same time thankful I wasn't getting shot at regularly as were our chopper crews in the landing zones and my Special Forces and advisor friends out in the field.

SAIGON
WED
16 JAN 63

Gen. Harkins, MACV commander, received the official after-action report on the Battle of Ap Bac from senior American advisors in the Delta. It was highly critical of both the ARVN performance and the course of the war in the Delta.[18]

SOC TRANG
FRI
18 JAN 63

The VC announced a three-day truce for the Vietnamese New Year celebration called Tet. It would begin January 24. Tet, I learned from Duc at the O-Club, was short for Tet Nhat, which meant first day of the return of spring. This would be a big national celebration, family event, and time to honor the dead. Ancestor worship and superstitions were popular religious beliefs throughout the country.

The province chief invited six of us to be his guests at a gala benefit stage performance on Saturday evening. It wouldn't start until 2100. The major decided we should go, so we would all break curfew to attend. I wondered which group the show benefited. The schools, hospitals, orphanage, and leprosarium could all use the help.

We had a late-night med evac to somewhere. Flying after dark spooked me.

TAN SON NHUT
FRI
18 JAN 63

The joint chiefs of staff ordered a team to investigate and

report back whether South Vietnam was winning or losing the war. Led by a four-star army general, the team consisted of five generals and an admiral. Included in their entourage were colonels representing the three major military branches and the Marine Corps. The committee arrived in Saigon for an eight-day inspection.

Gen. Harkins was acutely aware of the importance of this investigation. In keeping with military custom, it was his duty to arrange the itinerary. Instead of sending the team to the Delta, where the action was heaviest, they spent most of their time in Saigon, the mountains of the Central Highlands, and the coastal areas of central Vietnam. The committee was in the Delta for only one day.

In Saigon, they interviewed the field officers who had been at Ap Bac and written the scathing after-action reports. The team discounted these reports.

The twenty-nine page report prepared for the joint chiefs concluded that the war would undoubtedly be successful. This would be, in large part, due to the inspired leadership of Gen. Harkins. The field officers critical of Ap Bac were mentioned once in the report—deemed "overreactive." Heavy blame for the negative press about Ap Bac was placed on the press and its irresponsible reporting of the battle. The official report concluded things were going well.[19]

SOC TRANG
SAT
19 JAN 63

Our greeting party stood at the side of the tarmac: Maj. Ewald and pilots PBD, Slick, Trey, Billy T. Witt; the engineers; the entire staff of the 134th Medical Detachment; and assorted others. At the side, several black-clad Vietnamese laborers working for the contractor on the O-Club addition stopped to watch. We all looked toward the Air America C-47. It taxied toward us. After the engines shut down, the cargo door opened. The dark interior seemed empty.

Suddenly, with a leap, a golden flash with dark stripes jumped toward us from the plane.

Everyone pretty much scattered, and the Vietnamese workers ran, yelling, "Ai-Yee! Ai-Yee!"

A heavy chain, which no one noticed, went taut. The Royal Bengal Tiger stopped, stood on his huge paws, and with bright eyes, stared at us staring at him in the sunlight. The crew from the C-47 had a big laugh when they saw how scared we all were.

PBD, who had kept his distance, stepped forward and saluted. "Welcome to Soc Trang, Tuffy." PBD always was the most adventurous of our crew.

The crowd cheered, except for the Vietnamese workers, who increased their distance by slowly backing off even further. The C-47 crew chief undid the end of the chain attached to the interior of the plane, and we all walked a respectful distance behind the tiger, the airman using the chain as a leash.

Tuffy, a beautiful animal indeed, was sleek and handsome. As we ambled slowly down the company street to his new home next to headquarters, he looked in all directions. We reached his enclosure: a yard fenced-in by a mostly symbolic three-foot white picket fence. At the far edge of the yard next to the headquarters building, the engineers had placed a large metal shipping container. They removed the doors at one end, and this made his lair. Fresh water filled a nearby large tub, and a sturdy table made a great place for him to perch. From there, he could see what was going on up and down the street.

Once Tuffy was inside the enclosure, the engineer shortened the safety chain and attached it to a stake in the ground. He made sure it was long enough for Tuffy to have full benefit of the yard.

Someone shouted, "How old is he?"

"Tuffy is nine months old." The tiger looked up when PBD called his name.

The admiring crowd slowly dispersed, and thirty or so sweaty men reluctantly returned to the hot hangar or other daily duties, the welcome break over. Tuffy yawned, took a big drink of water, and then stretched out on his table in the sun preparing for a catnap.

I watched his great eyes take in his new surroundings. Immobile, absolutely as still as a statue, only a quick switch of his tail revealed life. Seemingly satisfied, he closed his eyes and dozed in the warm sun. Soc Trang's proper mascot was officially signed in at headquarters and on duty.

In my mail was a letter posted at Ft. Ord from my old friend Scott Mitchell. I had not thought of him in some time. He did not like his duty and wished he was over here. He wondered if I had seen Frank, and I had not, since he was so far to the north. Scott asked me to write him back. I decided to hold off answering him for a while. My morale was too bruised and sensitive; I didn't want him to think I couldn't take it.

Late in the afternoon, while relaxing on my bunk, I read the latest *Stars and Stripes* and tried not to feel sorry for myself and my predicament. Trey came by my room. Just getting off standby, he was sweaty and still dressed in his flight suit.

"Get off your butt, Doc, and get over to the dispensary," he yelled at me.

"Trouble?" I asked.

"*Au contraire*, good physician; your ship has come in," he laughed as he went down the hall to his room.

Dressed in our standard casual uniform of shorts and T-shirt, I sprinted over to the dispensary as fast as I could in flip-flops. Standing at the front door, I saw four medics surrounded by a mound of boxes.

The good Col. Montjoy was as good as his word. My ship had indeed come in. The four medics, stationed in Saigon, would be on-loan until permanent replacements arrived. The boxes contained the long-awaited supplies. This was absolutely the only good thing that had happened in this new year so far.

"Doc Hoyland," said a sturdy sergeant, who appeared to be a Native American with dark brown eyes and hair, "where do you want us to start?"

"Tomorrow is Sunday. Let's clean the dispensary first thing. It's a mess. Then we'll unpack the supplies."

"You've got it, sir," he replied, and they quickly stacked the boxes in the waiting room.

"Welcome to Soc Trang. I'm glad you're here," I said in understatement.

That evening, the dusk had turned to night before our jeeps left the airfield for Soc Trang. It seemed strange and unnatural to leave the airfield so late and in the dark, but at about 2045, six of us arrived in two jeeps in front of the large Soc Trang movie theater.

The city, as always, was bustling but much more festive than usual. Banners and decorative colored lights were hung in preparation for the upcoming Tet holiday. I had passed this theater many times and always noticed the huge graphics they used to promote movies. Often, they were American movies with well-known film stars. I loved the fact that I could not read one word of the advertisements.

Inside, the theater appeared much like any large theater back home with a big stage and red curtain. Shortly after everyone was seated—I noticed it was a full house with every seat filled—a small live band played. The popular Vietnamese music seemed haunting—foreign and exotic to my Western ears. The anticipation from the audience proved infectious.

The curtain parted in the middle and revealed a huge stage. The large cast of forty or so singers and dancers in the opening number were dressed in beautiful costumes of reds, yellows, and purple. The audience loved the extravagant beginning. This was rapidly followed by many solos, dances, and comedy skits. They must have been clever and fun, as the crowd laughed and applauded freely. This was a true variety show. They sang three popular American songs in English. This both impressed and touched me. Even though I enjoyed the performances, I was so tired that I dozed off. I hoped no one noticed or thought I didn't appreciate the talent.

The finale woke me; the entire cast performed a beautiful dance of the Rice Harvest. The show—as long as it was varied—did not end until 0030. We joined the entire audience in giving hearty applause; the musical had been a great diversion for both the military and civilians in this time of war. The benefit must have been a huge success.

Outside, the refreshing air, humid and about sixty degrees Fahrenheit, smelled of the dank river. We thanked our hosts, and our two jeeps, in caravan, returned to the airfield. On the way, I wondered how many VC had been in the audience. One thing for sure, they knew there were six Americans there. How did they feel about our presence at this event—intruding on their space? Or maybe they watched to see if we had a sense of humor or seemed to like their music. I again hoped no one caught me dozing off.

We saluted at the front gate, and our jeeps returned to a dark, silent compound, quite a contrast to the bustling activity and bright lights of festive Soc Trang at Tet.

SOC TRANG
SUN
20 JAN 63

The morning sky was completely clear, and the temperature was in the seventies. I slept well after we had finally gotten home from the big musical. This fine weather matched my much-improved mood. I went to the dispensary for sick call. The place was spotless. It had never looked so good since I had arrived.

After a light sick call, I tracked down Maj. Ewald. He had been my support and knew all of my gripes. I brought him over to the dispensary and introduced him to the four temporary men. He congratulated them. They had done fine work.

One of our young lieutenants came from St. Paul, and he wrote a letter to his hometown zoo about how we had obtained our mascot, Tuffy. The zoo sent a copy of the letter to their local paper, which published a lengthy article about the tigers of the Ninety-Third with a cartoon. This depicted Maj. Ewald, our CO, as a tiger. It also mentioned our monkey, Charlie, and our little brown dog, Tiger. The dog had never been the same since Sput was gone; he missed Sput.

SOC TRANG
MON
21 JAN 63

I finished FAA paperwork for a flight physical and had it ready to put in the mail when the on-loan medic sergeant from Saigon came back to my desk. "Sir, more help has arrived," he laughed.

Two medics with their gear stood in the waiting room. They had just arrived from Okinawa and were assigned temporary duty to the 134th. With a staff of six, I felt flush; my esteem for Col. Montjoy rose even higher.

An odd thing arrived in the mail, a large, fancy box of dried dates from Knott's Berry Farm in California. The gift—clearly addressed to me—had been mailed 1 Dec 62. The enclosure card had names I couldn't recall. I wracked my brain. Who were these people; why did they send me this package?

SOC TRANG
WED
23 JAN 63

This would turn out to be the best day since I arrived in Soc Trang. But first it was Keystone Cops time. Early in the afternoon, not one, but two permanently assigned sergeants arrived. They were accompanied by two medics and a medical clerk. With the arrival of these five long-awaited permanent staff, the personnel for the 134th had gone from zero to eleven in four days! We could now get caught up and keep current with our duties. The dispensary had come to life.

Sgt. Patterson, the more senior, would be our new NCO. Pat Patterson, an amiable man I judged to be in his late thirties, was a large man with prematurely graying hair. He reminded me of a friendly bear with dark eyes taking it all in. He came from Ohio, where he had had some college and worked as an assistant to a veterinarian before going into the army at the end of the Korean War. His wife and three children were staying on at Ft. Hood, Texas, his last duty station. Quick to smile, I felt immediately at ease and knew it would be easy to work with him.

The other sergeant was equally impressive. Sgt. Tom Thibedeaux, originally from Louisiana, had come from Ft. Lewis in Washington, where he left his wife and two children. He was close in age to Sgt. Patterson. Sgt. Tibbs, as he asked us to call him, had black skin and a handsome face. His broad smile lit up his brown eyes and reflected a great sense of humor; his speech, slow and deliberate, inspired confidence.

Of the two medics, Bob Bennett—called Brooklyn because of his marked home accent—was the designated ambulance driver. John Harris, the other young medic, was from a farm in Iowa and had a quiet manner. Tony Alessi, our clerk with dark hair and rosy cheeks, came from a large Italian family in the Bronx.

Brooklyn, Harris, and Tony were all new to the service. None had served any duty overseas, and all were unmarried in their twenties.

I had a good feeling about all five of these men. Finally, the 134ᵗʰ could become an effective team. Permanent staff meant we could get to know and depend on one another. This would make a tough situation better. When the other three medics arrived, we would be fully staffed and could accomplish our mission to provide medical care for the Ninety-Third.

SOC TRANG
THUR
24 JAN 63
TET

Without fanfare, the U.S. Air Force plane landed at mid-morning and taxied to the near side of the Soc Trang airfield. In front of the large maintenance hangar, the officers and men stood in straight lines dressed in fresh khaki uniforms with close haircuts, spit-shined shoes, and gleaming brass.

General Earle Wheeler, chief of staff of the U.S. Army, emerged from the plane along with some journalists, TV reporters, and cameramen. General Wheeler had come to honor Soc Trang heroes of the Ninety-Third from the infamous battle at Ap Bac.

These decorations would be among the first to be awarded for service in Vietnam. None had been authorized previously by President Kennedy or Congress; they wanted Vietnam to have a low profile and not call the public's attention to the fact that this conflict was already a war. The ceremony would be brief but meaningful and historic.

"What's this?" one of the CBS cameramen asked as he looked toward headquarters and saw Tuffy luxuriating in his yard by his pool.

Maj. Ewald said, "Our mascot, Tuffy. Come on. I'll introduce you."

The cameras rolled, and the photographer expended as much or more footage on this tawny Bengal tiger as on the award ceremony. He assured the major pictures of both would be shown on the nightly news in the United States. Tuffy would become famous. One of the journalists got too close, and Tuffy took a light swipe at his right arm. The grazing scratch, very superficial, brought great respect. We went to the dispensary, and I cleaned the small wound.

"Where'd you go to med school, Doc?" the newsman asked.

"Missouri University," I replied.

"Small world. I went to Mizzou for journalism." He filled me in on the end of the season for the football Tigers, which I had missed, and caught me up on basketball season. We agreed the weather was very different from the Midwest. In mid-January here in the Mekong Delta, we were enjoying eighty degree highs in the day and sixty degree lows at night.

We returned to the enclosed yard next to headquarters and found a cautious General Wheeler having his picture taken with Tuffy. Several of the news crew also posed with the handsome tiger. The ceremony over and the news filmed, the crew packed up their gear and returned to the plane. General Wheeler boarded, and the entourage departed quickly. Soc Trang airfield resumed a normal routine.

That afternoon, Maj. Ewald, PBD, and I went into town as guests of the province chief for a Tet celebration, the biggest of their week-long celebration.

We observed the women of Ba Xuyen Province hand out new clothes for the poor, in keeping with the custom for the Tet festival. Hundreds of the needy gratefully received these donated garments to begin the new year. Candy, donated by the Americans, proved to be a popular treat. Children dressed in rabbit costumes performed a dance for proud families. A good band played popular music, and a dragon-headed figure paraded, much to the delight of all of us in the large crowd.

In the early evening, we attended a dignified tea on the province chief's lawn. The refreshing tea was of excellent quality, and the little cookies proved tasty. I had to mind my manners and not eat too many.

Nearby, a huge dinner had been laid out on long tables for the cyclo-drivers. This open-air feast, an annual event, was to thank the wiry men who peddled people all over town in bicycle-powered pedicabs. The drivers, very noisy and happy, ate a large meal and washed it all down with some fermented rice drink. One of them got the idea that the three visiting American officers should share in this potion. The friendly crowd challenged us. I took a glass. It burned all the way down my esophagus—obviously an acquired taste. Even at the risk of losing face, the major and I declined refills. PBD drank three glasses. Ever the adventurer, he had mild regret later.

SOC TRANG
FRI
25 JAN 63

The medics on loan from Okinawa and Tan Son Nhut left today. None of them seemed unhappy about leaving our rustic Delta camp. Before they departed on the milk run this morning, they all agreed to celebrate with a night on the town in Saigon.

SOC TRANG
WED
30 JAN 63

An experienced instructor pilot crashed today. Nothing serious; thankfully, neither he nor the co-pilot suffered injury. The accident site was nearby the airfield, and our mechanics went out in trucks to the rice field for repairs. The Ninety-Third needs every chopper it has to be airworthy, and this proves a daily challenge. I have orders to be on an accident investigation board. Good old Ft. Rucker training helps me out again. The pilot reported the cause of this crash may have been a defective gyroscope—a vital component.

WASHINGTON, DC
WED
30 JAN 63

The U.S. Department of Army released a statement by Admiral Harry Felt, the commander in chief in the Pacific. He estimated the Saigon government controlled about 51 percent of the rural population, the VC 8 percent, and the rest were still uncommitted.[20]

SOC TRANG
THUR
31 JAN 63

Our contractor finished the addition to the O-Club this week. It didn't take long to build with such good weather and only light construction. A large, rectangular open room, it was built on one side of the original club. They took out some windows to make a connecting door. The pitched roof had an overhang for shade. Completely screened, the many and varied Delta insects should be less of a problem when we watch movies in the evening. We bought bamboo chairs, comfortable and cheap. In the old club area, there is now room for a card table and a ping-pong table. First-class.

Maj. Ewald stood up on one of the chairs to be seen above the crowd. "Men, since we have to spend most of our free time here, it's no secret we needed more space. I know you've been waiting quite awhile for this addition. We now have probably the best club in the Republic of Vietnam. Thanks to the building committee, to all of you for your support and contributions, and most of all, thanks to Charley Marr, club manager."

The boisterous crowd sang one of our three favorite songs:

> For He's a Jolly Good Fellow,
> For He's a Jolly Good Fellow,
> For He's a Jolly Good Fellow,
> Which Nobody Can Deny ... *Bullshit!*

Charley raised his arm in a victory salute. "And to you, gentlemen." Everyone laughed.

"There is one piece of business," Maj. Ewald continued. "In honor of Tuffy, from now on, the name of this club is officially the Tigers' Den."

The crowd roared approval.

Charley shouted above the din, "The Tigers' Den is open for business. First round's on the house."

Before he could get the words out of his mouth, the crowd roared even greater approval.

Trey opened the two new wide doors connecting the old club to the new addition, and the men crowded through. It would be a proper bash. In the meantime, we sent a large copy of the photograph of General Wheeler and Tuffy to the Pentagon in hopes we could get the general to sign the picture to hang up in a place of honor.

I couldn't help but smile as I looked at the high ceiling and spacious room with tables and benches. It was a barn of a space, but an improvement that should help morale—money well spent.

SOC TRANG
FRI
1 FEB 63

After a hearty breakfast of pancakes and sausage—our cooks made the best pancakes—I again appreciated the fine weather—a pleasant eighty degrees with balmy breezes that felt like the trade winds in Hawaii.

I arrived at the dispensary to find several men already in the waiting area. It was a hectic sick call—many soldiers with many different complaints and minor injuries. I treated two new gonorrhea cases from Saigon, and one from Bac Lieu. I saw four enlisted men with diarrhea. I asked each of them if they had eaten at the off-limits Chinese Palace in town. They denied it.

I made regular public-health inspections of the few approved small restaurants and cafes in Soc Trang. I always ate at the Chinese Palace, my favorite in Soc Trang, but kept it off-limits. The kitchen didn't have refrigeration and depended on an erratic supply of non-potable ice. To keep chicken fresh, they kept live chickens in cages next to the open-air kitchen in the back. These unsanitary coops were adjacent to the food preparation area. The slit over the river they used for a public toilet was adjacent to the man who washed dishes in buckets of river water.

The proprietor attempted to bribe me with his delicious Vietnamese food. Of course I declined anything raw. A nice, polite man, he would never do what I asked so it would be hygienic enough for American troops with delicate immune systems. Unfortunately, he fixed the tastiest food in town. For seventy-three piastres, about one U.S. dollar, they served crab soup, fried shrimp, rice, crab-meat rolls, and great French bread. I worried about food poisoning, or worse, some exotic parasite. But so far, so good. Unlike many of my friends, I had acquired a taste for *nuoc mam*. This fermented fish sauce was on every table. It didn't smell so good but added great flavor.

I finally finished seeing the last patient. He had a large, painful boil on his right buttock. When drained, the soldier gave a cry of immediate relief. I packed and dressed the wound. He readily agreed to a course of oral antibiotics and a return visit tomorrow for re-packing.

My last clinical duty of the morning would be to interview the pilot from the crash-landing two days before. I needed to complete my part of the accident investigation.

At the mess hall for lunch, I could tell it was payday, as everyone was in a good mood. The clubs would be busy tonight. I planned to try and collect some money for our fund to buy an electric clothes dryer for the orphanage but elected not to when I heard the guys were collecting for the young widow of the crew chief killed at

Ap Bac. I contributed and hoped they collected plenty. After PBD donated to the widow's fund, he gave me the rest of his pocket money for the dryer—135 piastres. Every piastre counted.

On my way to the Tigers' Den at about 1730, I saw tall, gaunt MAAG advisor Maj. Reagen crossing the street. Two of his American advisors had been out in the remote countryside for several days: Maj. Robert Bates, a tough man with a big heart from Minnesota, and Lieutenant Mark Myers, a young and energetic officer from Oregon.

"What have you heard from Bates and Myers?" I asked.

"They're still out there. Should have heard from them by now." Maj. Reagen lit a cigarette.

The duty officer appeared in the door to operations and yelled, "Major Reagan, we have Major Bates on the line!"

We ran over, and Maj. Reagan took the call. He relayed the message as he puffed on his cigarette. "Fourteen ARVN wounded. Need med evac—also ammunition. We're on our way." He hung up. "They've taken quite a beating."

I sent for Sgt. Patterson, and he soon showed up still in uniform. "We've got business," I said. "Grab an emergency kit. I'll change into uniform and meet you at the flight line. Looks like your first run's going to be one to remember."

I sprinted to hootch #4 and jumped into boots and fatigues. When I arrived with my emergency kit at the flight line, Sgt. Patterson was waiting on the tarmac.

"Ready?" I asked.

"Yes, sir," he replied. His face glistened with fine sweat and reflected an eagerness to be off. He was ready to go to work.

We climbed in the lead chopper and put on the armored vests. I showed Patterson how we sat on extra vests for extra protection. PBD told me we were going back to the isolated place where we had evacuated seven ARVN the day before yesterday, about twenty miles from Soc Trang down river.

We waited only a short time on the tarmac until Maj. Reagen, with an interpreter I had never seen before, and the province chief in army fatigues arrived from town and jumped aboard. We sat on facing canvas benches in the hold. It seemed odd to have American brass as well as the province chief on a run.

The crew chief and gunner quickly positioned their machine guns, PBD fired up the chopper, and we roared off. I was glad we didn't have far to go, as it was already evening. This dusky time of day was the transition zone from government to VC control. I felt uneasy. I also noticed the helicopter had some kind of unusual vibration. I was always alert to engine noises and vibrations, and there were plenty in these H-21s. I looked around the hold, but only the young aft gunner and I seemed to notice. He shrugged his shoulders and resumed looking out in the dusky Delta for snipers. From where I sat, I could see Capt. PBD and his co-pilot were not alarmed. That allayed my anxiety. I looked again at Patterson's face. He seemed to be enjoying his first med evac. He caught my eye and smiled a broad grin.

We arrived in the early dark as the tree lines in the distance turned black and the rice paddies looked like slate. The ARVN waiting on the dike were all badly wounded. Two had head wounds, one with skull and some brain exposed. Maj. Bates looked beat, muddy, and gray. I looked around but didn't see Lt. Myers. The ground troops eagerly unloaded the ammunition and carried it down the dike.

We loaded about half the casualties on one chopper. I asked Sgt. Patterson to fly back with the wounded on that H-21, while I would follow with the rest on the second chopper. There were so many we almost had to leave some behind, but Maj. Bates, the province chief, and the interpreter elected to stay for a later truck convoy pickup. That gave us enough room, but I didn't envy them. In this desolate VC country, it was an empty feeling watching a helicopter pull out, leaving you behind as darkness descended.

With the wheels and landing gear sunk into the rice paddy and soft mud, our chopper had a difficult liftoff. The engines must provide enough power for the twin rotors to overcome not only gravity but suction. Fully loaded as we were, that took a lot of extra power. H-21s weren't designed for this and don't have too much reserve horsepower. Trey, our pilot on this second chopper, accelerated the engine. The chopper shuddered but pulled loose with a jolt. Now free, he pointed nose down, and with relief, we gained speed and altitude. Takeoffs and landings were vulnerable times, and choppers made the best targets when slow or stationary. I breathed easier when we were at 1,500 feet altitude, headed back to Soc Trang.

The floor in the cargo hold was covered with wounded. Not on litters; they were lying on makeshift wooden slats and slabs. The ARVN with the severe head wound died just minutes after we took off. Another at my feet was restless and in severe pain. I took a morphine injection from my kit and gave him a dose. Only the most basic of first aid had been available for these men. Even in the dark hold, I could see the soldier with the other head wound was completely covered by a dirty blanket. The man at my feet was in pitiful shape; reddish foam came from his mouth. He was in delirium. I gave him some intramuscular morphine, hoping he would keep breathing.

We touched down in Soc Trang and were met with three ARVN ambulances. The man at my feet gasped his last breath as he was unloaded. With so many severely wounded, we had nothing to offer but transport. At least we would get them to the hospital.

With plenty ARVN help, our wounded human cargo was unloaded rapidly. After the three Vietnamese ambulances were filled, Brooklyn pulled ours up, and we filled it. I climbed in with Sgt. Patterson and medic Harris. We headed to the civilian hospital. As we speeded down the main street in Soc Trang, people at the side of the roads and in the streets stopped, silently watching our caravan of misery.

With Sgt. Patterson's help, I started two units of Dextran: one to the man in shock with the head injury and another to a man in shock from a leg wound. We arrived at the civilian hospital. We took the wounded to a long ward with wooden slabs for beds and mosquito nets overhead. While trying to start a unit of fluids on a man with a chest wound, the lights went out. A woman seemed to appear out of nowhere. She lit a white candle and held it close enough for me to see.

Our MPs had provided escort for the ambulances, and they joined in trying to help. They irrigated wounds, wrapped pressure dressings to stop bleeding, and moved patients at our direction. How many, I wondered, of these wounded would survive the night? Several women arrived and looked like relatives, but I realized they were volunteers—Soc Trang civilians helping out. Several nurses and some nuns arrived. This hospital had little or no equipment and very limited surgical capacity.

After we had done all we could, our crew piled back in the ambulance and started home with the MPs and their jeep escort.

We were all silent.

In the darkness, Sgt. Patterson said, "I've never seen anything like that before. Hope I never do again."

When I reached hootch #4, I took a shower and washed away mud and blood. I put on a T-shirt, shorts, and flip-flops and suddenly realized I had missed chow and felt hungry. I went to the club. The guys were watching the last half of the last reel of a Bob Hope and Lucille Ball movie, *Fancy Pants*. Everyone at the club seemed to be feeling mellow.

The carnage of the med evac made me miserable. I also felt a little sorry for myself. The grill had closed—too late for a sandwich. I felt even sorrier when they told me I had missed fried chicken, the best meal the mess hall prepared. I washed down a package of pork rinds with a beer and went to my hootch to read on my bunk. I felt disgusted about feeling sorry for myself, when downtown in the civilian hospital I knew there was incapacitating pain. I turned out the light and took comfort knowing I could get up for breakfast at 0630.

I drifted off to sleep. Some time later, the OD shook my shoulder, "Doc, Major Bates needs you. He's waiting in the club."

I went directly to the club. It was empty. The men had gone back to their hootches after the movie, and it was quiet. The truck convoy had returned, and Maj. Reagan was sitting at a long table with an exhausted and a grim Maj. Bates and Lt. Myers. They were all muddy, tired, and pale.

Maj. Reagan spoke first. "Just after you left with the med evac, Bates got hit in the head by a sniper round." He showed me the helmet with a large dent.

"It made a hell of a noise. My ears are still buzzing, and I've got a headache," Maj. Bates said in a flat tone. "I'm not complaining, you understand, 'cause I was lucky. Damn lucky."

"Doc," Maj. Reagan said, "could you give him something to help him sleep tonight? He's pretty keyed up."

I went across the company street and unlocked the dispensary. I brought back a sedative and some oral analgesics.

"Thanks, Doc."

"That was some med evac this evening," I said. "What happened?"

"We were out on a two-day operation, returning to the outpost by boat," Lt. Myers said. "The VC laid in ambush. They zeroed in on our lead boat and blitzed us. I thought it was all over. The unit got beat up bad, but I guess it wasn't our time, right Bates?"

"Right. But now let's drag our sorry asses into town. I could use a shower and bed."

The MAAG officers left. As harrowing as the evening had been, I felt relief; our guys were back relatively unscathed. I looked at my watch. It was 0100. I wouldn't have too long to wait for breakfast.

SOC TRANG
SAT
2 FEB 63

A busy sick call all morning, but pretty routine. I removed a cast from the right forearm from one of the MPs. We washed the smelly, scaly skin on his arm, and he flexed his arm, glad to regain his freedom. A private ran into the dispensary front door yelling, "Emergency on the flight line!"

Sgt. Patterson and Sgt. Tibbs grabbed the emergency kits, and we took off. Brooklyn ran to the ambulance and soon followed. We found a MAAG jeep at the side of the tarmac. Next to it, Maj. Bates, on all fours, was bent over, vomiting. The MAAG sergeant was standing by, wanting to help, but looked green himself, as if he would have sympathetic vomiting any moment. He looked up with relief as we arrived. We put the major on a litter and into the ambulance.

The MAAG sergeant said, "Major Bates seemed all right, and

we were going to fly to an outpost this morning. Suddenly, he told me to stop and got sick."

I sat next to the major in the ambulance. He gave a few heaves but produced no more vomitus.

In the treatment room, I checked him carefully, fearful this might be a sign of a subdural hematoma after getting hit in the helmet by that round yesterday. His retinal exam did not reveal any pressure on the optic nerve, thankfully. I could find no signs of a central nervous system injury.

"Take Major Bates back to the MAAG house," I said. The sergeant retrieved the jeep from the flight line, and we assisted the unsteady major back into the jeep.

"Major, when you get back to town, go to bed. I'll be in to check on you later. If there is any change, any at all, come back out here. Understand?"

"Yes, Doc. Imagine that. A doctor that makes house calls," he said with a feeble smile.

"Keep your eye on him," I said.

The sergeant nodded as the jeep headed toward town.

By now, it was 1000. I went to the club for a coffee break. I needed it. The usual morning quiet at the Tigers' Den was interrupted by two pilots from the Fifty-Seventh stationed in Saigon. They had been at Soc Trang the last two weeks on temporary duty and were scheduled to go back to Tan San Nhut tomorrow.

"You tigers are in for a real barbecue." The tall pilot accented each syllable. Gaunt, with dark hair and bushy eyebrows, he had broad shoulders and looked more like an outlaw in a Western movie than a white-hatted cowboy, as if transported directly from the 1900s to this southeast Asian frontier. Instead of boots and faded blue jeans, he was dressed in our standard causal garb: shorts, T-shirt, and flip-flops. "I'm from Memphis, and I know my barbecue."

I felt sure he did. I also realized the Tigers' Den was like an old-fashioned saloon in the Wild West. Cowboys drifted through, coming from somewhere, going somewhere. They all collected here, like at the mythical Long Branch Saloon—the only social hall for miles around.

His partner, small and wiry, was from New York. "I don't know much about grilling, but I know good food. You're gonna dine fine tonight."

The Tennessee pilot's father was a meat dealer and had sent 120 pounds of pork. I wondered how he managed to get it here, but by now realized if somebody wanted something bad enough, there always seemed to be a way.

The two pilots showed me the hole they had dug early that morning in a patch of ground outside the club. The fire in this pit already contained glowing coals. They had plenty of wood stacked nearby.

"The secret's in the fire. Not too hot. Long, slow cooking. That's what it's all about. You can tell when the fire is ready by just looking. This baby's almost ready," the tall pilot chef said.

His partner nodded agreement and added wood to the fire. Soon, the smell of grilling meat, haze, and smoke would fill the air. With beers in hand, and sweaty from the heat and exertion, they pulled up chairs to watch the fire and the meat. Squirt bottles at the ready, they put out flare-ups when fat would drip into the fire. Occasionally, they squirted each other or an unsuspecting passerby.

This could be a community barbecue in anytown, USA. Long after I returned to work, I could see from the dispensary window a lot more foot traffic than usual on the company street; curious GIs and civilian Vietnamese employees walked by the fire to watch the progress.

About 1530, I went into Soc Trang to check on Maj. Bates at the MAAG house. I found him in his upstairs bedroom. He looked much better. I repeated my neurological exam. It remained normal.

"Any headache? Vision problems?" I asked.

"Nope, I'm feeling a little weak but otherwise fit," he said.

"Reflexes are all normal, and I can't find anything. Unless there is a change, I'll see you in my office tomorrow morning. By the way, I recommend you skip our barbecue tonight."

"It doesn't even sound good." He rolled over in bed and groaned. "See you tomorrow."

As my jeep passed the front gate, Maj. Ewald was headed out. He stopped and asked about Maj. Bates.

After giving my favorable report, I said, "You're headed in the wrong direction for barbecue."

"Unfortunately, duty calls. I have a command invitation to dinner with the province chief." He added, "The guys said they'd save some. At least they'd better." He saluted the guards as he left the gate and yelled over his shoulder, "Have fun."

By the time I returned, the Tigers' Den was jumping. The mess hall furnished slaw, potato salad, and spicy baked beans. By the time the meat was crispy brown, the starved troops charged the serving table. As fast as the meat was carved, it was consumed. It did not take long for all 120 pounds to be devoured.

After the great dinner, Trey came over. "I have some business in town this evening. Care to go along?"

Traffic on the road to town was light, but in town, the streets, busy as usual, took on a glow at night. Pedicabs, bicycles, and old trucks belching smoke made the city at night come to busy fitful life.

"Where are we headed?" I asked.

"To the little hotel. I'm meeting the Vietnamese contractor who built the O-Club addition."

At the hotel, the thin, intense contractor welcomed us, and the waiter brought beers. We sat on a balcony upstairs overlooking the street.

"Kinda like the French Quarter in New Orleans at Mardi Gras." Trey motioned toward the passing crowd.

Before he could begin the business discussion about another project at the airstrip, a U.S. military jeep pulled up at the sidewalk below us and stopped. The driver looked up and yelled over the noise, "Doc! You're needed back at base."

The second MP jumped in back, and I climbed in the passenger seat. The driver made a U-turn in the heavy traffic, and we headed toward the airfield. I watched the people streaming by. Several looked up and smiled; most did not even notice us in the traffic.

"What's up?" I asked the driver.

"A GI got stuck in the arm with a poison dart."

That's a new one, I thought as we speeded from town traffic to the open highway. MPs waved our jeep through the front gate. I returned a salute.

Lights were already on in the dispensary. Sgt. Tibbs had opened up and was standing by. I saw Spec. 4 Jensen, an enlisted man from North Carolina who worked in the car pool, white-faced and scared, sitting on the treatment table.

"What happened?" I asked.

"I was downtown 'bout 1900, and a kid stuck me." He extended his right forearm to reveal a small puncture wound to the dorsal aspect of his left forearm.

"It's 2200 now," I said, somewhat more sternly than I wished. "What kind of symptoms have you had?"

He only shrugged.

"How are you feeling?" I noted he did not have any alcohol on his breath.

"I feel glassy-eyed," he said.

"What's that like?" I asked.

He shrugged his shoulders again.

I checked vital signs: blood pressure, heart rate, respiration, and temperature were all fine. Pupils normal and reactive; a quick neurological screening proved normal as well. If he had been poisoned, there should be some signs or symptoms by now. I knew it hadn't been curare—the substance favored in South America for poisoned arrows—if so, he'd have been dead long ago.

"I'll give you something to take by mouth right now." I handed him an antihistamine with some water. He swallowed without difficulty. I applied an antibiotic cream to the wound and gave him a tetanus booster. "We'll have the MPs keep an eye on you in your barracks. If you notice any change, any at all, have one of your buddies get an MP pronto. Understand?"

Jensen nodded in agreement and got up easily from the treatment table.

"See you first thing tomorrow at sick call."

He nodded his head again in agreement. One of the MPs escorted him back to his hootch.

I bid Sgt. Tibbs a good night, turned out the lights, locked up, and headed to the Tigers' Den to see what the action might be. An MP walked with me across the street.

"You know there have been reports of VC using poison darts in the field. I sure as hell hope they don't start doing it in town."

"You and me both," I replied. Whatever had punctured Jensen, I hoped it had not been a poison dart. We had enough scary stuff to deal with already.

Outside the club, PBD waved me over. "Where've you been? You've missed out on all the fun!"

"What's happening?"

"Look for yourself." PBD pointed as a truck pulled up in front of the club, motor rumbling. The door to the club opened, and out came MaMa from the Bungalow and several of the girls I recognized from my rounds downtown.

"What's going on here?" I asked.

PBD's laugh sounded sinister. "Some of the guys hired a civilian band, and they brought along the girls for dancing. The CO just got back from dinner in town, and he is not happy. Not one bit."

I saw Maj. Ewald, red-faced and angry, open the door. "You girls, on the truck. Back to town where you belong."

MaMa and the girls, looking out of place, loaded aboard the back of the truck. Dressed in their simple *au dais*, their dark eyes sparkled. Playfully, they blew kisses and yelled, "Good night, GI!"

With all of them loaded, the truck took off in a whirl of dust.

"After you." PDB held the door for me as we entered the club.

Inside, a local civilian band I had never heard before was playing "Satin Doll," an American standard. They played it well, but to my regret, the party was over. Also to my regret, Maj. Reagan was singing. Not too bad, but too loud. When I left after a couple of beers, he was still singing.

I went directly to my bunk and quickly fell asleep. About thirty minutes later, the OD rousted me out. "You're needed at the dispensary." This phrase, now numbingly familiar, seemed to me to be overused.

At the dispensary, Van, one of the civilian helpers in the kitchen, stood at the front door with his young wife. They both looked to be about twelve years old, but I realized this was a trait all the young Vietnamese seemed to share.

"Good evening," I said, bowing slightly.

"No English," the young man indicated.

I went to the club. Loc, the reliable bar boy and assistant to Duc, came over when I got his eye. "Could you help me out? I need a translator."

By now, the band had left, and the club was winding down. "Sure thing, *bac si.*" he smiled.

The small, fine-featured young woman was actually twenty, her husband, twenty-two. Both appeared frightened. The man related to Loc several lengthy sentences accompanied by hand gestures.

"She headache," Loc said finally. "She sick, cold."

In the treatment room, I took her temperature and vital signs. All normal. I didn't have any luck getting any more symptoms from the worried pair. I did a physical as best I could with the husband and Loc at my side. She did not have any abdominal tenderness or rebound, so I felt sure she did not have appendicitis. An ectopic pregnancy also seemed unlikely. I had no plans to do a pelvic exam.

After some reassurance, I gave her a mild oral analgesic. They agreed to return if there were changes or progression of symptoms. The young couple bowed deeply to express their thanks. I wished I had been able to communicate. It is so hard with an interpreter to know if what you ask is relayed accurately and what they tell the interpreter is accurately told to you.

I remembered as a kid playing the "telephone game." I only hoped I wasn't missing something important. They had such faith in me. I again thought how difficult it was for a new doctor without the support of a lab and all the things we took for granted at med school and Harbor Hospital. Without good communication, the symptoms were unclear and the medical history almost non-existent; the likelihood of a missed diagnosis was high. Not a comfortable feeling.

The young couple and Loc left in the night. As I turned out the lights to the treatment room, several civilian-clad GIs came in the front door.

A tall, thin soldier—I didn't know his name but had seen him around and always worried he may have some wasting disease because he was so gaunt—spoke first. "Doc, Lafferty here has cut himself."

Now what? I thought to myself. This was a never-ending night. I looked at my watch. It was 0100 hours.

"How'd it happen?" I asked the soldier.

Lafferty, awkward-looking with light hair and freckles, answered. "Uh, I was practicing my karate. I hit a board and the damn thing flipped up and cut me." He extended a blood-soaked T-shirt that covered his right hand.

I removed the improvised bandage, exposing a clean, shallow laceration on the lateral aspect of his right hand and wrist. After a thorough cleaning, thirteen sutures, a dressing, and tetanus booster, he and his buddies were on their way back into the black, humid Delta night.

"Thanks, Doc," Lafferty called out as he left.

"Anytime, soldier," I lied. "That's my job."

I walked back slowly to my hootch through the dark and now silent compound, abandoned and eerie. I hit the sack and immediately fell asleep.

UNAMED OUTPOST
SUNDAY, FEBRUARY 3, 1963
0130

Forty miles from Soc Trang, a Delta outpost echoed with small-arms fire. Immediately alert, the civilian Self Defense Corps, armed and trained, rushed to their stations. This outpost had American advisors. An advisor radioed for air support and sent up flares to light the flat paddies and black night. T-28s soon arrived and attacked the surrounding area. At dawn, many VC were pinned down, and an unusual daytime battle continued. The advisor called in a B-26 from Saigon for more firepower.

SOC TRANG
0830

The sparse late breakfast crowd buzzed with excitement as I entered the mess hall. PBD and Slick left their trays and ran out the door. Something was definitely going on.

One of the five new pilots who had arrived recently looked up as I went through the food line for my eggs. "Doc, did you hear? B-26 down, two Americans aboard!"

That was the bad news rippling through the room.

"What happened?"

"All's we know is it crashed and burned over some outpost that was getting hammered since early this morning," he added as he took a last swig of coffee before heading out.

My appetite lost, I sprinted to operations to find out the latest.

The lieutenant reported, "We don't know if it got hit or what. It went down a little after 0800 in a wooded area, here." He gave coordinates and pointed to the map. "One report said it crashed first, then burned."

"Any word on the crew?" I asked.

"Not yet, but it doesn't look good." He added tersely, "They're unable to take troops directly to the crash site, so Vietnamese soldiers will be dropped here, as a blocking force." He pointed again to the map. "They're also sending a six-man air force team to try and reach the plane."

He paused briefly to listen to a radio transmission, then resumed. "The Fifty-Seventh already has four choppers out there. They're calling for more. We're going to send the three we can spare."

H-21s cranked up on the flight line; the familiar thump-thumps echoed across the airstrip.

"VNAF is sending two H-34s, and six Hueys are firing away. It's turning into a big operation."

He stopped again to listen to a radio transmission. "Some of the VC tried to take off in waiting sampans. That's their bad luck. They're getting zapped by the Hueys."

The morning dragged on. The two T-28s stationed at Soc Trang made five missions, returning only briefly for refueling. Bad news: Ground troops could not get to the crash site, so they were unable to remove the three bodies from the B-26. If they couldn't reach them by nightfall, flare ships would light the area from dusk to dawn and try for recovery tomorrow.

In the early afternoon heat, our three choppers returned, cargo holds full of the injured. All were civilians. We transferred them as quickly as we could to waiting ARVN trucks for transport to the local hospital. I learned from Slick that over one hundred VCs had been reported killed in the sampans.

"Hey, Doc!" CWO Witt yelled. "It's our turn." He explained we had a new request for a med evac. I grabbed the emergency gear, threw on my helmet, and sat on a flak jacket. Witty gave me a thumbs-up, and we were off. Another outpost had been overrun.

At the still-burning hamlet, we loaded a small woman, about six months pregnant, shot in the right arm. The crew chief lifted aboard a girl, who looked to be perhaps eight years old, with a wound in the left shoulder. I handed him a boy, probably ten years old, with a wound over the right hip. Four men were loaded last. One had a terrible left maxillo-facial injury—the whole left side of his face torn and exposed. The final man aboard had been shot through the left ear.

The ARVN trucks were still tied up with the earlier evacuation carnage, so Brooklyn raced to get our ambulance when we arrived back at Soc Trang. We transferred the wounded to the ambulance. Two of the men rode with Sgt. Patterson and me in our jeep. We arrived at the civilian hospital. It was chaos.

We did all we could. After we had used up the medical supplies we had brought, the day was fading and the setting sun was a blaze of orange. We picked up our litters, loaded the ambulance, and in tandem drove back to the airfield—a long day. At the front gate, the MP saluted smartly and said, "Sir, the officer of the day asks you to report to him first thing."

Sgt. Patterson and I looked at one another, unsure of what that request would mean.

At headquarters, we were told another med evac had been

requested but subsequently cancelled. I felt relief with this news. I didn't have much energy left, and night flying intimidated me. I couldn't help but imagine how it would be to have a chopper shot up and forced to crash land, how it would be in a dark alien rice paddy, hoping help would arrive before the enemy, looking at the flares that would give away your position to the VC—necessary, but troubling, flares. They, alone, afforded any hope of rescue from the sky.

Back in the dispensary, Sgt. Patterson and I finished re-loading our emergency kits with fresh supplies. "So, Sarge, you've been here almost two weeks. What do you think about duty at Soc Trang so far?"

"I have a lot to learn—but doing okay." After a pause, he said, "I sure miss my family."

He took out his billfold from his back pocket and flipped through plastic sleeves holding photos. He selected one, stared at the picture briefly, and handed it to me with a smile. "That's Shirley and the kids. They got it taken just before I left."

A pretty dark-haired woman smiled in the picture, but her eyes looked sad. Two boys stood on either side of her, and she was holding a young girl with brown hair and dark eyes.

"That's a fine family." I handed the billfold back.

"Thanks. I'm pretty proud of them." Sgt. Patterson flipped through several more pictures and selected one. He stared at it briefly, then handed it back to me.

It was a picture of a boy, about twelve years old, dressed in camouflage fatigues and wearing a cap. He had an infectious smile, and with brown eyes directly looking into the camera, he saluted.

"That's Patrick Junior. He can't wait to be old enough to enlist."

"I hate to tell you this, but he's a lot better looking than his old man."

Sgt. Patterson laughed. "He's a champ." After taking a last look, he replaced the billfold in his pocket. "They all are."

We closed the dispensary for the night.

After a quick bite to eat at the O-Club, I headed to the showers and an early bedtime. I looked to the southeast toward Camp Dutah.

I often did, as the Special Forces team there were my buddies. They rarely came in to Soc Trang airfield for a hot shower and well-deserved break. I noted flares in the distance in the approximate place where the camp was located. I sent up a prayer that they were not under attack tonight—this day from hell. I noticed the moonlight softly bathing the land and felt a gentle warm breeze on my face. Wonderful weather seemed so paradoxical to all that was going on around us.

B-26 CRASH SITE

From dusk to dawn, flares lit up the area where the bomber went down. ARVN troops, placed in blocking positions, guarded the wooded site in an effort to keep the VC away from the dead American crew and the weapons aboard the plane.

SOC TRANG
MON
4 FEB 63
0130

The OD rousted me out of the sack as I had memories of being summoned from deep sleep at Harbor General when on call. I didn't know then how good I had it there—another world, distant and remote. This wake-up call: another med evac. Quick response meant quick response. I threw on my fatigues, laced my boots, and grabbed the ever-ready emergency kit. We flew about forty minutes from Soc Trang and descended in the darkness toward four small fires, which designated a pickup area. Two American advisors and several black-pajamaed Vietnamese civilians were standing by. They helped us load eight wounded civilians who lived in the village and belonged to the Self Defense Corps ; fortunately, none were too severely wounded.

A three-quarter moon was clear in the sky, and below us, the flat Delta glittered with small fires from innumerable hamlets and villages—a beautiful, tranquil scene. The night was warm. I saw some tracers and knew the VC were shooting at us. I thought back to the night infiltration course and the tracers at Camp Bullis; that was a picnic compared to this. Even though I knew tonight we were too high to be hit by ground fire, my fear marred the joy of flying on this fine night; our chopper was great for VC target practice.

We returned to Soc Trang without incident, and the wounded were transferred for transport to the civilian hospital. I thought of that hospital, which lacked facilities for all this definitive emergency care, and wondered why the Vietnamese didn't have military hospitals to care for the wounded civilian Self Defense Corps and Civilian Defense Corps who, it seemed to me, fought more than the ARVN. Why didn't they treat all those wounded in combat at military hospitals? This country was at war. Many of their men, young and not so young, were being hurt, maimed, and killed. Something just wasn't right. I returned to my bunk at 0135. No worry about counting sheep. I only needed to close my eyes.

SOC TRANG
1030

Sgt. Tibbs and I loaded aboard one of two choppers and took off from Soc Trang. Our dreadful mission would be to retrieve the bodies at the B-26 crash site. We now knew there were three officers: two Americans and one Vietnamese. The punishing Delta sun made this grim task harder. Working as a team, we again made records of our findings for the crash investigation. All weapons were accounted for. We loaded our silent cargo.

Another team would come out next and dismantle and take away everything that might be of use to the VC. Glad to leave this place of disaster, we boarded our choppers, gained altitude, and headed home.

In the noisy aircraft, my thoughts were of these three pilots, lives lost in their prime. They carried within them the hopes and dreams of their parents and friends, now forever extinguished.

The ARVN ambulance took the Vietnamese officer's body, and Brooklyn had the ambulance ready for the two Americans. Sgt. Patterson was right there when we landed. We did not talk but loaded the two olive-drab canvas bags in the back of the ambulance.

It was hard to find relief from the unforgiving Delta sun, but Brooklyn parked the ambulance in the shade of the hangar. The heat of the day turned this makeshift morgue into an oven.

At 1500, the plane arrived to evacuate the fallen warriors. We loaded the lonely bags aboard the plane for Saigon and watched the plane take off.

We had to leave the ambulance doors open for several days to rid it of the stench of death.

The dead weight of sadness permeated the air. Fortunately, I had a quiet afternoon and some time to reflect.

At 1730, the OD alerted me to a possible med evac, but the VNAF took it; I was glad.

A bad day; I was now tired of flying. I didn't think that would happen. It wasn't the flying—that was still a thrill—it was where and how we flew. At high altitudes, I felt safe from the ground fire, but when we were up there, about 2,500 feet, I thought of Sput and the others, what their last minutes were like. Those H-21s were old and shaky. The mechanics worked miracles, but the machines were stressed and wearing out. Replacement parts, new or used, were hard to come by. Sometime they had to "cannibalize" parts from choppers that were down for routine maintenance and use them to keep enough going to fly our missions.

When we came in for a med evac and bullets hit the chopper, or when we flew into an unsecured area and needed real power because we were overloaded, I got anxious. I remembered Doc Greene telling me about the flight surgeon up north who died in that crash last year. I felt sorry for him, and then I felt guilty about feeling sorry for myself.

The men here needed me, and I could control most of my fears pretty well. I had confidence in these pilots and mechanics and their abilities. They needed to have confidence in me and my abilities. We were all at considerable risk, but that came with our mission. That was our life. I knew my family and friends would have missed me if anything happened, but I didn't have a wife and children, so it would have been better me than them. It was an honor to take care of the Soc Trang Tigers.

I needed to get downtown to the orphanage. They could use

some supplies by now, but I wondered if our interventions made any real change for them in the cosmic sense. Couldn't give up, though; there was hope—the only antidote I knew.

I took out my diary from its accustomed spot in my duffle bag. In the distance, I heard explosions, now routine. I thought of home. So far away now, it seemed almost difficult to remember.

WASHINGTON, DC
MON
4 FEB 63

JFK received the report he requested in December 1962 for a fresh look at the war. This account indicated a long and costly war and suggested the VC were so successful recruiting in South Vietnam they would not need any infiltration from North Vietnam.

The rules of engagement were changed: Americans could now "shoot first" at enemy targets of opportunity. The order expanded the U.S. mission. This change, almost imperceptibly, meant the role of the American military was no longer to just advise, support, and defend the ARVN.[21]

SOC TRANG
THUR
7 FEB 63

Morning sick call was heavy. Sgt. Patterson and crew helped out so efficiently that we soon finished, leaving time to attend to our other tasks. I inspected the kitchen and water point and had time to complete the documentation.

I asked Sgt. Patterson to come back to the treatment room/ office. He sat on the chair next my desk and we reviewed how the crew was doing. We decided on the supplies we needed to order and concluded things seemed to be going pretty well.
When we finished, I asked, "What are your plans? After Vietnam?"

"My next duty station should be my last. I'll have my twenty years in soon. The army's been good to me, but I hate to be away from Shirley and the kids. We'll move back to Ohio. I plan to get certified to become a physician's assistant. I'm thirty-eight, and I figure I've got lots of good years ahead of me."

"Sounds good. Being a PA with your experience, you can get work anyplace."

"How about you, Doc?"

"I've got another year to put in after I get back. I'll apply for residency training of some kind. Undecided right now. It seems just too far off."

"Single and no attachments—you'll be free to go wherever you want."

"True, but it must be great to have a family like yours to go home to."

"Doc, I couldn't agree more."

In the late afternoon, we had a med evac to Bac Lieu to pick up nine severely wounded ARVN soldiers who had been traveling in an army truck that drove over a mine. They were not stabilized, but we loaded them in the choppers anyway. Thick dust swirled from the rotor wash.

"Slick," I yelled over the engine roar, "call ahead and let them know we're going to need to go to the dispensary before we can evac these men anywhere."

"Roger, that." Slick relayed the message.

We gained altitude, and I looked at the land below. It was dry and brown. When I first came to Soc Trang, the land had been green. Now the rice had been harvested, and there had been no rain. The fields were parched and cracked open, the paddies dusty. I wished for rain, but when it had rained and the mud proved so tough for our landings and takeoffs, I'd wished for dust.

We were not far from Soc Trang, and ambulances, including our own with Brooklyn at the wheel, met us to take the men to our dispensary.

This would be a test of our new team. They had been well-trained and went to work. The injured were given first aid and moved to the hospital. I felt pleased; my men handled this challenge very well.

When things quieted down, I took Sgt. Patterson and Tibbs aside. "Great work." They nodded.

Finally, I had some good help. What a relief—medics to share the never-ending demand. Even though right now, we still did not have enough aircraft available for ARVN assault missions, we were doing lots of med evacs all over the Delta.

In the mail, I found a letter from my old friend Scott Mitchell. He was still at Ft. Ord in California, but, as predicted, he had received orders to come to Vietnam. He hoped we could get together in Saigon before he started his duty station. I thought back to our days at Harbor General Hospital, Ft. Sam, and Ft. Rucker.

I had changed since then. It was hard to understand or put into words, but I felt somehow different. Back at Ft. Rucker, flying in helicopters had been an adventure. I assumed Scott's stint at Ft. Ord had been more of the same. I had three months under my belt at Soc Trang, but it seemed much longer. What had I accomplished? What had I learned? I could hardly understand my thoughts, much less write them in a letter. I decided to put off writing anything, at least for awhile. Things would become clearer, but I definitely knew I looked forward to seeing Scott, hopefully in Saigon, before long.

I looked again at the pinup pictures of our California stewardess friends—so blond, so round-eyed, and so very far away.

SAIGON
THUR
7 FEB 63

MACV reported both progress in the war and weakening VC morale.[22]

MY THO
FRI
8 FEB 63

A field advisor detailed for MACV in Saigon how Gen. Cao, IV Corps commander, used intelligence supplied by the United

States to purposely plan ARVN assault missions in areas where there were no VC to engage in battle.[23]

SOC TRANG
MON
11 FEB 63

"Last one." Sgt. Patterson ushered the Spec. 4 in for suture removal.

Glad to see the end of a busy morning sick call, I finished removing the last stitch and admired the clean scar.

"Good work, Doc," Sgt. Patterson said as the young GI left the treatment room.

"Thanks. I try." I put the instruments on the tray to be sterilized in the autoclave. "What's the news from home, Sarge?"

"Not much. Shirley's got her hands full, but her younger sister's moving from Ohio to stay awhile. That'll help. A lot."

We were interrupted by the clerk, Tony, who rushed into the treatment room.

"Doc Hoyland—a med evac. Outpost got overrun last night. Four wounded. Several dead."

"We're on our way," I said. "Ready, Sergeant Patterson?"

He smiled his agreeable smile. "As ready as I'll ever be."

We both picked up our emergency bags and jogged together to the flight line.

It was a short flight. When we were going in for the landing, I recognized the hamlet. We had been here before. Now smoke was in the air; it was in ruins, almost totally destroyed. The small palm-thatched huts were burned. Bamboo poles, forlorn without walls to support, were upright under the tall palm trees singed and brown. Smoke, pungent and gray, hung in the still air. The peasants looked ashen and desperate. Grim-faced American advisors helped load the escort chopper with the dead.

It was horrifying to see these strategic hamlets after they had been overrun. Mostly, the peasants got shot-up at night trying to defend these desperate little fortified hamlets surrounded by a sea of VC. It was no secret; the Communists wanted them dead to get their hands on new U.S. weapons.

We loaded so many wounded onto our chopper, I quickly lost count. Sgt. Patterson, blood on his uniform, helped lift an old man with a chest wound up into the hold. He took up the last space on the floor. I placed a young boy with an injury to his left arm on the bench seat. I didn't see any tears in his enormous eyes; they were too filled with fear. The injured now completely filled our chopper; we had no more room.

The crew chief gave a thumbs-up to Trey, and the overloaded chopper labored mightily to get airborne.

The floor was covered wall to wall with wounded. I sat on the bench seat on one side of the hold, and Sgt. Patterson and the young boy sat across from me. I looked at the suffering cargo and felt some relief to know we were close to the airfield. It wouldn't be a long flight. These wounded would soon be in the Soc Trang civilian hospital—better there than in a destroyed hamlet.

We landed, and our chopper shuddered to a stop on the tarmac. The engine whine began to wind down. I looked out the back door to see how many Vietnamese ambulances were standing by, when the inside of our chopper ripped with thunderous machine-gun fire. By reflex, my hands covered my face, and I curled into a protective fetal position.

The machine-gun rounds were inside the hold with us. They were so fast that they ran together; they were so close, my nose instantly filled with the stench of the hot gun, blood, and burned flesh. I assumed I had been shot. Blood and flesh covered my left side, but I had no pain. The rounds stopped as suddenly as they started. I quickly checked myself. Except for a piece of metal shrapnel in the back of my left hand, which had covered my face, I was fully functional. I was not shot and not injured. I couldn't comprehend what had just happened.

After a momentary stunned silence, a soft moan came from across the hold. It was not coming from the two Vietnamese who had been lying on the floor at my feet. Both had been shot and were now dead. I looked across the hold. Sgt. Patterson moaned again.

Motionless and slumped forward, his uniform was shredded and bloody from multiple wounds at close range.

A deadly accident in our chopper—the gunner had routinely swung the supporting bar and machine gun into the cabin and toward us to get the weapon out of the doorway for off-loading. As the machine gun was pointed toward us inside the cargo hold, the trigger caught on the improvised mounting and automatically fired directly at us and our wounded passengers. Eleven automatic rounds exploded in the instant it took the gunner to disengage the trigger.

In the emergency, activity blurred. Sgt. Tibbs and medic Harris, already standing by to help with our wounded cargo, immediately put Sgt. Patterson on a litter. Brooklyn and the ambulance were at the ready; tires burned rubber on the tarmac as we took off for the dispensary. In the treatment room, airway secured, we started two Dextran IVs, one in his left arm, one in his right leg. He had been shot in the right arm, groin, and left leg. Pressure dressings on the wounds halted further blood loss.

Maj. Ewald cleared a plane for immediate takeoff. Brooklyn and Harris carried Sgt. Patterson's litter to the Otter, and within minutes, Sgt. Tibbs and I were flying with our injured colleague north toward Saigon. Sgt. Tibbs and I took turns providing CPR and pushing the IVs. In less than forty minutes, our plane landed at Tan Son Nhut. A waiting ambulance rushed us to the hospital, where the receiving doctor, my old friend Doc Lemmon, pronounced what Tibbs and I could not accept: Sgt. Patterson was dead.

Numb and still unable to accept what had just occurred, Sgt. Tibbs and I climbed back aboard the Otter for the return flight to Soc Trang. We sat in silence, the drone of the engine the only sound. The pilot took the familiar heading toward the Delta. I looked out from the window at the flat rice paddies and tree lines, my thoughts filled with Sgt. Patterson.

I thought of his family back home; I remembered the picture he showed me of his wife and their three young children. I remembered the picture of young Patrick Junior, saluting. Would he want to join the army now? Unlikely. It would be hard, knowing it took his dad. And I thought of the young gunner whose weapon had malfunctioned with such dreadful consequence. This would be pain he would carry forever. I thought of our new, small dispensary team—our family here. This accidental loss was inconceivable.

Late that night, alone at the typewriter in the dispensary, I struggled over what to write to the Patterson family. I counted the days he had been here—only nineteen. As his commanding officer, I agonized about finding words for a meaningful condolence letter. I tried, but I knew my words would be of little comfort. I knew life was unfair, but why did it have to be so merciless to the kind and good?

SAIGON
WED
13 FEB 63

All H-21s were grounded to modify the gun mounts. We could not tolerate a repeat of this disaster.

We closed the dispensary long enough for all of us to attend plane-side services at Tan Son Nhut. Chaplain O'Brian said a few words. We stood at attention, saluted the coffin draped in an American flag, and watched in silence as Sgt. Patterson was loaded aboard for his flight home to Shirley and three young children, who would only be left with memories.

SOC TRANG
FRI
15 FEB 63

A fair amount of good scrap lumber remained from the new O-Club addition. Since it belonged to the officers—we had paid for it after all—we knew what we wanted to do with it.

PBD borrowed one of the trucks, and several of us loaded the good-quality boards and plywood. PBD drove me to the Tigers' Den and we picked up Duc, our loyal translator. The three of us rode to the leprosarium.

The elderly chief of the colony, with tears in his eyes, was thankful for this gift of hard-to-come-by wood. He bowed low in appreciation.

Their work at the compound consisted of light woodworking, manufacturing clay roof tiles by hand, and repairing fishing nets. He told Duc tomorrow would be an anniversary of "Leprous Day," and he hoped we would come to the celebration, which would start at 1700.

Pleased the gift would be used for a very good cause, we returned to the airfield and dropped Duc off at the club.

SOC TRANG
SAT
16 FEB 63

Another balmy, beautiful day. PBD, Hartley Davis, and I loaded some cartons of cereal and two big cases of dried milk into my jeep.

Maj. Reagan pulled up beside us in an open jeep, driven by a young sergeant. "Don't forget, you three musketeers, dinner tonight at the MAAG house. We'll see you at 1830."

"We'll be there." I stopped to wipe the sweat from my brow. It was a treat to be invited to eat with the MAAGits, as we loved to call them. Because they were few in number, they hired a civilian chef for their mess at the villa in town. The food was served in a regular dining room and tended to be like a family dinner. It was a nice change from both the mess hall and the Tigers' Den.

We loaded the rest of the provisions in the jeep, and PBD sat next to the cartons in back. I drove and Hartley sat in front. We headed toward the leprosarium in town. Graceful arches, made from palm fronds for the celebration, decorated the dusty lane from the highway leading to the colony. Many colorful Republic of South Vietnam flags, yellow with three red stripes to signify North, Central, and South Vietnam, also lined the drive and flapped in the wind. The patients and their families were in a festive mood. They greeted us warmly. The children who had attended the Christmas party rushed up to us, laughing and welcoming. The residents bowed. Everyone was freshly scrubbed and wore their best clothes.

The chief, a slight, gaunt man with a wispy white beard, stepped forward to receive us and the cartons. He was dressed in white pajamas of celebration instead of the usual black ones. Several men quickly unloaded the supplies and took them to the kitchen. This food would supplement their steady diet of fish and rice.

Many local people gathered for the event: several Sisters from the Orphanage, who stood out in the crowd dressed in their black habits; a group of ARVN officers and the province chief and his deputies; and dozens more officials and people from town I had never seen before.

After several speakers, the chief stepped up to the microphone. He somehow held the formal speech even though the disease had claimed all his fingers on both hands, and only small mounds were left where his thumbs should be. He read the brief speech in the musical Vietnamese language, but even though I didn't understand the words, he communicated the message with sincerity and clarity. I looked at the residents as the chief spoke. They all had various stages of the disease; many had distorted faces, noses, ears, and limbs. In spite of all this deformity, they had a genuine, gracious quality.

The speaker finished to generous applause, and a little band of five patients played Oriental music on a stage erected for the party. The nuns from the orphanage nursery came over and greeted us like old friends.

Before we left, the chief handed me a letter typed in English. He bowed politely. I felt touched, as I knew this had taken great effort. It was his brief address:

"Tenth Anniversary of BA XUYEN LEPROSARIUM

On behalf of all the patients of BA XUYEN LEPROSARIUM, I would like to welcome you to the ceremony of our tenth anniversary. I want to express to you our deepest appreciation for your attendance. Your presence here today is a great

*honor, a tremendous comfort and encouragement
to all of us. Your presence makes us feel that we
are no longer outcast. It warms our hearts to know
that there are still people who are interested in
our welfare. Again, I want to thank you for your
attendance and your many donations."*

We bowed our good-byes, climbed in my jeep, and headed down the lane. The setting sun lit up the flags as they snapped smartly in the wind, adding to the celebration. We turned toward town. I looked forward to dinner at the MAAG house, which had some charm, at least to those of us living in the barracks. It was a house, and the officers had trained their civilian cook to prepare foods they liked. I enjoyed the MAAGits' company, and this was a mighty welcome invitation.

We drove up, and Maj. Reagan came out. "Doc, we just received a call. They're looking for you. Someone got cut at the airfield."

PBD said, "I'll go along. No sense going it alone and tempting fate."

Davis climbed down, and Maj. Reagan added, "Sorry. We'll keep some chow warm."

The MP sentry waved us through the front gate to the airfield, and I drove directly to the dispensary. I went through the back door into the treatment room and found Sgt. Tibbs and Spec.4 Mosby from the water supply point.

"What happened?" I asked.

"Bad luck," Mosby said with disgust. "I was working on the water storage tank. Slipped somehow and caught my elbow on a metal support strap that holds the stand up."

The edge must have been as sharp as a razor. My examination revealed a severe laceration to his right elbow. The ulnar and cutaneous nerves were both severed. This required surgery. I dressed the wound and made quick phone calls to operations and the field hospital. Fortunately, a transport was preparing to leave; they agreed to take Mosby along for the med evac.

Problem resolved, PBD, waiting in the driver's seat, started the jeep's engine. "Record time, Doc. We're gonna have dinner with the MAAGits after all."

The dining room smelled of pungent Italian spices—spaghetti with long-simmered meat sauce. They also had the excellent local French bread I loved, and red table wine to wash it down. This dinner had been worth the wait.

After dinner, we all drove over for a warm beer on one of the barges in the river. The Japanese bottled beer was very good, but without refrigeration, it had to be served warm. Locals used ice in their beer glass to cool it, but the water to make ice was untreated and not safe for our delicate immune systems. Thirsty after the spaghetti, the warm beer would be fine.

Since the MAAG people lived here in the Soc Trang community, many customers on the barge knew and greeted them as neighbors. As I sipped my beer, I looked around and again wondered how many of the black pajama-clad people surrounding us were VC. I knew they knew, again, exactly how many Americans were here tonight.

SOC TRANG
SUN
17 FEB 63

A beautiful, sunny, quiet morning with no missions scheduled. A day of rest. Since the disaster at Ap Bac, we did not have many choppers flyable, so not many missions. I understood, though, that the fleet had now been repaired, and we were about ready to resume regular duty.

The chaplain finished with a prayer, and about twenty of us filed out of the Sunday service.

"I'll be here full-time next week," said Father O'Brian, bright blue eyes twinkling.

"Good news," I said. "We need all the help you can give."

I flopped on my bunk and re-read a letter from Frank, up in Pleiku. He had been busy, it seemed, doing pretty much what I did. He also had been treating some tribesmen in the mountains up there. He hoped we could get some R&R together to go to Hong

Kong in March. It sounded good, but I wished I'd saved up more money. You needed plenty of cash, as that was the place to buy great stuff at great prices. Custom clothes were a particular bargain.

PBD's yell startled me. "Doc, old buddy, grab your gear!"

I couldn't help but groan, "Where to this time?"

"South, where else? You didn't think we'd be going to the 'ville?" he laughed. "Father Hoa's place. We're picking up somebody who's sick and taking in some supplies."

I had heard of the legendary Father Hoa. He and Father Phuoc were two of the few Catholic priests who had organized militias loyal to the government. President Diem personally supported the priests. He also made certain these loyal civilian volunteers, who bravely defended their hamlets and fought the VC, had arms and supplies.

I had never been to either of these outposts, but I knew Father Phuoc's stronghold was on Gung Island in the Mekong. Choppers were the only safe way for re-supply, as the VC owned most of the island and the river.

Father Hoa's outpost, about eighty miles from Soc Trang, was located at Binh Hung near the southwest tip of the Delta. His compound had been run over by the VC in May, and of the three hundred who lived there, over thirty had been killed. His troops called themselves the Sea Swallows. They gave anyone who visited their compound a small ornament of a swallow, fashioned from used brass shell casings. These artful swallows were pinned on the caps of many chopper pilots and crews and were a desired souvenir.

Once aloft at high altitude, my doldrums at having Sunday interrupted immediately lifted. It was a great day to fly, not too hot and not too humid. The chopper hummed; the flight was smooth; the countryside looked clean; and the watery world sparkled in the bright sun.

As we started our descent, I saw a bright flash from the ground near a clump of luxuriant coconut palms. It flashed again. I realized it was a mirror reflecting the sun—a signal for PBD. I remembered that's how they did it in all those cowboy movies in my youth; the mirror reflected in the sunlight saved many a day for the cavalry.

We touched down near the riverbank on a flat, dry stretch of land. A group of black-clad peasants clumped together at one side of the field surrounded a young Vietnamese soldier lying on a military stretcher. Many other civilians appeared from nowhere after we landed and quickly off-loaded the supplies. Four others carried the wounded soldier on a litter to the chopper.

One of the younger men in the group came over to me and, in English, explained, "He have pain. It bad." He pointed to the soldier's right lower abdomen.

"We'll get him to Can Tho hospital," I said.

"Thank you, *bac si*." He gave me a swallow pin and bowed politely.

"Thank you," I echoed and bowed my head.

When we had the litter secured in the hold, another wounded soldier came hobbling over. He had a large, bloody bandage over his left thigh. After he boarded, many civilians came over and wanted to climb aboard; the crew chief had to limit the passenger load. Several were disappointed to miss out on this free taxi service to Can Tho but seemed to understand the limitation.

PBD fired up the engine, and the passengers smiled, giddy with excitement. They were all talking to one another at once until we lifted off and they fell into absolute silence—their first flight.

We reached cruising altitude quickly. The crew chief came over to me and shouted in my ear, "Doc, ARVN transportation will be standing by."

When we landed at the Can Tho airstrip, an ARVN ambulance, as promised, drove up. We rapidly transferred the two soldiers. In the meantime, the civilians scattered in all directions across the tarmac.

Some MAAG personnel drove up in a jeep with coffee and an unexpected surprise. This was the only time anyone had ever brought us chopper crews coffee, and the only time anyone brought along an American girl as well.

Attractive, with a bright smile, she introduced herself. "Hi, guys. I'm Beverly. Beverly Deepe."

PBD, as always, recovered from his sense of surprise first. "And what brings a nice girl like you to a place like this?"

She laughed. "I'm a correspondent. For *Newsweek*."

We introduced ourselves, and the MAAG people enjoyed our delight at meeting this attractive round-eyed girl dressed in a white blouse and blue skirt. Her light blue silk scarf blew off in the prop wash, revealing dark brown hair. The crew chief retrieved the scarf as it tumbled over the asphalt. She smiled and thanked him. He blushed when he handed it to her.

PBD said, "Miss Beverly, you are the news here. How about flying back with us to Soc Trang? Maybe we could make some headlines."

She laughed her pleasant, soft laugh again. "I've heard about you Soc Trang Tigers. I'd love to, but I'm in the middle of something here."

"How long have you been in-country?" I asked.

"One year and three days." This impressed me.

The crew chief pointed to his watch to let us know it was time to take off. We finished our coffee and thanked the MAAG guys profusely.

"Unfortunately, duty calls," PBD said. "But come down our way if you get a chance, Bev."

Once our chopper was in the air, PBD did a quick flyover. Beverly waved, and we waved a good-bye as we headed back south.

PBD yelled over the noise, "Doc, I think I'm in love."

SOC TRANG
WED
20 FEB 63

"*Bac si*," Duc said as I walked in the O-Club, "you want see Chinese doctor?"

I almost misunderstood, but he quickly clarified he was asking if I wanted to see a Chinese doctor at work. I readily agreed.

He smiled. "I take you."

After dinner, Duc and I headed to town in my jeep. We climbed narrow stairs in one of the downtown hotels and stood at the end of a long, dark hallway lined with closed doors. About two-thirds of the way down the hallway, I saw a bony, elderly Oriental man dressed in shabby white pajamas. He was blind, eyes open and opaque perhaps from cataracts, glaucoma, or trachoma, all prevalent in this country.

Holding his right hand, a young boy, who appeared to be about eight years old, acted as guide. The boy had a canvas backpack of sorts filled with some equipment. In his left hand, the doctor had a wire strung with bottle caps. When he shook these, they made a loud, distinct sound, advertising he was available for patients. He also cried out in a chant, both mournful and piercing.

No one could miss his presence.

The boy stopped when Duc approached and told the doctor I was an American army doctor who wanted to observe his work. The old man's face lit up, and he smiled, revealing mostly gums and a few yellow and brown stained teeth.

"*Bac si.*" He bowed politely and seemed pleased we were there.

One of the many doors along the hallway opened, and a man's hand beckoned toward the doctor. The boy immediately steered the doctor toward the room. Illuminated only by a bare overhead light bulb, we entered the dark room interior. The sparse furnishings consisted of an old bed with a mat, a saggy reed-bottom chair, and a small bedside table. The man, a youngish to middle-aged Vietnamese, stripped off his loose shirt to reveal a thin, bony ribcage and chest. Going over to the bed, he laid face down. He must have had previous treatments, I surmised, as he definitely knew the routine.

With amazing dexterity and speed for a man who could not see, the doctor took supplies from his young assistant: glass cups, an alcohol burner, and long matches, which he set on the little table next to the bed. The old man, sightless eyes vacant and unfocused, gave an amazingly vigorous massage to the patient's upper and lower back. He pulled up the man's pajama legs and massaged his lower legs and feet.

After completing the massages, the doctor lit the alcohol burner and briefly heated the inside of a glass cup. Quickly, he placed this on the upper right side of the patient's back. Suction pulled skin up into the glass cup for at least two inches. The skin turned bright red and faded to purple as the oxygen in the tissue became depleted. The old man soon had covered the patient's back with ten cups filled with purple skin.

After several minutes, the doctor determined the treatment had been completed. He expertly and rapidly removed the cups with a snap of his thin wrist. Each cup gave a sound as the suction released, and the skin flattened. Left behind were deep purple bruises where the edges of the cups had caused the most pressure on the capillaries under the skin.

Duc said, "He treat back pain. For headache, one or two here," he pointed to his forehead.

Fascinated, I said, "Duc, ask the doctor how this treatment works."

Duc and the old man had a lengthy conversation. Duc turned to me. "He say pull out evil and poisons."

I remembered seeing people walking along the street with dark bruises between their eyes. I asked about this.

Duc replied, "That another treatment headache. Same sore throat."

The old doctor, who seemed pleased by the questions, began talking to Duc again.

"He do four or six treatment on good night. He doctor twenty-one years. He ask how long you doctor?"

"Almost two years," I said.

Duc translated, and the blind man gave me a kind smile and bowed.

The doctor quickly pocketed the fifty piastres the patient paid for the treatment. The young boy efficiently put the glass cups, burner, and matches back in the cloth bag and picked it up by the strap. He put the bottle-cap noisemaker in his mentor's left hand and took the right hand to lead him away.

We said good night, and the boy and blind doctor resumed their trek down the hallway. When we reached the bottom of the hotel stairs, I could still hear the rattle of the bottle caps and strange sing-song chant echoing in the hallway above. I hoped the Chinese doctor, ready for the next patient, felt good about adding to my medical education. I now understood more about all the odd bruises I had noticed on so many people.

SOC TRANG
THUR
21 FEB 63

The news was good and bad. The good news: Capt. Brewster was on the promotion list. A fine officer; he deserved it. Unfortunately, the Ninety-Third as an organization had room for only one major. That would be the CO, Maj. Ewald. Consequently, the bad news: The soon-to-be new Maj. Brewster would have to be transferred.

I remembered the last night in Saigon before I came to Soc Trang in November. Doc Lemmon, Frank, and I met up with Brewster at the *Cercle Sportif.* He gave me the "secret" POL message. Could it be only three months ago? It seemed longer, much longer to me.

With the news of promotion comes celebration. I put in an enthusiastic appearance at the Tigers' Den, but even though I knew there was no mission scheduled for the next day, I felt so tired I retired to hootch #4 early. I knew Brewster would throw a proper party later on before he was transferred, and I certainly wouldn't miss that.

At 0030, the OD roused me with the old familiar, "Doc, you're needed right away." He added urgently, "At the O-Club."

Now what, I wondered. Had someone had too much and had a problem? That had never happened yet. An accident? A fall? A tussle with Tuffy? I rushed over, following the OD.

The Tigers' Den reverberated with a party atmosphere.

"Look at these, Doc," the new Maj. Brewster called me over. He and Maj. Ewald were both holding brand new state-of-the-art flight helmets. These APH-5 models were the envy of every helicopter pilot. Pristine white, they came equipped with the best headphones and microphones available—the Cadillac of flight helmets. Both of these babies had been personalized with the majors' names and gold insignias. The men had surprised Maj. Ewald and the new Maj. Brewster with these coveted helmets.

Before I could congratulate these deserving officers, out from beneath the bar came a third helmet. It was exactly like the majors' but had captain's bars, a medical caduceus, and my name! My throat burned, and my eyes stung; fortunately, the guys began to sing our old favorite, "For He's A Jolly Good Fellow … Bullshit."

Before, when we were in-flight, I had no radio contact with the crew. This new helmet had a mike and headphones for internal communications. I could talk to the pilots and crew without trying to shout over the engine noise. I could also hear the pilots on their radios and know what was going on between pilot and airfield and pilot and crew. An unexpected, superb gift that would help me do a better job.

I saw someone come in the side door but paid little attention, basking in my new helmet.

"Tell Doc to meet me at the dispensary."

I looked up and saw an MP leaving the club. Party over, it was again time for work. Carrying my treasured flight helmet, I crossed the dark street. An MP and a PFC were standing at the front door.

"What's up?" I asked.

"I woke up to take a piss and walked right into the latrine door," the young soldier said. His left hand held a white T-shirt to his forehead, soaked with blood.

The MP, wearing a crisp uniform and highly polished boots, added, "We brought him right over, sir."

When I removed the shirt, I saw a clean laceration about one and one-half inches long perpendicular to frown lines, pumping blood from a small severed artery. After local anesthetic, cleaning, clamping, tying off, and stitching, the closed wound looked good.

The PFC thanked me. His voice had a pleasant twang.

"Where're you from?" I asked.

"Little Rock, Arkansas."

"I'm from not too far away, myself." I laughed, "But you better come up with a better story on how this happened for the folks back home. A latrine door is pretty lame."

"You're right, sir. I even dread the ration of grief I'll get from the guys in the barracks."

The young PFC headed back to his hootch, the MP resumed his

duties, and cradling my helmet, I walked back to the club to see if anyone was still up. It was dark and quiet. I looked at my watch: 0230. TGIF was over for this week. Glad tomorrow would be a Saturday with no flying scheduled, I went to hootch #4. PBD was coming back from the shower room.

"Hey, Doc, great helmet," he said.

"Thanks," I said.

He slapped me on the shoulder. "You deserve it, good doctor." He went into his bunk.

Standing in the night, outside hootch #4, my throat again ached. Thankfully, I was alone and unobserved in the dark.

SOC TRANG
FRI
22 FEB 63

Strong, gusty winds swept the Delta. It buffeted our two H-21s as we circled Long Phu.

Before we left Soc Trang, I had checked to be sure I had vasopressors and an emergency airway in the first-aid kit. We were on a flight to med evac a U.S. Special Forces sergeant reported to have suffered a head wound. I plugged my new helmet into the aircraft communications jack and heard all the communications. What a gift; it was great to be able to communicate with the pilots and crew by headset.

In spite of the wind, PBD had a smooth touchdown. I jumped out of the back cargo door and ran under the rotor wash. He did not plan to turn the engine off, as we were going to make a quick pickup in this known bad area. A group of Green Berets were clustered under the shelter of a line of palm trees.

"What do we have?" I shouted to be heard over the grinding engine noise.

The medic tending the sergeant on a litter answered, "A leg wound."

Better than a head wound, I thought.

The medic continued, "His .45 discharged while it was in his holster. A through-and-through wound." He removed the dressing to reveal a bullet wound.

"Went through the fibula, looks like," I said, noting fat globules glistening in the sunlight.

The Special Forces medics were well trained, and he had done a good job of immobilization. We replaced the dressing and ran to the waiting chopper. We traded litters and the aft gunner helped load the patient aboard. With his machine gun quickly back in place, a wave to the Special Forces team, and a thumbs-up from the crew chief, we took off.

Through the telecom, I asked PBD to call Soc Trang and request a med evac. A few minutes later, I heard PBD say, "There's an Otter available to take him to Saigon. The medical officer at Tan San Nhut, a Capt. Lemmon, requested the patient should be sent with medical escort."

I smiled. Old buddy Lemmon. A real pal. I hadn't been to the city in a very long time.

When we approached Soc Trang, I saw the waiting Otter. Sgt. Tibbs and Brooklyn were standing by to help transfer the wounded sergeant. I quickly briefed Sgt. Tibbs about the plan and sprinted to hootch #4 to pick up overnight gear. By 1530, the wounded Special Forces sergeant and I were airborne. I looked out at the flat Delta, anticipating the unexpected few hours of glorious respite.

The Green Beret sergeant waved good-bye to me from the litter and was transferred to the receiving area. It was great to see Doc Lemmon. All physicians have a kinship, but doctors in the Medical Corps have a special bond. We talked the same language.

"Tonight, it's La Cigalle for dinner," Doc Lemmon announced.

I had heard this was one of the best restaurants in Saigon and served fine French cuisine. It could have been New Orleans, as far from the military and mess-hall food as could be imagined. We were not disappointed.

Christmas Day 1962: Picking up children from the lepers' colony for the party.

Christmas party for children from orphanage and lepers' colony.

Sisters at orphanage showing off new washing machine.

Cardinal Spellman arrives for Christmas Mass
at Soc Trang Airfield.

134ᵗʰ Med Det ready for duty.

Tuffy at ease.

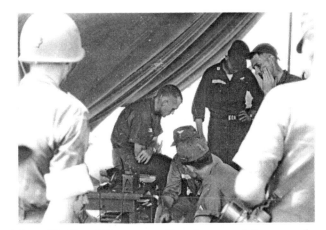

2 Jan 63: Tan Hiep; standing by, awaiting word on twelve downed crewmen at battle of Ap Bac.

Wearing my new APH-5 helmet.

ARVN soldier guarding VC.

VC detainment area.

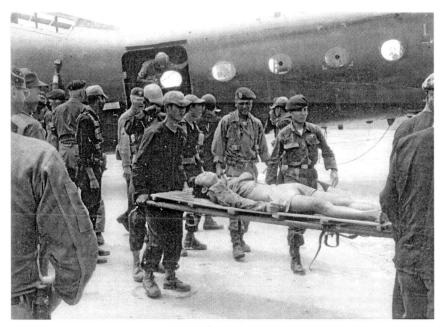

ARVN med evac.

Typical H-21 hit by VC gunfire.

TAN SAN NHUT
SAT
23 FEB 63

Early in the morning, the winds still gusting, I boarded the "milk run" headed south. A short time in Saigon had been just what the doctor ordered. I would never forget Doc Lemmon looking out for me.

SOC TRANG
MON
25 FEB 63

Up at 0530, we greeted the dawn and scrambled for early takeoff: a mission to Cam Mau. This morning, I lucked out. An Otter going down to the staging area in Cam Mau had some room, so I got to ride in the luxury of this quiet, smooth, fixed-wing plane instead of the usually rougher chopper. This proved particularly welcome today, as the winds had continued to be an annoyance.

As usual, I saw hundreds of ARVN troops standing by, waiting to be transported. With the first lift, the choppers reported taking heavy fire at the landing zone but no hits on our aircraft. It took five additional lifts to move all of the men. Oddly, there were no reports of any additional fire after the first lift.

The ARVN radioed back to the command post the discovery of a hastily abandoned headquarters and a twenty-bed VC field hospital but little or no contact with the VC. They had melted away again.

A small party of ARVN officers returned with some of the spoils of the day: several bottles of Dextran from the hospital and large jars of antibiotics manufactured in New York; from the well-equipped headquarters, there were many papers, photos of Ho Chi Minh, and propaganda for the peasants in the countryside. They also brought back a typewriter made in Germany. An American officer quipped, "If they're using typewriters for reports and memos now, they're sure to lose the war."

Back at the airfield by 1600, I learned we would take off again the next morning for Cam Mau. I also learned a USO show was scheduled for Soc Trang that evening. That would sure help cut the tedium of the routine.

WASHINGTON, DC

JFK forwarded a report to the Senate Foreign Relations Committee. It concluded: "There is no interest of the United Sates in Vietnam which would justify, in present circumstances, the conversion of the war ... primarily into an American war to be fought primarily with American lives."[24]

CAM MAU
TUES
26 FEB 63

Strong winds tossed us around on our way to Cam Mau. They made a rough ride rougher. Helicopters were tricky to fly when the winds were this strong.

We landed at the staging area and there were not many troops lined up for transport. This operation was failing or scaled back.

The H-21s made three lifts to move the troops out into the field. Our choppers radioed back to the command post they had taken only sporadic sniper fire. The ARVN troops made no contact with VC in this sweep, and soon the choppers returned the troops to the staging area. They reported the peasants in the villages they had searched used VC currency and had not seen anyone from the official Vietnam government since 1954.

We left early, and I was glad to be back in Soc Trang by 1500. I found it all quiet at the dispensary. I went to my bunk for a quick nap. So many early mornings and long days had taken a toll, though I had not done much lately but stand-by. The winds gusted to thirty mph and were so strong that the USO show scheduled for this evening had to be canceled; it was a big disappointment for me and all the troops. Even Mother Nature seemed to thwart us.

Tonight at the O-Club, we had a great time. Maj. Brewster and a young pilot just promoted to captain bought the bar. This eased the pain of the cancelled USO show.

SOC TRANG
WED
27 FEB 63

Good news. The wind had died down, and the USO show would be going on that evening in front of the hangar for sure.

I hurried through my paperwork and realized with satisfaction all my reports were current—a good feeling. I always seemed to put this task off to last in spite of my resolutions to the contrary.

Sgt. Tibbs brought me a message from Sgt. Runnion at the Special Forces camp at Dutah. "They need some antibiotic ointment, bandages, and a few other items."

"Collect what he asked for, and we'll get it out there." I had never forgotten the generosity of the Green Berets last Christmas when Sgt. Runnion and Copt. Clay gave me the Tetracycline I needed.

Since the good Colonel Montjoy's visit, my initial supply problems had resolved. We now had dependable delivery of medical supplies, and I had long ago replaced those bottles of Tetracycline.

I asked the captain in operations about getting the supplies out to Dutah. Two choppers were going to Can Tho tomorrow. If I wanted, they would drop me off on the way and pick me up on the way back. I agreed, although I was not too keen to be left alone in this isolated hamlet of Dutah. I could handle a few hours, but I did not want to spend the night as Capt. Clay had suggested last Christmas. I liked to sleep. Out there in the VC dark with no electricity and no perimeter protection, I would be awake on alert all night.

At 1730, I sat down to one of the mess hall's specialties, a Salisbury steak dinner. The OD entered. "We have a Mayday."

When we reached operations, the radio still crackled, "Mayday! Mayday!"

The radio operator said, "One of our H-21s with a load of VIPs developed engine trouble. Gone in for a crash landing. About ten miles out."

"Shot down?" someone asked.

"Don't know yet," the OD answered.

Choppers rarely, if ever, traveled alone; they were always in pairs. If one developed problems, the escort would be right there to help out. The second chopper shortly radioed that the Mayday had been a soft crash. This rescue chopper landed next to the crippled one and took onboard the ten passengers, four crew, and all weapons. No word on injuries.

After agonizing minutes, the rescue ship radioed they left the stripped chopper in the field, had liftoff, and were in the air, bound for Soc Trang.

Our alerted dispensary crew and ambulance raced into action and prepared for the emergency. Standing by on the tarmac, we didn't have long to wait before we saw the solitary H-21. It rapidly approached and touched down near us.

We went into action. Six had injuries—three Americans and three Vietnamese. Our medics rapidly placed them on litters and loaded the ambulance—Trey and Billy T. among them. The remaining eight were brought by jeep to the dispensary for triage.

Trey had a back injury and a lacerated right elbow. Billy T. suffered a hard blow to his right upper abdomen. Although he had tenderness to deep palpation, the liver did not seem enlarged, and the base of his lungs seemed clear. I hoped he was not bleeding internally. The third American, a Catholic chaplain I had never met before, had a back injury and was going into shock. We started fluids intravenously. A Vietnamese army officer had a back injury. A Vietnamese civilian official had a dislocated shoulder. On the sixth litter, a lieutenant commander, one of two Vietnamese naval officers aboard, had a back injury and lacerated finger.

The other naval officer had no injury. An American captain, who served as a division advisor, had bilateral contusions over his tibias. Of the two American naval officers aboard, one had a lacerated finger, and the other had no injury. The rest of the crew from the downed chopper, the crew chief and gunner, were uninjured.

Finally, there were two American advisors, both colonels, neither of whom suffered injury.

With our dispensary full of human distress, Operations called to ask what we needed for transportation. A Caribou had arrived and was on the ground. They were holding it for medical evacuation transport—the first and only good news I'd heard all evening.

After our team had evaluated, stabilized, and patched up the injured, the three injured Americans were placed on the Caribou to be taken to Eighth Field Hospital in Nha Trang. Soc Trang cleared two choppers to take the Vietnamese injured to the military hospital in Can Tho.

We were a tired, beat group of medics by the time the dispensary was cleaned up and the ambulance was parked back in place. After congratulating one another for getting a tough job done, we turned out the lights and left for the night.

I realized I was starving. I went to the O-Club for a cheeseburger. The grill had already been shut down, so I had a cheese sandwich and beer. When you're hungry, anything tastes good. Charley, our faithful club manager, saw me come in.

"Well, Doc. You missed a great USO show. Sorry 'bout that," he said. "Your sandwich and beer's on the house."

"Thanks, Charley. You're a pal." I meant it.

I felt too tired for a shower but had no choice. On my way back from the shower room, I heard the familiar artillery and mortars and saw the flares light up the sky in the distance. The mortars were becoming a nightly lullaby. I suddenly realized the dispensary would be three litters short. I'd have to worry about that tomorrow.

SOC TRANG
THUR
28 FEB 63

Good news. The Field Hospital called; Trey and Billy T. had no serious injuries and would be back in a day or two.

I received a letter from Knott's Berry Farm in response to my inquiry about the box of dried dates that arrived in January. The secretary in their preserving office wrote:

FEB 26, 1963

Dear Captain Hoyland,

We thank you for your very interesting letter concerning the box of dates you received recently. The senders, Rev. and Mrs. Wright, had intended this shipment for their nephew who it happens is now either on his way to Vietnam or is already there.

We certainly do not expect you to pay for the dates; we are glad you opened the package. When Mrs. Wright has the correct address for Lt. Jay Hoyland, another package will be mailed with our compliments.

Thank you for your courtesy.

One of life's little mysteries solved.

I picked up the supplies for camp Dutah and got aboard Hartley Davis's chopper. We didn't fly long before we circled an approach over a small field near a clump of palm trees along a canal. I saw a few huts made of bamboo with palm fronds for roofs. PBD piloted our escort ship, and it remained aloft while we descended. Hartley Davis did not land but hovered low briefly so I could exit out the rear door. The rear door gunner helped unload the supplies. When I was clear, the crew chief gave a thumbs-up, and with nose down, the chopper picked up speed and altitude. I watched the two choppers rapidly disappear as they headed toward Can Tho.

The engine noise faded, and the first thing I noticed was the deathly quiet out here in the country. Sgt. Runnion called out and walked toward me.

"Welcome to Dutah," he said. "Thanks for bringing the supplies. I really need them."

"We aim to please," I said.

"I've got something I need to finish up," he said. "Captain Clay is still out on patrol. Should be back shortly."

I helped him put the supplies on a rough table sheltered by a palm frond lean-to. "The rest of the team won't get back until tomorrow. Look around. I'll just be a minute."

In this isolated hamlet, looking around would not take long. Dutah, a small compound, was typical of the many villages I had seen at a distance flying above. The huts were simple, built of bamboo with mat siding, and had hard, dirt-packed floors. The roofs were palm thatch to keep out the monsoon. They had no doors, but panels of bamboo could be placed at the entry for privacy. The huts were grouped in an irregular circle, and an open fire burned in the center of each one.

Two women, squatted on their haunches, cleaned fish. Another older woman used a palm frond as a broom and swept the ground in front of her hut. Several children, young and naked, ran around in a group. So did a scrawny flock of chickens.

Everyone was aware of my noisy arrival, but they seemed shy. No one looked at me directly. They did smile, though, as if they shared a secret about this stranger in their midst. They talked to one another in a steady stream of musical language and occasionally laughed. Someone must have told a joke. The only word they used I knew and could understand was *"Di,"* which meant "Go." I had no idea of the context.

There were no roads, only hard-packed dirt paths. I saw one bicycle propped against a hut—the only machine I saw in the hamlet.

On the bank of the canal were a few primitive boats with fishnets drying in the sun. There were some small bamboo traps I thought they must use to catch shrimp. The landscape seemed immense, with rice fields, ditches and canals, and tree lines on all sides. The quiet seemed almost complete and oppressive except for the women talking and scaling fish. This was a primitive, peaceful place—a lot like camping out back home without a forest or camping equipment. It would not be a bad way to live if the country had not been at war. They had a temperate climate, fertile fields, and plenty of fresh fruits and seafood.

Instead of feeling peaceful, I felt threatened. What would it be like here at night, totally dark except for fires, lanterns, and GI flashlights? How did the Special Forces get by?

I ventured to the side of a canal, crossing on a felled log used for a bridge. Down the bank of the canal, I saw a few canoes and open ground across the canal. To the right, I saw bamboo cages with a few VC prisoners inside. I turned and went back across the footbridge.

Sgt. Runnion joined me, and in the distance, I heard the return of the foot patrol. The Self Defense Corps were much less formal than the ARVN and dressed in a variety of shorts, thongs, neck scarves, and hats. They all carried rifles properly, I noticed. Activity in the village picked up when the men returned.

Capt. Clay had a lean, handsome, fresh-shaved face. His boots and fatigues were wet and muddied from the patrol, but he looked like the poster boy for Special Forces in his Green Beret. He spoke to the men in fluent Vietnamese, and they disbanded to go back to their huts. I shared JFK's admiration for these soldiers.

"Doc, you got out here for a visit," he said. "We don't welcome many visitors. In fact, you're the first." He washed his face and hands from water dispensed from a canvas bag hanging from a tree branch. "Stay for dinner? We'll heat up the ham and lima beans. Make some real coffee. Or we could always have some fish, rice, and *Nuoc mam.*" He pointed toward the fire, where the women were preparing to cook the fish.

"Spending the night?" he asked.

This isolated team would welcome any new diversion and American conversation. I thought again of cowboys on the range. When a stranger rode up, they were welcomed to eat beans, drink coffee, and warm themselves around the campfire. Now I understood why. They wanted company, a diversion. But I didn't want to be here after dark. My sense of adventure was not that keen.

"No, but thanks. They need me for sick call in the morning." I tried to sound casual, but the thought of spending a night out here was downright terrifying. Maybe if I had more training, I silently rationalized. Darkness out in VC country, where they owned the night, might be the life for Special Forces, but it was not for me.

"Thirsty?" Capt. Clay must have sensed my discomfort and laughed softly.

We went over to a bamboo table with benches on either side. "This is our mess hall." Sgt. Runnion opened three bottles of warm Japanese beer. It was cool in the shade of the palm grove and oddly peaceful.

We had just about finished our beers when I heard the familiar thump-thump of rotors.

"My taxi," I said, hoping my relief was not too obvious.

"Come back for another visit anytime," Sgt. Runnion called out. "And thanks for the supplies."

"See you in Soc Trang," Capt. Clay echoed.

I waved and climbed aboard the hovering chopper. The crew chief gave pilot Hartley Davis a thumbs-up, and we were out of Dutah. I took a deep breath of relief. This experience had been an eye-opener. Soc Trang airfield suddenly seemed downright urban. I admired this team of men; they had guts to live out there—a different breed. For sure, I would not take Soc Trang for granted any more. We lived like kings.

SOC TRANG
FRI
1 MAR 63

"Yes sir, I understand," I overheard Maj. Ewald say into the telephone. "I report to Saigon next week."

His back toward me, he was unaware of my presence. I had come into headquarters to ask a question about one of my men, and it was unusual that no one but the major was around. The question could wait. This was not the time for talk. I left quietly; he never knew I had been there or overheard his conversation.

I surmised he had been re-assigned. Probably moving up to Saigon for some desk job, I thought. This news hadn't been announced, so I would keep it to myself. I regretted his leaving, and I wondered if it was fallout from the Ap Bac disaster. That would be unfair. It had not been his fault. A good leader and commander, the men liked and respected him. I didn't know his story, but I had the feeling he had pretty much seen it all. I knew he had seen action as an enlisted paratrooper before he became a helicopter pilot, so he must have been very young when he enlisted.

We would face a challenge with change in leadership. Captain—now Major—Brewster would soon be leaving for his new assignment at Battalion. With the loss of these two men, we would lose a lot of skill and experience.

I noticed the sky, clear in the twilight, as I headed back to hootch #4. My head was filled with thoughts of this place and the war, what was happening and what wasn't. The distant rumbling sounded like thunder, but it was the usual booming of mortar and gunfire. I looked across the airfield toward the Soc Trang radio station antenna located about one mile away toward town. Standard red lights routinely beaconed a warning to aircraft.

Something seemed different, and then I realized the blinking red warning lights were not on. I knew that the radio stations, like the newspapers, were all controlled by Diem's government. Getting perhaps more insecure the longer I stayed here, I wondered if not having the lights could be a signal of some sort? If a signal, could it be from the government? Covert VC? Could I just be getting paranoid?

Suspicions came from a lack of trust in anything here except our U.S. Army. I had been told, and I felt certain it was true, many Vietnamese in the government and military were really VC or Communist sympathizers. Even our civilian employees were suspect: Lydia, the young war widow who cleaned our hootch; Duc; Hannah from the Tigers' Den; Loc, the barber who cut our hair. I wondered about the contractor who built the O-Club. These were all good people, but where did their political allegiances lie?

They were all friendly, helpful, and seemed honest and uncomplicated. I assumed they were all pro-government and anticommunist, but they worked here where the information was to be had for the looking. They could be—at least some of them probably were—VC spies. We were told never to talk in front of them, but just as I overheard the major, secrets are hard to keep in such close quarters.

Of course, guerilla war does not encourage trust in the Vietnamese government or our relationship with the military or civilians. But then, how did they feel about us being here? How could they trust us? They were just probably trying to do the best they could. Would I feel differently if the roles were reversed? I don't know; I think not.

NEW YORK
FRI
1 MAR 63

A Times article by correspondent David Halberstram reported senior ARVN officers were using intelligence to avoid the VC, and American advisors could not get Diem's army to take the initiative.

His article charged that operations were often faked and ARVN action reports were fabricated and unreliable.[25]

MEKONG DELTA

"Ap Bac" was the new VC rally cry. They forged ahead with preparations for revolution in the Delta, which they called the "Ap Bac Emulation Drive." VC cadres did not need help from the north; they recruited all the volunteers they needed from the failing Strategic Hamlet program.[26]

SOC TRANG
SAT
2 MAR 63

"Why the hell couldn't the Ninety-Third have a mythical mascot like the Purple Foxes or Thunderbolts?" the U.S. Air Force veterinarian from Saigon muttered under his breath as he approached Tuffy's enclosure. "But no, you have to be the Soc Trang Tigers." He saw the inadequate three-foot picket fence and eyed the chain that fastened the tiger to a secure stake.

"We appreciate your coming down to do this routine checkup, Doc," I said.

"Save the thanks until the job's done." The vet shook his head with emphasis. "He's a fine specimen. I'll say that."

"I've treated one tiger wound," I said, "but even that is one more than I ever imagined during med school."

"I don't intend to be your second." The vet laughed uneasily. "But it's good to know you've had experience. It gives me confidence." He added with a wink, "I think."

Tuffy yawned, exposing his maw of a mouth and great teeth.

"At least his teeth look clean." I chuckled.

"Basically, a cat's a cat. Vet school prepares you for animals large and small. You just don't surprise them and do your job. They won't surprise you."

Lazily stretched out on the table placed in his yard for a platform, Tuffy's golden eyes watched the two of us watching him. The vet opened his black bag and took out a small 35 mm camera and handed it to me. He took out a large needle and syringe and filled it with a clear fluid. "Feline enteritis vaccine," he told Tuffy, as if he could understand.

Except for the occasional movement of his tail, the tiger did not move and appeared disinterested.

As agreed earlier, CWO Billy T. Witt entered the enclosure slowly. He took hold of the chain as the vet entered Tuffy's yard.

Talking to me, but looking at Tuffy, the vet said, "There's a whole roll of film. Be sure to get plenty of pictures. They'll make a good story for my grandchildren one day, if I live to have any."

"You got it." I began snapping picture after picture as soon as the vet entered Tuffy's yard. I hoped, to myself, not to get any bloody ones.

The vet approached the animal confidently, saying, "Atta boy, Tuffy." Very quickly, but with no sudden moves, the needle was in the left haunch. When emptied, the vet removed it gently. "That's a good soldier, Tuffy." The vet backed away and climbed over the fence. CWO Witt followed.

"He looks more surprised than angry," I said. The tiger continued to watch the three of us as we stood by the fence.

"All's well that ends well," the vet said. "Sure hope you got some good pictures."

"I'm sure I did. How about some coffee at the Tigers' Den before you head back? It's a little too early for lunch."

"I'll take a rain check. The pilot flew me down as a favor and has to get back." The vet took a last long look at Tuffy.

Maj. Ewald approached on his way to operations.

"Tuffy's now certified grade-A, Major," I said. "The U.S. Air Force to the rescue."

"Thanks." The major shook the vet's hand. "He's gaining on us. Captain Jones, the guy who had Tuffy as a cub, said he was born about a year ago."

"Looks about right," the vet said. "Like any teenager, he's growing fast. I'd say he's about 175 to two hundred pounds now. He'll weigh in at about 650 when he reaches maturity."

The air force pilot signaled they were cleared to fly back to Saigon. "This was my first house call in-country. It'll make a great story when I'm back in Homestead, Florida, taking care of house cats!"

Tuffy switched his tail slowly back and forth to chase flies, his eyes half-closed in the warm sun.

SOC TRANG
MON
4 MAR 63

It was official: Maj. Ewald had been reassigned to a job in Saigon. A new officer, Maj. Steve Saunders, would assume command here in Soc Trang. I would miss Maj. Ewald. He was an officer and a gentleman and a friend. I admired him.

I received an invitation for a going-away party for Maj. Reagan, my MAAG friend from downtown, on March 9. The party was to be given by the chief lieutenant colonel of our local ARVN sector at the Ba Xuyen meeting hall starting at 1930. It was always tough to tell the good guys good-bye. I wouldn't miss his singing at the

Tigers' Den, though. The party would also welcome the new senior advisor, Maj. Cutter.

"Sir, there's someone here to see you," Tony, the clerk, announced from the open doorway.

"Be right there," I answered as I finished wrapping the elastic bandage around a corporal's sprained ankle. I knew I had only two more patients left to see from morning sick call. I secured the bandage, and the patient went out the back door for limited duty.

I entered the waiting room, and there stood Capt. Scott Mitchell with a big grin. He looked even more tan and fit than when I last saw him in Alabama.

"Scott, my man, how long has it been?" I asked as we shook hands.

"Four months. We left Fort Rucker in November."

"It's seems more like a year." I laughed. "Time flies even when you're not having fun."

"Looking good, Captain Hoyland."

"Glad to see you, Scott. I mean it."

"I've got lots of questions," Scott said. "Have you seen our buddy Frank?"

"Not once. We're hoping to get some R & R to Hong Kong next month. I'll finish sick call real quick, and let's head over to the Tigers' Den for coffee."

We entered the empty club. After getting coffee, we sat at the far end of the bar.

"Nice club." He looked around. "What's it been like down here?"

"The worst and the best. I've learned a lot, but I've missed having another doc just to talk to. Mostly it's been me alone down here; it's really isolated medically. The thing that makes it worthwhile is the pilots. They're great," I said. "Where are you assigned?"

"I may luck out and be the battalion surgeon. I don't know for sure yet. I'll find out tomorrow." Scott added, "The way I hear it, Max Schmitt, our old friend from Harbor General days, is in the army now."

"Yeah. I got a letter from him. He's at Fort Sam right now and has orders to Rucker for flight surgeon training."

"He's as good as on his way over here."

"That's just what he wrote, too," I added. "He wanted to know what to bring." Too soon for me, the pilot summoned Scott to get on board the Otter to go back to Saigon. As he headed across the tarmac, I couldn't help but yell, "You're in for it now, Scott!"

He flipped me the bird and got on the plane with a grin.

SOC TRANG
WED
6 MAR 63

The officers gathered in the O-Club annex as Maj. Ewald stood in front with another major at his side. "Gentlemen, as you all know, I will be going up to battalion in a couple of weeks. Tonight, I want to introduce Major Steve Saunders, who will be taking over as the new CO of the Ninety-Third."

The group applauded politely.

Maj. Saunders, who appeared to be about the same age as Maj. Ewald, had short, cropped rust-colored hair and ruddy sunburned skin about the same color. He stepped forward. "I just want to say I am pleased to join the Soc Trang Tigers. Maj. Ewing has done a hell of a job, and I hope to continue in his footsteps." His husky voice sounded sincere. He had big shoes to fill, but the army, like life, keeps evolving. This man wanted to do a good job.

"You have a proud history. The Ninety-Third has the reputation as one of the best outfits in Vietnam. I am looking forward to working with each and every one of you." I figured this was his first command, and he wanted it to be successful.

Maj. Ewald yelled, "All right, men. Set 'em up, Charley. This round's on me."

After enthusiastic applause, the crowd gave three cheers for both majors and gathered in a rite of passage at the bar.

SOC TRANG
FRI
8 MAR 63

Stretched out on my bunk, I looked at my watch. It was 2030. The day was over—time for a shower before hitting the sack early. There weren't any mortar rounds exploding in the distance, so I hoped for a good night's sleep.

I unlaced my scruffy combat boots, noticing they could use some polish, when the OD came to my door. "Doc, we've got to make a run to Bac Lieu. A GI's gone berserk. Six men brought him down, and they've got him in cuffs."

I re-laced my boots and grabbed the emergency kit. I checked to see I had an airway tube and went by the dispensary to pick up some antipsychotic medication and a litter. Who knew what I'd need? At the flight line, I saw a full moon in a clear, blue-black sky. Our choppers would make good targets tonight.

We flew at an altitude well over 1,500 feet, but the VC fired anyway for sport and harassment. The night, unusually clear, would be beautiful anywhere except here. We had not flown long when the pilot spotted a flare in the distance. He maneuvered the chopper into a clearing near a tree line and hamlet. While the twin rotary wings continued to turn, I jumped out into the dark field. A small group of soldiers surrounded a litter occupied by a young, unconscious enlisted man.

A medic stepped up, yelling over the sound of the rotors and engine, "I gave him a whopping dose of IM pentothal."

Two soldiers helped load the litter into the hold of our chopper. I gave the medic my litter in exchange.

In the dim cabin light, I gave the crew chief a thumbs-up, and the pilot revved the engines for a quick departure. We gained speed and altitude and soon were headed for Soc Trang. The Delta below had a few clusters of electric lights, but myriads of small outdoor fires lit the dark countryside. Primitive but effective, these fires provided hamlets with light as they had since man first settled here.

We landed at Soc Trang, and Brooklyn drove up to meet us

with the ambulance. At the dispensary, I attempted to examine the lethargic young man. He was in his mid-twenties, a private. I detected alcohol on his breath. We took off the handcuffs, and finding no injury other than scuffed knuckles, I decided to let him stay in the dispensary overnight for watchful waiting. Tomorrow, I would reevaluate.

I sent Brooklyn back to his hootch and sat down in the chair beside the soldier's cot. His breathing was deep and sonorous. He had dark hair, needed a shave, but had unremarkable regular features. He may have been uncontrollable a few hours ago, but now he was asleep and peaceful. Chemicals can do amazing things. I wondered where he came from. Where would his family be right now, and would they be worried about him? Did he have some psychiatric problem? Psychotic? Probably not. Probably stressed beyond endurance, he had briefly disorganized.

The bright moon shone through the shutters, casting striped shadows on the cement floor. The empty dispensary seemed larger at night without anyone around. Military police on patrol checked in on us several times. It was quiet except for the soldier's regular breathing. I still hadn't heard any explosions in the distance; that was a relief, as we had been hearing them every night for a long time.

Lying on the treatment table next to the young soldier's cot, I could not sleep but dozed off and on. He slumbered all night. In the morning, when Sgt. Tibbs arrived, we roused the still-drowsy soldier, and Sgt. Tibbs brought breakfast from the mess hall.

"Here, soldier," I said. "Some coffee and chow."

He was still a little dazed from the huge dose of sedative.

"What happened?" he asked. "Where am I?"

I explained the events of last night.

"Oh, God!" Embarrassed, this young man clearly felt he had let his unit down, a good sign.

"What's your name?" I asked, to check orientation.

"Winston, sir."

"Where're you from?"

"Nebraska." He added, "My folks live on a farm not too far outside Omaha."

"How old are you?"

"Nineteen, sir."

This was the first time he had been away from the family farm for any period of time. Neither he nor his family had any history of mental health problems, and he didn't drink.

"I don't remember much," he said slowly. "Yesterday, my best buddy stepped on one of those damn VC bamboo stakes. Then, when we finally got our mail, I had a letter from my girl back home." He began to cry. "Breaking up with me. I don't remember what happened after that. Oh God, I'm so sorry."

With some coaxing, he ate breakfast and drank the coffee. That helped. I couldn't return him to duty, and he couldn't stay. I would send him to Saigon for further observation and a brief respite. He could use a little time off. If he checked out as I thought, I recommended we return him to his unit as soon as possible. That would minimize the consequences of an unfortunate incident and keep it from becoming a bigger problem for him and the army. Later that morning, he saluted smartly when he climbed aboard the med evac chopper bound for Saigon.

I received a letter from my family in Missouri; on March 1, I became an uncle for the tenth time. Welcome to the world, little Carole Ann. Life goes on.

SOC TRANG
SAT
9 MAR 63

This would be my first time at the province meeting hall. It was a large room, and many people, both military and civilian, had been invited to the party. From all I observed, Maj. Reagan had been popular and well-liked by the Vietnamese military he advised and by his fellow officers. The event started promptly at 1930.

The ARVN lieutenant colonel host welcomed the diverse crowd. A long table held refreshments: small sandwiches with some sort of tasty meat; small portions of chicken with a soy-based barbecue sauce; pieces of pork with unknown spices; my favorite, shrimp in a thin rice wrapper; a delicious meat-filled pastry from Saigon;

and olives in a lime-pepper marinade. We drank the ubiquitous Vietnamese rice beer, which I had come to like, warm.

We all applauded several speeches. The lieutenant colonel presented Maj. Reagan with a picture of a bucolic scene of Vietnam to remember his time in-country. The other gift was a teapot. It came with a hollowed-out coconut shell which, when filled with straw, made an ingenious insulator to keep the tea hot. Maj. Reagan thanked everyone, made a few remarks, and received a long round of applause.

Maj. Cutter, the new MAAG advisor, was introduced; a little younger than Maj. Reagan, he had a sturdier build. With his very short gray hair and fresh uniform, he looked ready for his new duty.

I had a chance to spend a moment alone with Maj. Reagan.

"Thanks, Doc, for being here. This has been quite a year, and there's a hell of a lot left to do." We shook hands and he added, "Best of luck. Tell Tuffy good-bye for me."

SOC TRANG
MON
11 MAR 63

"Hey, Doc Hoyland," Billy T. Witt greeted me as I came in the Tigers' Den, "did you see this?"

He handed me the *Stars and Stripes*, March 8, 1963 edition, and pointed to a large picture of Tuffy on the front page. The caption read, "A Cool Cat." The AP photo showed one of the enlisted men holding a hose, with a stream of water spraying on Tuffy in his pool; he appeared to be smiling.

Witt continued, "Did you hear about the guy from Saigon who came down here last week? Tuffy was lounging in his spot at the door to the XO's office. Tuffy seemed to be asleep, so this guy, to get in the door, had to put his foot between Tuffy's front paws. Tuffy grabbed his leg, and the guy about passed out."

Everyone in the club laughed, as they always did when the many stories were told and re-told about Tuffy. He had approached mythical status and proved, indeed, good for morale.

SAIGON
THUR
14 MAR 63

MACV reported VC activity 50 percent less than in 1962.[27]

SOC TRANG
FRI
15 MAR 63

"We have to do it; we have no choice," I told Sgt. Tibbs.

"It'll be a big deal, but you're right."

The problem of the health of civilian employees was not new. We gave physicals to all the Vietnamese we employed at the airfield, and this included a skin test for TB. The challenge was a new directive to document clear chest X-rays.

With the list of civilians employed at the airfield, I used Duc to help me explain to them what we required. The civilian hospital had X-ray capability, so it was more a logistics than a medical problem. The widows who cleaned the hootches were transported by trucks to the hospital; the employees who lived in town would go on their own.

I had read somewhere there were seven hundred physicians in the country of South Vietnam. Soc Trang, a city of forty-two thousand, had two doctors, both on the staff of the civilian hospital. One was a Vietnamese doctor who had trained in Saigon, but I did not know where the other, a Chinese physician, had gone to school. They were genuinely capable and caring. I regretted our need to burden them with our X-ray request. Understanding and cooperative, they agreed to the plan.

The project took less time than I thought. The good news: Everyone had clear X-rays.

PBD and I took supplies to the orphanage: powdered milk, cereals from the mess hall, and some laundry soap. I wiped the sweat from my forehead as we unloaded the goods. The weather was definitely getting hotter.

"Thank you. Thank you. Thank you," the nuns repeated, bowing at the waist.

We bowed in return. "We'll be back. We'll be back."

The five nuns waved farewell.

PBD did not speak for a long while on the drive back to the air base.

Finally I broke the silence. "That's always overwhelming. Where to start?"

"And why start? What chance do they have?" He added, "That's one of the most depressing things I've ever seen in my life. Those kids. They didn't ask to be born."

"Well, they're here. And so are we." I stopped at the guard gate. After our salutes, the jeep was cleared for entry. "PBD, how old do you think that Sister is? The one in charge? And how long ago do you suppose she left France?"

"Hard to tell, but she's old and left a long time ago. You know the French used Catholicism for power and control more than any other European colonials."

"She's given her life to this country. Next time we go in, I'm going to take an interpreter," I said. "The washing machine has sure been a big hit. They use it all the time. Hope we can get them a dryer."

"You can count on me for some bucks, but I don't think I'll be going back." PBD sank lower in his seat and stared straight ahead.

"That's what you said the last time, and the time before that." I said. "On a lighter note, I got orders today for another medic. We'll still be under strength, but Sergeant Tibbs is doing a great job."

PBD said, "Maybe there is some justice in this world. I hope so, anyway."

SOC TRANG
SAT
16 MAR 63

I entered the back door of the dispensary to begin sick call, and Sgt. Tibbs greeted me. "We have a VIP today."

"Who?" I asked.

"Major Saunders. He's not feeling well."

"Maybe having second thoughts about being CO of this outfit." I laughed.

"No, sir. He says he hasn't been up to par for some time."

"Have him come back," I said.

Maj. Saunders entered the exam room, and I could tell he was ill.

"What brings you in?" I asked.

"I don't really know. I'm just tired. No energy when I need it."

"How long how have you been feeling like this?"

"Oh, looking back, I'd say the last week, two weeks. I'm usually in great health."

After a brief physical exam, I said, "You may have hepatitis. I want to send you up to Saigon. They have a lab and can confirm or find out what it is. Something is wrong, for sure."

"This couldn't come at a worse time. My first command." The major frowned. "Sure you couldn't just wait a few days? See how I do?"

"No. If it is hepatitis, they'll need to get on it right away. The sooner you get bed rest, the sooner you'll be back."

"Are you sure?"

"Whatever it is, you may be gone for a while. Plan on it."

"Okay," he said. "Whatever you say, Doc."

"I'll make arrangements for a med evac today."

Feeling worse than when he came in, the major went across the street to headquarters; two hours later, he was on a plane bound for Saigon.

Later that day, I received a call from Saigon. The bad news circulated quickly: Maj. Saunders would be hospitalized at Clark Air Force Hospital in the Philippines for six to eight weeks.

Capt. Joe Andrews would be acting CO until Maj. Saunders could get back. Capt. Andrews, although he hadn't been with the Ninety-Third very long, had flown several missions. A good pilot and leader, it would be business as usual. The army always seemed prepared with capable men to back up the organization.

That evening, the Tigers' Den hosted a big "shipwreck party"— the officers' going away celebration for one of their own, Maj.

Ewald. Although he had been here for only four months, a lot had happened during that time.

SOC TRANG
WED
27 MAR 63

"Doc, meet one of our new protectors," Slick drawled. "This is Nick Parsons. Platoon leader for the gunners who just arrived from Hawaii. He's West Point," Slick added with some disdain. "You know I'm Texas A&M."

Young Second Lt. Parsons still looked like a West Point cadet, athletic with great posture.

Over beers at the club, I learned Lt. Parson's father had been a colonel in the army during World War II. Nick had excelled as a quarterback in high school. A fine student, he did well at West Point. It turned out he was as proficient in English literature and Shakespeare as he was in gunnery. An excellent marksman, this would be his first opportunity to lead a unit. The fact that it was in a war zone was a detail his former classmates envied.

"We're all tigers here," I said. Nick would be a welcome addition to our Soc Trang fraternity.

Slick said quickly, "And glad for the firepower."

I had not known the gunners were coming. Trained to shoot, these troops and their machine guns would boost protection. They would stand in the choppers at one hatch, while the crew chiefs, with their weapons, would cover the other.

"Having our gunners should make troop drops a little more secure," Nick said. "Our mission is to primarily protect U.S. aircraft and personnel."

At least for the time being, I thought. "Where are you from?"

"Louisiana. Evangeline country. Down in Cajun territory," he said.

It turned out Nick's girlfriend, Ellen, lived in the same town and was a good friend of Barbara, the new wife of my old intern buddy from Harbor General Hospital, Harold Baxter.

"Small world," Slick said, "a very small world."

SOC TRANG
FRI
29 MAR 63

A routine sick call can be pretty routine. The hot, humid conditions always promoted skin problems. One pilot had a severe sensitivity to the sun, and his burned lips were swollen and painful. One of our good cooks had painful recurrent hemorrhoids, which would require sending him back to the hospital where he could get more help. I had excised several purple external clots, but he had more, worse, further internally than I could go with my equipment and experience. I set up a med evac.

I was startled when the back door to the treatment room flew open.

"God, Doc. I need help!" A MAAG captain, gray with anxiety, stood in the open door.

Outside, his jeep motor was running, and when I got outside, I saw a black-clad Vietnamese woman holding a boy in her arms, seated in the passenger side. She pressed an old cloth shirt to the boy's head.

The captain blurted out, "He darted out in front of me as I rounded a corner. Oh, God, I hope he's going to be all right."

The mother sat silently, unmoving.

Sgt. Tibbs and I carefully transferred the boy onto the treatment table. He seemed so small; all the patients on this table had been burly men.

The dispensary staff had collected in the hallway to see what was going on. "Tony," I said, "run over to the Tigers' Den. Get Duc over here right away."

Duc arrived immediately. The previously silent mother became animated when Duc arrived, and they talked the melodic Vietnamese language too difficult for me to learn. It was a great relief for her to communicate. Duc told us that the boy's name was Doan. He was seven years old and in good health prior to the accident, which she said happened just as the captain had related to me.

She began to softly whimper, and tears rolled down her cheeks.

Doan, a nice-looking boy with fine Vietnamese features, did not cry or whine at all. Stoic, he seemed almost curious about what we were up to. He was bright and his senses clear. The medical assessment revealed an intact neurological system and no broken bones. His only major injury was an alarming laceration across his forehead, which exposed the bony table of the skull. The only other injuries were four lacerations on his right arm. They were superficial. Fortunately, he was not in pain.

I wanted the mother to stay in the room with us to reassure the boy, but I could see that the laceration would require stitches and a lot of them. For a good cosmetic result, I would need to use fine suture material and place many tiny stitches close together. This would be a big challenge for me. Fortunately, the scar would follow his frown lines.

I asked Tony to run another errand. "Go over to hootch #4 and ask Lydia to come over here and stay with the mother while we sew him up."

Lydia, a sweet-faced civilian employee, cleaned our hootch, and like most of the women employed at the airfield, had been given an American name. They seemed to like having this new identity, even if only at work. They were all poor and uneducated, the widows of Buddhist peasants killed in strategic hamlets. They lived together in a barracks at the edge of the base. We all contributed money for them to work for us, and the pay was very good for the standards of the country. GIs treated them well, and they had food and security. They liked their jobs.

I knew nothing about Lydia, but she always smiled politely even though very shy. She came over quickly, and she thought it best if the mother went to the waiting room. The mother went willingly.

Sgt. Tibbs scrubbed first, donning a mask and cap. I scrubbed while he opened the sterile surgical tray. I put on sterile gloves, covering the little guy's face with sterile sheets. Duc, wide-eyed at our rituals, sat next to Doan's head to let him know what we were doing and to reassure him.

Doan asked only one question, "Am I going to die?"

Duc explained that he would be good as new before long, and this proved to be enough to satisfy him.

Brooklyn, standing by to help out if we needed anything, adjusted the light. I was thankful for the excellent surgical light in the treatment room. After injecting the local anesthesia and irrigating and cleaning the wound thoroughly, we went to work. Sgt. Tibbs proved to be a good OR scrub nurse, and I liked suturing both in medical school and internship, where I'd had lots of experience. This deep wound would require closure in layers.

For me, the time flew, but when we finished and put the bandage in place, the boy's mother ran back to the treatment room. I am sure the time seemed long to her. Little Doan didn't flinch when Sgt. Tibbs gave a tetanus immune globulin shot intramuscularly in one arm and a tetanus toxoid in the other. Mother resumed her tears. Someone found a candy bar and presented it to an uncertain but smiling boy hero who looked none the worse for wear except for a bandage.

We gave the mother a bottle of oral antibiotics, and Duc explained carefully the importance of taking the full ten-days' supply. I explained he should have two follow-up tetanus booster shots a month apart. I then told her we would want to observe him overnight in the Soc Trang hospital, but he could go home tomorrow if everything checked out.

Doan did not seem happy at this news, but his mother told him, apparently, that she would spend the night with him. He relaxed, and I thought this was a good system indeed. A child in the hospital needed a mother nearby. A good practice.

I promised to come by the hospital the next day to see how he was doing.

The MAAG captain, still a little gray, was summoned back to the dispensary from headquarters. He was relieved with the outcome and plan. Mother bowed deeply and they got back in the jeep. This time, the mother rode in the back, and the captain lifted a beaming Doan into the front passenger seat where he could ride shotgun alone.

"Doc," the captain said, "thanks a million. I owe you one."

"Glad we could help."

I watched them drive off and hoped to myself Doan would not develop a subdural hematoma. He had suffered quite a blow to the head, and there could be delayed consequences. Brave little guy, he had been at the wrong place at the wrong time. I just hoped he didn't have any more bad luck.

That evening, we had a meeting of the officers to discuss improving the Tigers' Den. There were now seventy officers, and our old club, even with the new addition, seemed sparse.

"All in favor, say Aye." There was a loud vote. "All opposed say No." There was silence in the hall. Charley, the club manager, then announced, "Then good ol' Doc Hoyland is the new president."

I understood I had probably set myself up for this job by doing all the collecting for the orphanage and leprosarium. It would, however, be a different kind of job, and I accepted. What else could I do? I would appoint some committees to get the club fixed up the way the members wanted. They had big plans, including the number one request: an air-conditioner. The rainy season was coming. With heat and intense humidity, the already sweaty room, when crowded, could be miserable. We also had many requests to install a grill and deep fryer in the new addition. We collected the money, and Charley went to work immediately: He ordered air-conditioning and grill equipment from Okinawa.

SOC TRANG
SAT
30 MAR 63

Two dentists arrived today to tend the troops. We set up our treatment room for a dental office. They brought their own equipment, even chairs. These nice guys seemed to like their work and had the benefit of not being stuck in one location; they kept moving and got to see the whole country. I wouldn't want to swap places with them for anything; while they did get to see a lot of the country, they didn't get to know the guys the way you do if you live with them day in and day out.

Footloose dentists made me realize I had cabin fever, though. I had not been away from the airfield for six straight weeks and would sure like to get up to Saigon for even one day. At least the army knew I was still alive and on active duty. I received preliminary orders for my next duty station; in November, I would report to Ft. Huachuca, Arizona.

Long after having gone to my bunk that evening, my pilot friend Witty, thankful to be off duty the next day, had enough to drink at the club. He left, feeling no pain. Walking past Tuffy's yard, he had a lapse of judgment and decided Tuffy was probably lonely and needed company. Tuffy, surprised by this late-night intrusion, gave a swipe to Witty's right arm.

"Doc." The duty officer gently shook me from slumber. "Billy T. needs you."

At the dispensary door, I found a bare-chested Witty holding a bloody T-shirt to cover his right arm, a sheepish grin on his face.

I scrubbed the forearm, examining the wound. Fortunately, it was a clean slice, and the small bleeding artery was easily located and controlled. I put in some sutures and finished with a pressure dressing.

"And now, CWO Witt, keep your wits and please don't try this again. Ever. Okay?" I gave him a tetanus booster.

"Right on," he answered. "I owe you one, Doc."

On our way back to hootch #4, we looked in Tuffy's yard. Lying on his table, awake and content, he was as still as a marble statue in the moonlight.

SOC TRANG
SUN
31 MAR 63

Sick call was thankfully light. "Sarge, what do you know about Fort Huachuca?" I showed Sgt. Tibbs my orders.

"Not much, but I know it is a base for the signal corps."

"Sounds better than the infantry or Fort Benning and being out in the field all the time. That wouldn't be too different than here," I said.

"Doc, begging your pardon, but I'd take Benning over here any day." He laughed.

No missions were scheduled today, so after sick call, I took the jeep for a run into Soc Trang and the civilian hospital to check on Doan, our littlest soldier.

In the dim light of the hospital ward, I found the dark-eyed, stoic youngster lying on a slat hospital bed with a bamboo mat. His mother, lying beside him in her black pajamas, quickly stood as I approached and bowed politely. Worry and fatigue lined her face. I thought she could be twenty or thirty years old. I could not gauge. A Vietnamese hospital aide came up, smiling. She bowed politely and reported, "*Bac-Si*, Doan, good boy; do good."

As best as I could, I communicated to the boy, his mother, and the aide that I would conduct another examination to see how he was doing. They seemed to understand and were both watchful and respectful. Doan moved easily, and there were no new findings other than more bruises than I noted yesterday. He was definitely bright and alert. There had been no abnormal loss of consciousness. His sleep had been normal, according to his mother. He presented no evidence of a subdural or other brain injury.

The wound looked clean—no sign of infection. The lesions should heal well, and the scar would pretty much disappear into a frown line. I put on a new bandage I had brought with me.

"Doan," I said as he looked up at me with enormous brown eyes, "you brave. You be fine."

The aide translated by repeating these words, and both Doan and his mother smiled. Mother again bowed. She agreed to bring him back for the follow-up tetanus immunizations and even sooner if she saw any changes or complications. The sutures would be removed in one week. We all bowed, and I left, thankful it had not been a worse accident. The last thing we want to do is antagonize these good people.

I drove to the MAAG compound and again noted how daylight turned the once graceful building, after years of neglect and mold, into a gothic villa.

In the dining room, I found the MAAG captain who had been driving when the boy was struck.

"Any news? How's the boy?" he asked as I walked in, unable to mask his anxiety.

"Looks good this morning. He'll be fine. I just left the hospital, and his mother is taking him home."

"Thank God." His breath escaped softly. "I've been worried sick about him. Just ran out of nowhere."

"Accidents happen." I poured some coffee and sat down across the table. "But we're lucky. That little guy's a trooper. The wound looks good."

"Thank God he's okay."

"He'll have his own war story to tell now."

Back at the airfield, while driving down the company street headed toward the dispensary, Slick stood at the side of the dusty road and waved for me to stop.

"Treat tonight, Doc. Barbecue! Smell that?" he said.

"Sure 'nuff." I smelled the early smoke from a hardwood fire.

I drove on to the dispensary, and Sgt. Tibbs came out.

"Glad you're back. Brooklyn is out on the flight line with the ambulance standing by." He threw the gear in the back of the jeep and jumped in.

"What's up?" I asked.

"T-28 got a wing shot up. Due any minute."

Fire trucks and crews were already lined up on either side of the runway when we pulled up.

For about five very long minutes, every eye in the large, silent group was trained toward the north, searching the cloudless Delta sky.

Someone down the line shouted, "There she is!"

I could not see anything, but in moments, I located the outline of a plane. It rapidly pulled closer. The left wing had been ripped open and had sustained obvious heavy damage. The pilot nailed a perfect approach and landing. The crowd let out a loud, boisterous cheer.

Brooklyn pulled the ambulance up to the aircraft. The pilot, uninjured, helped a Special Forces major riding in the second seat behind the pilot down from the plane. One arm bloody, he had suffered a hit on his left side. We loaded both in the ambulance and sped to the dispensary.

I cut away the sleeve of the major's uniform. This exposed a large, jagged laceration to his left elbow caused by a sharp metal fragment from the wing. He would need X-rays to fully assess the extent of the injury, but it looked to me like he had escaped with only a clean laceration. The exposed tendons and bone appeared undamaged. We stopped the bleeding with a pressure dressing.

We called Dust Off. The team arrived in record time, and the major was quickly on his way to the field hospital in Nha Trang.

When I returned to my desk, I found a set of orders with my name.

I opened the envelope. My next duty would definitely be as a flight surgeon at the hospital in Ft. Huachuca, Arizona. November seemed like a long way off, but at least I had a future.

Tony, the clerk, came up to my desk. "Sir, you're not going to believe this—there's been another traffic accident in town."

Sgt. Tibbs came in behind Tony. "Two Special Forces were in a jeep and hit a couple of Vietnamese men crossing the street. They want you down there ASAP. I'll drive."

He gunned the motor. "I'll be careful, I promise," he said as our jeep sped out of the gate.

In front of the MAAG house, a captain met us and yelled, "They're all over at the hospital."

Two or three MAAG vehicles were in front of the small hospital. Standing next to them, in a cluster, were several MAAG advisors and two men wearing green berets and camouflage combat fatigues.

"Either of you hurt?" I asked.

"No. Just shook up," the taller one said. "The guys we hit are inside."

Sgt. Tibbs and I took the now-familiar route to the emergency area. We arrived, and the aide bowed as she smiled. "*Bac si*, back so soon."

Two men waited for us, both dressed in standard black pajamas with flip-flop-clad feet. They looked sullen.

"How are they?" I asked the aide.

"No hurt," she said.

More detailed examination confirmed the aide's diagnosis—only a few superficial bruises and abrasions, which we cleaned. When we finished, the men pulled on their shirts and with dark eyes unfathomable, they quickly left.

On our way out, we told the waiting soldiers the results, and they were visibly relieved. "I couldn't help but wonder if they're VC," I said. "Their attitude seemed hostile."

"A good hunch," the taller one said as he put out a cigarette. "I'd agree, for sure; and they're military age."

"VCs or not, we need a crossing guard in this part of town," Sgt. Tibbs said as he flashed his big smile.

"Military traffic and civilians are always trouble," a major said. "We'll redouble our efforts."

Sgt. Tibbs and I got back in our jeep, and the Special Forces men called out, "Thanks for helping us out."

Back at the airfield, Sgt. Tibbs dropped me off in front of hootch #4.

"See you, Doc," he said.

"Not until tomorrow morning, if we have any luck."

The unmistakable aroma of barbecue filled the air. I hadn't eaten since breakfast and felt starved. I changed clothes out of my fatigues as quickly as I could, washed up, and went to the O-Club.

Slick, holding a beer, was hot and sweaty as he bent over the fire and smoke. "Doc. I was afraid you might miss out on my secret Southern basting sauce."

The chicken halves were mahogany and golden. The troops had gone through a lot of food and beer to wash it down, but there was more than enough.

After digging into my share, I said, and I meant it, "I've never had better, Lieutenant Slick. You make the best."

After being well-fed and entertained by this event, the Tigers' Den was still festive at 2000. In the distance, booming mortars started up. The boisterous crowd fell silent.

"Those babies are close," Trey said.

They sounded closer than ever before. Small-arms fire started. "That sounds like the Fourth of July. And about as close as main gate," Slick said.

This action put a quick damper on the revelry; the party dispersed.

I sat alone outside hootch #4 for awhile. The small-arms fire had not amounted to much, and now mortars were only in the distance, much further than the earlier ones. I reluctantly got ready for bed, as I had to get some sleep. Tomorrow, an air force surgeon, major-general type, would be at the dispensary at 0940, making an inspection to see for himself how the 134th was treating the air force personnel assigned here at this army installation.

SOC TRANG
MON
1 APR 63

The air force inspection went fine. They were pleased with the dispensary and expressed appreciation for our support—good to get their feedback.

This might be an April Fool's joke, but Slick, not a totally reliable source, swears he heard Madame Nhu has added twist songs to her music ban. Busy lady.

SOC TRANG
SAT
6 APR 63

At 0200, that time of night when dream-filled sleep gave pleasant respite from reality, a sudden explosion, loud and nearby, ripped all of us in our hootches awake.

Someone down the hall yelled, "I'll get those bastards!"

Trouble. I dressed faster than usual, including boots. The OD showed up as I headed toward the dispensary.

"An MP got it in the leg," he yelled.

A small crowd stood at the dispensary front door by the time I arrived.

Two MPs entered the treatment room; one assisted the other, who had been wounded.

We put the injured man on the treatment table. I had seen this MP on guard duty at the front gate many times, but I did not know him by name. He was fully conscious and seemed somewhat embarrassed by all the commotion.

"What happened?" I asked.

"A grenade. From out of nowhere. We were patrolling on the inner perimeter road," the injured MP said. The driver of the jeep, who had no injury, did not say anything and left the treatment room.

"You are lucky," I said to the injured MP after giving him a careful examination. I cleaned the superficial abrasions to his right leg. "Here's some antibiotic ointment. Keep the area clean, and at the first sign of redness or infection, come back. Otherwise, you're good to return to duty."

A worrisome event—this was the first time the VC had penetrated the inner perimeter far enough to toss a grenade. If they meant this as a message to scare us, in my opinion, they had succeeded brilliantly. I cleaned up the bandage tray and turned out the lights.

The Delta air in the early morning felt cool on my face as the OD and I walked toward my hootch. I thought of how we were such an island of foreigners in this country. We had an inner perimeter we patrolled, and the Vietnamese secured the outer perimeter.

The OD said, "You know, Doc, that grenade was mighty close to the fuel dump. Can you imagine what it would be like if they hit that?" He thought for a moment. "How could they have gotten inside the perimeter? This is going to take some investigation— serious investigation."

I bid him good night as he went back to headquarters. I went to my bunk, unnerved by the thought of this security breach. The next thing I knew, the sky was pink and rosy with the dawn.

SOC TRANG
SUN
7 APR 63

A large new house has been built in Soc Trang for the children living in the leprosarium. I received an invitation to attend the dedication, and when I arrived, many people had already gathered. I saw some of the children who attended the Christmas party, and they came over, again eager to say hello. I did not know the number of children who would live here, but it was a spacious facility, very modern and different from the colony.

After many long speeches—I felt sure they did not seem so long to those who understood the language—the ribbon was cut, and we all explored this fine new residence. I worried about the parents back at the compound. They would miss the children, and the children would miss their families. There did not seem to be any good solutions to some problems.

In the crowd, I saw the two physicians from the civilian hospital in Soc Trang. They invited me to a medical meeting the next night. I would have liked to attend, but it would be too difficult, not speaking the language. In the crowd, I was shocked to see several American women. I went over and introduced myself. They were civilian nurses with the U.S. Public Health Service. They told me their agency had helped fund the building.

A tall, thin Caucasian physician joined us. "I'm an anesthesiologist," he said with a pleasant accent. From New Zealand, he was going up north to be part of a civilian surgical team.

These health workers made me aware there were many civilians in Vietnam. They had a very different life from the military— relatively free to come and go in the major population centers. I admired their motivation. At one point in my life, I briefly entertained the idea of working in the Foreign Service or as a medical missionary in some exotic locale. Now I realized I was not cut out for that work or lifestyle and had even greater respect for these idealistic and adventuresome people.

Seeing civilians made me wish again to have a break in Saigon. Since I arrived, I'd only been away from Soc Trang for two days, if you didn't count the missions, and I didn't count those as getting away. I had heard of a one-day R & R trip to Siem Reap in Cambodia. The Ankor Wat ruins nearby are a wonder of the world. I would like to go there. For the time being, though, I needed to just keep on doing what I could.

SAIGON
THUR
11 APR 63

With a policy change, the Army Combat Infantry Badge could be awarded to eligible U.S. soldiers fighting in South Vietnam.

Saigon reported 8,150,187 peasants were housed in 5,917 strategic hamlets. The goal for the end of the year: twelve thousand hamlets.[28]

SOC TRANG
FRI
12 APR 63

The project to resurface our airstrip was well underway, and the dusk-to-dawn noise and dust made living next to the airfield difficult. It made my room in hootch #4, almost on the runway, unpleasant while they worked. But it wouldn't last forever. The construction crew came by the club after work. These civilian workers were Americans who worked for a large U.S. contractor and traveled to jobs all over the world. Mostly single, they were a hard-working, fun-loving, footloose breed of rugged individuals.

I received an invitation to my tenth high school reunion, which will be next month. I'll need to write a letter, as I won't be able to make it.

SOC TRANG
SUN
14 APR 63

"Missed you last week at services," Father O'Brian said, ever-present twinkle in his eyes. "I'm counting on seeing you today. It's Easter, you know."

"I'll be there, Father," I answered. I didn't remember it was Easter or why I hadn't gone last week. I started to tell him I had been in town for the dedication of the children's home, but the event had been later in the day. I usually tried to attend Sunday services when we weren't flying. I wanted to support the chaplain, and we needed his support, but with so many missions on Sundays, I missed a lot. However, that was no excuse for last week; we hadn't flown that day.

Easter Sunday in the Delta was like any other Sunday, but the chaplain had some good words about how to make the best of things. I liked him, and he provided some positive stability in this very unstable setting.

HONOLULU
MID-APRIL 1963

During a meeting with McNamara in Hawaii, Gen. Harkins reported things were going so well in the fight against the VC, the war might be over by Christmas.[29]

SOC TRANG
FRI
19 APR 63

Through my helmet microphone, I heard the crew chief yell, "There he is: Buffalo Man. Still waving that damn torch." I looked toward where he pointed and saw a figure in the rice field below.

It was early morning, and we had just left Soc Trang airfield. I had heard of Buffalo Man; the crews had noted this peasant in black pajamas out in his field every time we left for a mission. He carried a torch, and when we took off, he lit it and waved toward the west. He got his name from a water buffalo that was never too far away. At first, the crews thought he might be driving off insects from his buffalo, but he persisted even in the dry season when bugs were scarce. Sometimes, the buffalo would be at a great distance from the farmer.

Everyone now assumed he was a VC and used his torch and smoke to signal someone, perhaps the direction we were headed. The CO complained about him to the province chief, but this did not stop Buffalo Man.

After that, I knew where to look. I determined to keep my eye on him. I could not help but think of the smoke signals used by the American Indians to communicate, at least in those old cowboy movies.

We were going to a new airstrip. With these missions becoming almost routine, it was good to go to a new part of the country. Rather than south, we were going west to an area near the cement factory. This plant produced most—if not all—of the cement for the whole of South Vietnam. There was a reliable report the VC wanted to sabotage the plant to hamper the war effort.

Maj. Saunders returned from the hospital. He looked fit and said he was fully recovered and raring to go. Our missions had picked up again. The current mission proved uneventful. The ARVN made no contact around the cement plant. No VC even spotted. Another assault was planned for the following day. Those VC the ARVN didn't get on the first day, they probably won't get on the second.

CEMENT PLANT
SAT
20 APR 63

After a second long day at the cement plant, we were not released until the early dusk began changing the landscape to a rust color. I looked at my watch. It was 1845. A long way from home, I was glad we were finally headed back.

I rode in Slick's chopper, the lead for this mission. We rapidly reached altitude on a heading east toward Soc Trang when I heard a sudden radio communication from the chopper to our right.

"Trouble." I heard PBD's familiar voice, but with an edge. I looked out the aft door toward his aircraft.

His chopper, I could see, headed down; it had lost power. PBD and his copilot were forced to perform auto rotation. A difficult task at best, all helicopter pilots are well-trained in this maneuver for just this rare emergency. After a brief agony, which seemed much longer, the silent engine coughed back to life and caught hold. With return of power, the chopper could be airworthy—or not—but unsafe for continued flight.

"Good work, Captain PBD," said Slick, relief in his voice.

"Thanks. Now what?" PBD said.

Slick, as the lead pilot for this mission, radioed Soc Trang about the situation. He broke in, "Captain PBD, Soc Trang advises landing at Rach Gia strip," and he gave coordinates. "We'll fly escort."

"Roger that," PBD said and changed his heading away from Soc Trang.

Slick continued as we changed direction, "Chalk 3, lead the birds home and don't bother to leave the porch light on for us."

Hartley Davis's voice echoed, "Will do. Better call ahead for reservations at the Rach Gia Hilton." The rest of the formation now followed him. "Have fun." I saw him wave from the cockpit as they headed for home.

Slick and our copilot, CWO Witt, both waved back, and the rest of the choppers disappeared in the evening sky.

Rach Gia was close by. As we approached, I could see the coastline and dark Gulf of Siam in the distance to the west. PBD had no more engine trouble and executed a perfect landing. We settled down nearby. It was now dark. The only lights were in the distance from town. We did not know where we were, as orientation is difficult at night.

"This ground is not secure, my friends," Slick said as we stood next to our choppers. "Little Lee Roy didn't exactly just sneak in here, so keep your eyes open."

I couldn't see much in the dark, but there was a glow in the distance indicating a sizable city not too far away.

"Soc Trang contacted the MAAG outfit here. They should be along shortly. Rach Gia's only about seven kilometers that way." Slick pointed toward the west.

"Hope they get here before the VC," PBD muttered under his breath.

Amen, I said to myself silently.

In the distance, we heard rumbling truck engines.

"I hear the sound of hoof beats. The cavalry is arriving to save our sorry butts," Witty said with relief.

Sure enough, two ARVN trucks came roaring up.

"A thing of beauty," said the crew chief.

The headlights from the trucks lighted the pitch-black area, and ARVN troops jumped off and deployed themselves in a circle around the two choppers. They were going to spend the night guarding this malfunctioning U.S. property. Mechanics would fly out from Soc Trang first thing tomorrow to find out what was wrong with PBD's ailing chopper.

An American MAAG captain came over to greet us. "Welcome, mighty Soc Trang Tigers. Welcome to our humble station." He added, "Be sure you bring all the machine guns and ammo with you, then climb aboard. Our limos will take you into town."

After a short ride in the dark countryside, we were driving through a city that looked to be a little larger than Soc Trang. It felt even more humid, if possible. We pulled up at a moderate-sized derelict French villa.

The captain came back to the second truck to talk to us. "We aren't equipped to take care of all of you. We can only feed and house the first truck. We've made arrangements for the rest of you down at a nearby hotel."

Unappreciative groans came from the dark insides of our truck. We all knew this meant less than class-D accommodations.

"You bunch of ingrates," PBD yelled toward the back of the dark truck. "Would you rather spend the night out there with the choppers?" I sensed he was feeling down that he was the pilot of the machine that failed, causing this whole misadventure.

Our truck stopped next at a dingy, dirty, run-down hotel unaccustomed to Western travelers. We piled out, and the friendly Vietnamese proprietor, a small man with a pockmarked face, showed us where to bunk. He made his reluctant kitchen staff stay late to prepare us something to eat.

They served tough, stringy chicken, rice, and a thin soup that provided little more than calories. They also had that fresh French bread that was so excellent. Those baguettes made up for the rest of the meal. We drank warm beer from the bottles. I hoped our delicate systems could handle this indigenous fare. The men groused but all agreed they were thankful to be here and not out in some dark rice field; better safe than very sorry later.

PBD and I shared a room. We carried our gear up two flights of dark, narrow stairs. The room was small and had two bamboo mats on low, hard wooden cots, each covered with a dirty gray sheet. Mosquitoes, lying in wait, were glad for us to arrive. They flew in circles, as there was no netting to keep them in control. I hoped everyone was up-to-date on their anti-malaria pills.

There would be no showers tonight. We flopped on the pallets, glad to at least be off our feet. It had been a long, long day. Too wrung-out to be finicky tourist, I went to sleep.

RACH GIA
SUN
21 APR 63

When I awoke, I could not place where I was. The sun was just coming up. In the dim early morning light, I looked around the small room; PBD sat on the edge of his cot.

"It's about time you woke up," PBD said. "I never closed my eyes. Didn't get a wink of sleep. Those damn mosquitoes. And you, prince charming, slept like a damn baby."

"Comes from practice. I could sleep standing up when I was an intern."

We grabbed our gear and climbed down the stairs. After we took turns relieving ourselves in the primitive toilet, we joined the rest of our crew, who had assembled in various states of alertness. For breakfast, we had black, bitter coffee and more of that great French bread. By 0800, our truck arrived, and we climbed aboard. Early mist hung over the cool landscape. The second truck joined us, and we were all soon back at the rice field where I saw not two, but four choppers looming large in the landscape.

I was astounded; our Soc Trang mechanics had already arrived and were hard at work on the errant engine. They had flown here in two H-21s at first light.

Trey piloted one of the rescue ships, and he greeted us, freshly shaved and wearing a spic-and-span flight suit. "They've got the problem fixed and your H-21s airworthy, PBD. That's the good news. The bad news—both for you and Slick—these choppers are needed back at the cement plant this morning to complete yesterday's mission."

My heart sank at this news.

"Doc," Trey said. "Our choppers have to get these mechanics back to Soc Trang. You can fly with us; the flight surgeon from the Fifty-Seventh is covering the mission today."

"Doc, you lucked out," PBD said.

Tired and faces lined with fatigue and unshaved stubble, the crews went through the checklists and routines. The engines roared, and both Slick and PBD waved as they took off for duty near the cement plant.

I loaded my emergency kit on Trey's chopper and we prepared for takeoff. Soon, we were in tandem on our way back home. When we arrived at Soc Trang, I thought it never looked so good. I was tired, smelly, unshaved, and didn't look so good, but I went by the dispensary to check in.

My medic team had taken care of business. "Not much of a sick call this morning. Nothing I couldn't handle." Sgt. Tibbs beamed. "The paperwork's on your desk."

"Thank you. Look for something extra in your paycheck this month," I laughed.

Sgt. Tibbs beamed again. "I'll hold my breath, sir."

Hootch #4 looked clean, neat, and inviting. I realized Americans aren't used to sweat or body odor, even in a hot country like this. After a long, soothing shower, I had the luxury of a nap.

I awoke to familiar surroundings and went to the mess hall for dinner. Good food, and wholesome. By 1800, I was at the O-Club. The pilots from the mission were just returning. PBD and Slick straggled in. They looked pretty bad.

"I think I'll put in for some R & R at Rach Gia," Slick said.

PBD said, "It kinda reminds me a lot of Hong Kong."

Slick rolled his eyes up. "Amen." He and PBD ordered drinks and food from the grill. They ate as if they hadn't seen food in two days.

SOC TRANG
MON
22 APR 63

I stopped by the mess hall for a late afternoon coffee break. Two pilots I had never met were sitting at a table, and I joined them. We introduced ourselves; they had just arrived in Vietnam and had come directly to Soc Trang.

Looking grim, Trey came in, got some coffee, and sat at our long table. After introductions, he said, "Two more outposts near Cam Mau were hit last night, real bad. Over 150 were killed at one, and one hundred or so at the other." He took a sip of coffee and continued. "A T-28 flew over there this morning. They reported bodies everywhere. Both hamlets completely leveled. Said it looked like they'd been hit with an A-bomb."

"I bet we'll head back to Cam Mau first thing tomorrow," I said.

"That's a pretty sure thing." Trey took another sip from his cup. "ARVN paratroopers went in early this afternoon. We'll soon find out. There's a briefing this evening." Trey smiled for the first time as he addressed the new pilots. "We might as well initiate you FNG Tigers properly."

CAM MAU
TUE
23 APR 63

As predicted, at first light, the choppers fired up, and we headed south to Cam Mau. As usual, Buffalo Man waved his torch. But today, the gunner standing shotgun in the aft door took aim and fired. The carefully placed rounds landed, as planned, near the farmer but did not hit him. Buffalo Man dropped the torch and took off running for the nearest tree line.

After we landed, the crew chief said, "I'll probably face disciplinary action, but whatever it is, it was worth it." Several other gunners and crew chiefs came by to congratulate him. We would not see Buffalo Man again, even though we regularly saw the water buffalo out in the field.

At Cam Mau, the government was building a new airstrip, not far from the one we had been using. It would be longer, wider, and bigger but would still look the same as all of them do; a strip carved out of the flat Delta earth, built up above the rice fields, and compacted with gravel and dirt to support helicopters, troops, and small fixed-wing observer aircraft. The strips were connected to basic roads for hauling in troops and refueling trucks. They were always in the middle of nowhere and away from villages and tree lines that might provide cover for VC snipers. You've seen one, you've seen them all. Even after all my frequent visits, I rarely could name a location by appearance.

The long lines of ARVN troops, in full battle gear and colorful unit neck scarves, were ferried, load after load, to the drop zone. After the choppers had delivered the last load, they returned to the strip in an orderly formation, and in a straight line at the side of the field, shut down their engines. A deafening quiet settled on the countryside. Time for lunch.

I strolled over to where the pilots had gathered in the shade of a truck. Olive-drab cardboard boxes containing our rations were in large cartons. I picked one up. It was the best—wieners and beans—my favorite and preferred by almost everyone else.

Slick saw I had scored, and he said in a polite Southern accented voice, "Sir, would you be interested in a trade?" He held his box toward me.

"And what do you have?" I laughed.

"The always favorite chicken in lard."

I politely declined.

He asked, "And Captain PBD, how about you? What do you have?"

"Sorry, Slick old buddy. The hamburger. Almost as good as weenies and beans."

We put our cans to heat up on a still hot truck manifold.

Witt came over. "One of the MAAG captains stationed near here told me about a grisly scene." Taking a can from the carton, he shrugged and put his container of chicken next to ours. "He told me he saw a humongous number of bodies floating downstream. Apparently, the VC overran a hamlet and threw the bodies of the farmers and their families into the river. Meant to scare all the villages and hamlets downstream."

"That ought to be pretty effective," I said.

"It's even worse," Witt said. "The guy told me they'd been dead over twenty-four hours and in the water all that time. His villagers stood on the river bank, watching in silence, absolute silence. He said it was surreal."

CAM MAU
WED
24 APR 63

Not much action reported from yesterday's mission, so we returned to Cam Mau for another attempt. The day seemed almost identical to yesterday.

I sat with Sgt. Tibbs, who had been going with me on many missions, at the side of the airstrip watching the choppers return from the second uneventful troop lift of the morning.

"What do you miss most about home?" I asked.

"Mostly my wife and kids." He took out his billfold and showed me a family picture. "But on a hot, dry day like this, I'd also have to say I miss Emma's—that's my wife's name—lemonade. What I wouldn't give for a glass right now." He replaced his billfold. "She makes the best. She says she doesn't do anything special, but she cooks up a syrup before she adds the lemons. It's the best, I'll tell you."

"It's been a long time since breakfast," I said.

"And can she make gumbo! Doc, after all this is over, come down and see us. She'll make you some. You can judge for yourself."

"Okay, Sergeant Tibbs. All your food talk has made me hungry. I hope we can snag some good lunch."

"I'd sure like to get my hands on a can of weenies and beans," he said.

"You and everyone else in this army. Maybe that's all they should make."

"The hamburger patty's not bad." Sgt. Tibbs grinned. "But it's sure not gumbo."

During the third and last troop drop, the command post radio crackled. "Chalk 2 taking fire," the radio operator repeated. "They're headed back. Have the ARVN ambulance on standby."

All thoughts of food now gone, I scanned the sky. Almost immediately, I heard the roar and saw the choppers returning, but not in a precise formation. The first to land was Chalk 2, Slick's plane. Immediately after touchdown, the crew chief hopped out, aiding a wounded ARVN soldier.

"He was the last one off. Got it in the leg just as we were ready to leave the LZ," the lanky crew chief reported. An ARVN medic helped the injured man into an ambulance, and it sped off.

"Doc," the crew chief continued, "look at this." He pointed to his left combat boot. The sole had been shot off.

The gunner ran over. When he saw the boot, he laughed with relief. "You lucky son of a bitch! That's too close even for government work." He patted the crew chief on the back and said, "They missed me by only about three feet."

Slick emerged from the chopper, unruffled. "I'd say we were all damn lucky." He inspected the several bullet holes in the fuselage.

"Are the ARVN troops running into action?" I asked.

"Didn't look that way to me. I think we just got unlucky and were in the crosshairs of a lucky sniper." Slick continued, "An area gets overrun at night; we bring in the cavalry the next morning; and there's no VC around. Just MaMa-san and PaPa-san doing their chores in their black pajamas. No action."

The crew chief laughed, "Begging your pardon, Lieutenant Slick, sir. But this has been enough for me." He examined the fresh bullet holes in the fuselage, then climbed back up in the chopper to assess the damage from the inside.

And that was the excitement for the day. Nothing more eventful occurred, and we were released to go back to Soc Trang.

When I had some free time, I looked at my mail. Along with pay, mail is critical to GIs everywhere; the U.S. Army does an amazing job in delivery of both. My family had been writing faithfully, and this evening, I found an airmail letter from my parents.

They enclosed a picture from an April 14 edition of *The Jefferson City Sunday News and Tribune*. I was as surprised as they had been to see a photo of me at work in the 134th Dispensary. I had forgotten a military photographer had been down here several weeks before. The picture, boring and posed, could have been taken in any office anywhere. In the photo, I am standing behind Tony, looking over his shoulder at a file on his desk. I realized, sheepishly, I would rather the picture had been an action shot of me getting in a chopper with my emergency bag. But boring to me or not, my parents were proud, and that was good. I realized, for the first time, the army had public relations at work back home.

SOC TRANG
SAT
27 APR 63

A day off. No missions scheduled, and a Saturday to boot. Sick call was light. It was a beautiful, sunny day. I headed for hootch #4 and looked forward to lying on my bunk to catch up on my reading: a new-to-me issue of *Time* magazine and the latest *Stars and Stripes*.

I read the first page of the paper when I heard Witt's familiar voice call out, "Doc Hoyland. Get a move on. PBD's got an American Special Forces evac."

The routine was now familiar. I tossed the paper and quickly geared up.

In the chopper, I put on one flak jacket and sat on one. I heard PBD say over the intercom, "This one is way out in the boondocks. Make yourself comfortable, Doc, it'll take about an hour to get there."

After about fifty minutes out, he switched to the ground frequency, and I heard communications with the Special Forces team. This area, deep in VC territory, could not be secured even in the daytime. Our crew chief and gunner kept keen eyes on the tree lines, which surrounded the area on three sides. VC were in there, and our noisy arrival would announce us as an easy visual target. I wished I had not been so lazy when we left and had put three flak jackets on my seat. Too late this time, but I would next flight, for sure.

The Green Berets had rigged up a landing site by placing orange-colored fabric panels on the ground. This area would be firm enough to support the helicopter. I could see the team standing by with the injured man.

My adrenalin pumped as the H-21 descended to the improvised landing area. The three American Special Forces were huddled behind a dike for protection. Even before we touched down, they sprinted toward us. An enlisted man had a splint protecting his right hand and forearm. He quickly boarded; the crew chief waved; and we were airborne. The rear end kicked up, and we gained speed and altitude. The Green Berets, left on the ground below, disappeared behind the dike.

The soldier advised me he had a bamboo-stake injury through his right hand. It had occurred earlier this morning. Through the intercom, I asked PBD to radio ahead to Soc Trang for emergency transportation to the field hospital. I felt thankful for this helmet that allowed me to talk to the crew. This injury needed prompt definitive care.

PBD advised me a C-47 was ready to take off from Soc Trang, but they could hold it until we arrived.

By 1100, I was back on my bunk, reading page two of the paper—still plenty of time to enjoy a quiet Saturday. When I read *Time*, I felt like a foreigner reading the magazine. A new singer I had never heard of, Barbra Streisand, seemed to be getting a lot of press.

America seemed far away, and the stories and events and movies they reported on had so little to do with the real world.

SOC TRANG
FRI
3 MAY 63

Clouds appeared in the clear Delta skies. The monsoon would

arrive soon—ever-present dust to be replaced with pervasive mud. But seasonal rains meant hope and the time to plant rice. The latitude and longitude made the Mekong Delta a marvel of terrain, water, and geography. No wonder it had a history of turbulence. Everyone in Asia coveted this land.

This area was so productive–the weather mild, water dependable, and the alluvial ground fertile. The peasant farmers and their families appeared well fed, and with so much rice production, they always had plenty for export. Fish and shrimp were abundant, and amazing exotic fruits grew everywhere. No wonder they called the mighty Mekong Delta the rice bowl of Asia. It must have been a wonderful country at peace.

The Provincial Hospital, as the civilian hospital in Soc Trang was officially known, had just completed a brand-new surgical wing. The United States Overseas Mission (USOM) built and equipped it. Where would they get surgeons and staff? Medical personnel were in short supply. Maybe with the new facility, they would find new help. I hoped so. They desperately needed it.

I received a letter from the CO of the Eighth Field Hospital. He suggested they send a physician down here for one month, and I could spend a month working up there. I appreciated his concern that I might be getting rusty in my medical skills. I would definitely take him up on the offer. I needed other physicians to talk medicine with, and it also would be nice to have a change of scenery. I'd miss the Tigers, but Nha Trang, on the beach, was a resort town; it would be quite a change from the Delta and Soc Trang airfield.

While having dinner at the O-Club, the talk turned to Tuffy.

"I hear one of our pilot's wives volunteers at the Toledo Zoo. He wrote her to see if they are interested in Tuffy," Witty said. "That tiger's over a year old now; I'll bet he weighs in close to two hundred pounds."

"All muscle." Slick started laughing. "Did you hear about that officer over in maintenance who was sitting on the john? He had the strange feeling he was being watched. Tuffy poked his head in the stall, and the captain's constipation cleared right up." Everyone in the club laughed at this familiar and often-told story.

I heard some good news from the club manager. The air-conditioning and grill equipment arrived and would be up and running soon—just in time for the muggy weather ahead.

SOC TRANG
SUN
5 MAY 63

Dust. Dust. The yellowish powdered dust made grit in my mouth and irritated my nose. It was everywhere. The dry period lasted from autumn to spring, so soon the monsoon rains should begin. I felt eager for the rains, and so did the Vietnamese. Even though the new Cam Mau airstrip was not finished, we used it as a staging area anyway.

After we set up our aid station, I watched the workers labor to build this new airstrip. A long line of perhaps one hundred men—all wearing cone-shaped bamboo hats and dressed in the ubiquitous black muslin pajamas or loose, short pants—carried a bucket in each hand filled with crushed rocks. In single file, they lugged the rocks to a designated place, dumped the buckets, and returned, still in line, to the immense pile of gravel, where other men refilled the containers. The men carrying the rocks wore only flip-flops on their feet. They were so adept, they did not miss a step and retraced their paths to dump the next load. Remarkably agile, they looked like a long line of worker ants. They did a great job, and their work looked as good as any made with machines. It amazed me.

When I looked back at the choppers, lined up on the already completed section, I could see the typical large number of ARVN troops standing in groups with their U.S. advisors. They loaded on board, and one by one, the giant flying bananas took off in heavy dust clouds. Hueys, circling, took off as escorts. For this mission, the landing zone would not be far from the airstrip.

The command post had been set up in the shade of a small canvas shelter, at some distance from the dust. I heard a major yell to be heard over the radio transmission, "They're running into ground fire!" He stopped as additional communications crackled on the radio. In the command post, both the Vietnamese and anxious American advisors listened intently.

Within minutes, I heard the distinctive whop-whop sound of a Huey, and the lone chopper landed. Dust billowed. One of the pilots made a quick exit and ran over toward our aid station. With his right hand, he put pressure on a wound to his left hand, which was bleeding profusely.

The Huey had been hit by ground fire, and a piece of aluminum fuselage had ripped off and lodged in the dorsum of the copilot's hand. These sharp metal fragments slipped out as easily as they went in. I cleaned and bandaged the wound with a pressure dressing. Only temporarily incapacitated, he and the Huey were soon headed back to provide cover for our choppers and the troops in the landing zone.

Strangely, the shooting suddenly ceased, and the rest of the mission proved quiet. No action. The VC had disappeared for the day. Released by early afternoon, we returned from Cam Mau over the now-familiar flight path. After we landed at Soc Trang, I headed over to the dispensary to reload my emergency kit.

PBD passed me on the company street. "We're in luck. There's a USO show today. If your social calendar permits, I asked one of the girls to have dinner at the club afterward. You're invited to join us."

"PBD, you are indeed an officer and gentleman," I said. "I'll clear my schedule."

The USO show was fun. The girls, wholesome and good-looking, sang, danced, and gave from their hearts. The band was terrific. The music and jokes—some clever, some corny—proved to be a great diversion. Everyone who could get free sat in the sun facing the truck-turned-stage parked in front of the hangar. The amplifiers worked, so we could all hear. After much clapping, hooting, and wolf whistles, the show concluded. A standing ovation was genuine and deserved. The crowd dispersed reluctantly to resume routines, morale buoyed because these talented people from home cared enough to come all the way over here to entertain us.

I went to the O-Club. As promised, one of the young entertainers sat with PBD at a long table. Slick was already seated across from her; both pilots had wide grins.

"Hi, soldier. I'm Patricia, but everyone calls me Honey," the unnaturally blonde girl with beautiful dark brown eyes said as I sat down.

I could only say, "Great show."

Honey, in response to eager questions from our table, told us she was a recent USC graduate hoping to get into show business.

"I heard about this trip and just had to come," she said in a musical voice, "to do my part."

Before we could find out more, a pilot came in and shouted, "T-28 ran off the runway."

We all left Honey sitting at the table and ran toward the airstrip. Across the broad runway, a plane was fully engulfed in flames. The men from our fire station were already at work putting out the fire.

"How about the men aboard?" I yelled to an officer returning in a jeep headed to report to the CO.

"They're okay. Got out before it caught fire."

As required, I gave them a checkup at the dispensary. Totally unscathed, they were physically fit to return to duty.

By the time I got back to the O-Club, Honey and the USO troupe had departed for Saigon.

"Doc," Slick said, "Have you noticed how something always happens around here when we're having a little fun?"

I could only nod my head in sad agreement. He was right. But I still felt good; I knew in eleven more days, my tour would be officially half over! Good feeling.

HUE
WED
8 MAY 63

The Buddhists were celebrating Buddha's 2,527th birthday in the old imperial capitol of Hue. President Diem's government issued a decree that no Buddhist flags were to be flown in the city. A large crowd gathered to protest.

A company of Vietnamese Civil Guards, led by a Catholic officer, tried to disperse the crowd. When the group refused to move, the guards opened fire. Nine protestors were killed, and fourteen others, including some children, injured. Buddhists monks, nuns, and their followers—suffering from nine years of what they felt had been government discrimination—were outraged.

The Vietnamese government's attack against the Buddhists was condemned by the American people and the rest of the world. President Diem and the Ngo Dinh family attempted to place the blame for the attack on the VC.[30]

SAIGON
THUR
9 MAY 63

A MACV spokesman reported all trends were favorable in the war effort.[31]

SOC TRANG
SUN
12 MAY 63

Although clouds were forming up, we still had not seen any rain. It was hot, dry, and remained always dusty. Today was a day off! The first Sunday in five weeks we had not been out on a mission. PBD and I joined the celebration in the O-Club.

"So, Captain President." He looked up. "The ceiling's finished. When will the air-conditioners get turned on?"

"A fair question," I said.

Before the air-conditioning could be hooked up, we had to install a ceiling and insulation.

"We will have air in the next two to three days, or I'll resign."

"And who do you think would want the job?" he laughed.

He did not know—and I did not tell him—we needed an additional generator to have enough electricity to power the equipment. It was scheduled to be installed in the next two days.

"PBD," I said, "I have a problem."

"So what's new, Doc?"

"No, seriously; it's a good problem. I need to run something by you."

"Shoot."

"I have received a letter from an officers' wives club. One of the guys wrote to his wife stateside about the orphanage. The ladies have adopted it for a project and are pledging 4,500 piastres a month for the next six months. They want me to decide how to spend it to help the most."

"What's the exchange now?"

"Still about seventy-two piastres to the dollar."

"That's pretty good money when you don't have any," PBD said.

"I have been thinking we could pay to install window screens to keep the flies out. Then the sisters could hire some young girls to come in and do nothing but give the babies baths with soap and water. That would cut way down on the infections and diarrhea."

Before PBD could answer, the club door opened, and with a grand flourish of his arms, Slick welcomed a new captain to the Tigers' Den.

"Hey guys, meet Captain Michael O'Malley, CO for the transportation company that's moving in to join our happy family."

Before we could shake hands, PBD interrupted. "MOM. MOM, is it really you, or do my eyes deceive?"

"Damn, PBD. You old SOB," Michael said. "Scourge of our class. I thought I was rid of you."

The men slapped one another on the back.

PBD explained, "Since flight school, friend Michael O'Malley here has hated to be called MOM. But it's not possible to call him anything else, considering his initials, unless he has a complete name change."

MOM groaned. His dark, curly hair framed a sensitive face with light skin shadowed by his closely shaved dark facial hair. Bright blue eyes glinted with good humor, and his chin had a small cleft, like my old friend Scott Mitchell from internship days. I wondered about his luck with airline stewardesses; probably good,

I thought, and briefly wondered again about plastic surgery for my ordinary chin.

"MOM is God's gift to women." PBD laughed. "He's left broken hearts all over the world."

"Captain PBD, you're still sore about that blond back in Dothan, aren't you?"

"Let bygones be bygones. She wasn't worth it," PBD said in his best Joe Friday dramatic voice. "I'm glad to see you! Welcome to our humble station."

"So this is where the Tigers hang out." MOM looked around the club. "What's Soc Trang like?"

"I plan to go in late this afternoon to inspect the Chinese restaurant," I said. "MOM, you're welcome to join me."

"The one you put off-limits because of everyone that got sick?" Slick said.

"The very one. They sent word they've cleaned up and want some business."

PBD and Slick shook their heads vigorously to discourage him from going.

Ignoring them, MOM said, "Doc, you're on. I could use some good Chinese, and I'd like to get the lay of the land."

Later that afternoon, I picked MOM up at the club, and we took off in my jeep. We parked in front of the small café. The owner came out, and bowing politely, seated us in the front of the small eatery.

We started with very good war wonton soup and then enjoyed a tasty local fresh fish with crispy grilled skin spiced with fresh lime and ground pepper. An MP arrived at the door.

"Doc, a med evac's coming in. One American and a couple of ARVN."

I rapidly paid the proprietor some piastres, even though he indicated he did not want any money. I tried to explain I would come back soon for the kitchen inspection. MOM and I jumped in my jeep and followed the MP for a quick return to the airfield.

Two H-21s were landing as we arrived. I pulled the jeep up next to Brooklyn in the ambulance. Sgt. Tibbs had gone on the flight, and he hopped off the chopper first.

"These guys were in a jeep leading a convoy. Struck a land mine," Sgt. Tibbs yelled to me over the sound of the engines. "They're lucky. Injuries aren't too bad."

In the dispensary, we cleaned and bandaged the wounds, none life-threatening. We had luck, as a C-47 was heading to Saigon. We loaded them aboard, and they were on their way.

I found MOM and PBD at the O-Club.

"MOM tells me you ate dinner at the Chinese place. I thought you went to inspect it?" PBD said.

"I planned to after dinner. I didn't want the inspection to spoil my appetite."

PBD laughed. "See, MOM, you've got to watch out for Doc Hoyland. He uses us as guinea pigs."

"The food tasted good. So far, I'm okay," MOM said, feeling his pulse. "How about the wounded?"

"Not bad for hitting a mine," I said. "By the way, PBD, did we ever hear any more about the MP who got injured on the inner perimeter a few weeks ago?"

"Yep. Turns out he wanted to be a hero to the folks back home in the worst way. But no Purple Heart for him. He threw the grenade himself and made up the story the VC threw it. Sent back to the states and disciplined. Poor bastard."

SOC TRANG
TUE
14 MAY 63

It was early evening, and I felt bored. Not much was going on. I didn't want to read, and I didn't want to write any letters or listen to the radio. How could I be bored? But life in Vietnam could go from tireless routines to exciting and frightening without much notice.

The isolation at Soc Trang airfield bred a certain sameness, and days tended to blur together. Sometimes, I almost forgot what I had done the day before. It wasn't critical; I just needed to be in the here and now; on-call and ready to go, prepared to do my job. But what were we accomplishing? In the large scheme of things—the history of this country and the world—how much difference would it make a year from now? Five years? Forty?

I didn't feel like going to the O-Club. Nothing was going on. I felt bored. Flopped out on my bunk half asleep, I suddenly smelled smoke! Jumping up, I looked down the hallway. Gray smoke poured from a room at the other end of hootch #4.

I dashed out the back door next to my room and ran outside around to the front. Apparently, someone had already reported the fire, as the fire truck arrived before I did. A small crowd watched as the smoke stopped, and the smell of wet, charred clothes filled the air. The young lieutenant who lived in the room came running back from the showers wearing only flip-flops and a towel.

"What the hell?" he asked, gasping for breath from his sprint.

The fire-suppression team, always at the ready to fight fire for aircraft crashes, had done their job. A spec. 5 firefighter said, "Lieutenant, the bulb in your closet heated up the clothes to the flash point. The officer across the hall found it early and called us. We're lucky. These hootches are tinder boxes; each one is a fire just waiting to happen."

The young officer said, "Thank you." He stared in disbelief at his trashed closet.

We all kept electric light bulbs turned on in our closets to dry them out in an attempt to cut down on mildew in this hot, humid climate. This excitement proved to be way more than enough to cure my bored state. We had a "fire party" at the club.

SOC TRANG
WED
15 MAY 63

"Coffee break," I announced from the treatment room. It had been a long morning. We had just finished a heavy sick call, and I looked at my watch: 1015, a reasonable time for a black coffee pickup.

"Doc, there's been a terrible accident on the perimeter," Tony said from the door, his face flushed. "Brooklyn and Harris have already gone for the ambulance."

Sgt. Tibbs made a run for the jeep. After executing a quick

U-turn, he stopped in front of the dispensary and picked me up. Over the noise of the wind in the open cab, he yelled, "Something happened at the outer perimeter. An explosion. Lots of ARVN reported wounded."

We followed the speeding ambulance down the dusty inner-perimeter road to the very farthest side of the airfield. I had never been out there before. We crossed over to the outer road, secured by the Vietnamese troops. Two ARVN trucks and two ambulances were already in place. The bright mid-morning sun etched a catastrophe. Several overwhelmed ARVN field medics were giving first aid to stunned soldiers with multiple injuries. Blown-up body parts were strewn in the ditch that served as a trench for perimeter defense.

The dispensary staff arrived in a U.S. Army truck. We triaged: leaving the dead, we tended the wounded. Those injured worst, we stabilized and carried to ambulances. We all helped bandage the walking wounded, assisting them onto an ARVN truck; the dead were placed in the second truck.

After the last of the wounded and dead had been dispatched, I told my men to take some time off for a shower and lunch before returning to the dispensary. Sgt. Tibbs and I followed the ARVN caravan of misery in our jeep, headed for the civilian hospital in Soc Trang.

When we arrived at the hospital, unloading went fast.

"Four dead and eighteen wounded," Sgt. Tibbs reported.

We did what we could to help. The overworked hospital staff again responded heroically. It turned out most of the injured were local civil guards who would be staying here at the civilian hospital. The news had apparently gotten out, as grief-stricken families began to arrive. The two injured ARVN soldiers would be transferred to the Can Tho military hospital.

Back at the dispensary after a quick cleanup and lunch, things returned to normal. The men cleaned our gear and replenished empty emergency kits.

"What a mess." Sgt. Tibbs shook his head.

Tony came to the supply room. "One of my MP buddies just came by; he heard the explosion was an accident. Someone unintentionally detonated a grenade. This set off two frag grenades. A white phosphorous grenade went off from sympathetic compression. That set off small-arms ammunition."

"What a mess," Sgt. Tibbs repeated, "and what a waste."

We silently continued to fill our well-used kits with fresh emergency supplies to be ready for the next disaster.

SOC TRANG
FRI
17 MAY 63

I arrived at the orphanage with the generous gift of piastres the wives' club had sent for the first installment. The old sister I believed to be Sister Mary Cecil was clearly delighted and agreed to use the money to buy screens for the windows and to hire some girls to regularly bathe the babies. I told her we would provide soap enough so that they all could wash their hands between handling babies. This, along with new screens, should make a big difference.

"The washing machine. A gift from heaven," is what I think she said in French. I could understand better than I could converse. But I clearly understood her words *"Merci, merci."* I waved good-bye from the jeep.

That evening, there would be another gift from heaven. At the Tigers' Den—with the ceiling done, the generators in place and running, and the newly arrived equipment installed—Charley had turned on the air-conditioners. The club, now dry and cool, was something to celebrate. It didn't take much to make a huge difference in our lives; this was absolutely quantum.

By the time I arrived, the place was humming. Slick caught my eye and ambled over, beer in hand.

"Can you believe it, Doc? Duc's flipping burgers. Hallelujah Hannah."

Slick looked skyward. "A burger and a side of fries. Little Lee Roy done died and gone to air-conditioned heaven," Slick drawled with a big smile.

Back in hootch #4, I took out the invitation to my ten-year high school class reunion, scheduled for May 25. I wrote a quick letter to my friends and hoped it wasn't sappy and too sentimental; so much had happened since we graduated from VHS in 1953. I looked at my well-worn friend, the 1963 calendar. I realized my tour was half over. Way too soon to start counting days, but I felt sure life was bound to be better on the downhill slope.

SAIGON
THUR
23 MAY 63

An Australian expert in guerrilla warfare questioned the Strategic Hamlet Program: The VC had control of vast areas to move about at will, and the program appeared to be overextended. Of the many thousands of hamlets set up by the government, probably only one thousand were viable. MACV spokesmen challenged these statements.[32]

SOC TRANG
FRI
24 MAY 63

Long-awaited rains arrived today; several drenching showers lasted from fifteen minutes to an hour. The lightning streaked the sky in spectacular light shows, and the thunder replaced the sound of explosions in the distance. Rice shoots would soon be transplanted in endless watery fields.

Duc explained, "*Bac si*, it rain every day now. More and more every day. Next five, six months."

The rains refreshed, but the humidity thickened in the heat. The Tigers' Den became even more of an oasis.

Today, we had a preliminary inspection, a trial run before the official inspector general's visit scheduled for mid-June. The 134th was ready, thanks to the hard work of my team. Sgt. Tibbs had been through many of these inspections, and things were in top-notch form. The dispensary floor gleamed; the reports were up to date; and all our equipment was accounted for and battle-ready—

including those precious litters Sgt. Tibbs had somehow scrounged from somewhere.

"This is for you, Doc." Sgt. Tibbs handed me two patches. "The Ninety-Third has a patch, so the 134th needed one too. I had these made for us in town."

He explained that he drew up a sketch of a tiger with smiling face, stethoscope, head mirror, and the words "134th Medical Detachment Soc Trang Tigers" around the edge. He had taken it to Vietnamese embroidery workers in town, and they had manufactured a round patch about four inches across.

"Sergeant Tibbs, this is terrific. It's great," I said. And it was. "There seems to be no end to your talent."

Maj. Saunders was very pleased with the preliminary inspection. And why wouldn't he be? Initial reports indicated the Tigers of the Ninety-Third and attached units had gotten the highest rating of any outfit in Vietnam.

SOC TRANG
SUN
26 MAY 63

I rolled over in my bunk and decided to give myself a Sunday treat by sleeping in, but MOM rudely came by my room. "Grab you gear, Doc. We've got a mission."

I groaned myself awake.

"And grab your swim trunks." He laughed.

I sat up in bed. "What?"

"I have to fly to *Cap St. Jacques* to pick up a part for one of the choppers."

He explained he would be piloting a two-seat fixed-wing aircraft, and he invited me to come along in the empty seat. "We'll have time for a good lunch and a quick dip. Have you been there?"

"No. I haven't been anywhere. They say it's great." I quickly dressed and grabbed my blue unused swimsuit and a towel.

Cap St. Jacques, a once-fashionable French resort town, was now called Vung Tau. This beach paradise—nearby but a world away—was located on the coast about fifty miles to the east and south of Saigon. In this fixed-wing plane, it would take us only about fifty minutes' flying time from Soc Trang.

We arrived at 1100. It did not take long for MOM to pick up the part he had come for. The sky was blue, and the water of the South China Sea looked like the Mediterranean. The broad, sandy beach truly seemed to be in another world.

There was no evidence of VC or war. I could understand how this area had been a favorite French retreat. Gracious villas with palm-lined streets gave the feel of the Riviera. It was the weekend, and I was surprised to see many French civilians enjoying the beach, along with some Vietnamese families and off-duty American military personnel.

After a refreshing swim in the warm South China Sea, we selected an oceanfront restaurant. There were several—all looked good. For lunch, I chose cold lobster mayonnaise. The French bread, as everywhere in the country, was wonderful—crusty on the outside and soft and chewy inside. I ordered a glass of white French wine; sitting there overlooking the beach and crashing surf, life was good.

"MOM, old buddy, I owe you one." I raised my glass.

Since he was flying, he only had mineral water, but he raised his glass in salute.

Too soon, we were back in the air on a southwesterly bearing for Soc Trang. We were back by 1630; the day seemed like a pleasant dream.

That evening, I told PBD about my day off.

"I've been there once, and it was great. A group of guys I know in the Thirty-Third pooled their money and rented a villa long-term. How about a bunch of us going together to rent one full-time? It couldn't be that expensive. It would be ours, and if two or three guys had a few days off, they could go there," he said. "A little R & R close to home."

"Now that, my friend, is your first good idea," I said.

"You're sore! You're just still sore we got Tuffy, right?" he laughed.

I didn't tell PBD, but the CO had heard from the Toledo Zoo— they agreed to take Tuffy.

SOC TRANG
SAT
1 JUN 63

The rice paddies were now flooded, and the rain came every day in heavy showers. Sure enough, we had lots of mud. This could be a serious problem with the choppers. If they settled too deep in the muck, far more power was needed to pull out and get liftoff. In the landing zones, that could be a problem, particularly when heavily loaded.

The weather had cooled, and that was good; the pesky insects were back, and that wasn't. There were many, many different kinds; some new to a midwesterner like me. At night, they could be so thick around the light in my bedroom, I just didn't turn it on. The company streetlights looked like there was thick fog from swarming bugs.

We went to Cam Mau again today. Little action reported. We will go back tomorrow. Logic suggests that the VC attacks would slow down with the monsoon, but logic is not necessarily reality during a war. One thing was that the insects wouldn't discriminate between us and them, but since the VC were used to these bugs and their troops didn't use much electricity at night, they probably wouldn't suffer.

I had a new office. Maj. Saunders gave me some space—a small room next to the barber shop. It was close to the dispensary. Although it had been convenient having my desk in the treatment room, I needed some quiet to write reports, and we needed more space in the treatment room when we got busy. After sick call, my guys helped me move the desk, chair, and a lamp to the new little space.

I drove down to the city market to get some things to make it look better.

"How much?" I held up a bamboo mat for the floor.

The thin, dried-up merchant squatting in his market booth said, "Eight hundred p's."

"Five hundred," I countered.

"Six fifty." He looked upset.

"Six hundred," I said and started to walk away as I'd been instructed by my more savvy friends.

He smiled and nodded. I had my first purchase. The bamboo mat would make a good rug for my new office.

I haggled for a black wooden box with the painting of a fish on the top and for three prints of the countryside. In the buying mood at the market, I also bought a small, smiling Buddha.

Happy with my purchases, I had no idea if the prices had been fair or not. It didn't matter. My new office would be fixed up.

The buying mood persisted even later in the day when I went to our small PX. I splurged on an eight-track reel-to-reel tape deck for my room in hootch #4.

I had seen this model in our PX many times. Although our PX was not large, it had some nifty things. The officer who managed it did a good job. The stock included necessities such as toothpaste and shaving cream and also some luxury items as well. The item I coveted most was a Rolex watch. I looked at it again, but it was way too much for my budget. I settled on a Sony tape deck with portable speakers and took it to my room. A friend of mine had the same model. Unfortunately, one of the channels on my set did not work. I took it back, and they agreed to fix it or give me a new one. Almost everyone had a sound system in his room, and it did help pass the time to have good music.

I faithfully read my medical magazines and medical texts, but it was hard when there were no cases in my practice to whet my interest; I hadn't seen one case of hypertension or heart disease, for example, nor would I have expected to.

I frequented our paperback library. Our collection appealed to a variety of readers, but I focused on the classics, good literature to fill in the wide gaps in my reading. Special Services also had basketball and volleyball equipment for checkout. I played some tennis, but a change in geography had not improved my game, particularly facing Nick Parsons, the recent West Point graduate and all-round athlete. He was a good sport, and I always enjoyed our tennis matches, even though I had few deserved wins.

Max Schmitt, my intern friend from Harbor General Hospital, sent me a letter to let me know he finished flight surgeon's training at Ft. Rucker and should be in Saigon very soon. He thinks he will be sent up north near our buddy Scott. I remembered that day one year ago in the cafeteria at Harbor when we learned interns would be drafted. Who would have thought back then the three of us would be in Vietnam at the same time?

SOC TRANG
FRI
7 JUN 63

After dinner, I wrote a letter to my family—I tried to write every week—and then strolled over to the Tigers' Den. Slick was already there, and I sat at his table. MOM came roaring in. "Victor Charlie's pulled a fast one," he said.

Slick, usually up on the news, asked in his drawl, "What, pray tell, this time?"

"We found booby traps in some of our choppers."

Slick's jaw dropped in surprise. We both were shocked. Rarely at a loss for words, all Slick managed to say was, "What?"

"This morning on the flight line, we found three choppers with trip wires attached to grenades. My men and I had to spend the whole fucking day fine-combing every one."

"How could that happen?" I said. "We've got all this security."

"It had to be one of our civilian employees. Someone who knew us and his way around. There's no other way." MOM ordered a beer and returned to our table. "As they say, the investigation continues."

He took a big swig and added, "Slick, you took time off today and missed out on the news." He took another swig. "And a T-28 went down this morning."

Slick and I looked at one another. His eyebrows went up, as they always did when he was surprised.

MOM continued in a flat tone, "Up north. On a strafing run. No one knows what happened exactly. After a low run, the plane started to pull up but then rolled over. Plowed into the ground. Their load had not been expended, so bombs were still aboard.

Kaboom. They bought the farm." He finished his beer and got up to get another.

He sat back down and took a drink from the fresh beer. "One American pilot and one VNAF observer, just like that," he snapped his fingers, "blown to smithereens."

We finished the evening in silence.

The air force lost a pilot, and someone, somewhere, lost someone they loved. That pilot, trained to extreme competence, gone. Years of dedication, study, practice to master the art and science of flight, now lost. At least the pilot and observer went fast; I hoped before they knew it was coming.

The assembly line would turn out another plane, an exact replacement. Flight school would turn out more pilots, but each was unique to family and friends—irreplaceable.

In this war, uncommon had become common; the surreal, real; the exotic, ordinary. The U.S. of A. seemed very far away.

This isolated airstrip was home—the men who lived here family. If I didn't get back, so be it. It didn't seem to matter much.

I turned out the overhead light; I found unexpected comfort in the dark, starless night.

SOC TRANG
MON
10 JUN 63

"Doc." MOM poured a cup of coffee. "Get a load of this." He sat down in the crowded mess hall across from me, holding up a copy of the latest *Stars and Stripes*.

"Tuffy's made the news again! Here's a picture. The headline says: '*Tuffy's Too Big; He's Got To Go.*'"

Everyone stopped talking as MOM read aloud in an official-sounding voice:

> "*Soc Trang, Vietnam: Tuffy the tiger doesn't want*
> *to leave, but he's got his orders. Tuffy, a Bengal*
> *tiger complete with regulation stripes, has spent*

*the last six months serving as the official mascot of
the 93d transportation Co. (light helicopter) here.*

*"But Tuffy, who now tips the scale at 250 pounds,
has grown too big for the job. Any day, he could
start working toward his full growth of six hundred
pounds. So Tuffy's now waiting to be shipped out.
His special orders read for one 'Pussycat,' Tuffy
with papers and cage to report for duty at the
Toledo, Ohio Zoo. Tuffy, who lived as a cub in the
American Embassy in Bangkok, performed his duty
in a manner that was a credit to the 93d, and to all
Bengal tigers."*

MOM paused to take a drink from his coffee cup. "There's more." He continued:

*"Tuffy gave impressive roars from time to time
and dutifully posed with generals and other high-
ranking officials for pictures.*

*"It was Brig. Gen. J.W. Stilwell, commanding
general, U.S. Army Support Command, Vietnam,
who realized it was time for a transfer for Tuffy. He
pointed out that Tuffy was fast growing and would
soon reach his full weight of six hundred pounds.*

*"Stilwell told the men of the 93d that if they would
find a new home for Tuffy he would give them two
tiger cubs to take the mascot's place.*

*"Tuffy got his hew home at the Toledo Zoo through
the help of the wife of one of the men in the unit.
The zoo will place a plaque on Tuffy's cage telling
of the Army men's contribution.*

"Although Tuffy has grown too big for his job here

*the men of the 93d point out with pride that the
powerful tiger engaged in many a playful tussle
with the men of the unit, knocking over a soldier on
occasion, but never seriously injuring a man.*

*"When Tuffy moves on to his next assignment, his
memory will live on here—for his picture is painted
on the side of every helicopter in the 93d as the
emblem of the unit."*

The room echoed with disappointed "Ahs" and "No ways." The rumors were now confirmed; Tuffy would be going to Ohio. Responses ranged from "Too bad" to "He's served his time."

"An answered prayer." I looked upward. "Thank you."

"Doc, you don't have a heart, do you? Let's face it," PBD said. "You've had it in for Tuffy since CWO Witt got into that scrape with him."

"Let's put it this way; in medical school, they never once covered how to treat a tiger wound. I'll be honestly relieved when he's onboard that plane headed stateside."

**WASHINGTON, DC
MON
10 JUN 63**

At the American University graduation ceremonies, JFK delivered a "Peace Speech," destined to be one of his greatest speeches. In an effort to reduce tensions and break the stalemate between the U.S. and Communism, he stated: "We all inhabit this small planet. We all breathe the same air. We all cherish our children's future. And we are all mortal."[33]

**SAIGON
TUE
11 JUN 63**

Seventy-three-year-old Quang Duc, a Buddhist monk, sat

down on the asphalt in the middle of a busy downtown Saigon street corner fingering holy beads. Another monk poured gasoline over his head and body. With a serene look, Quang Duc lit a match. His self-immolation ignited a Buddhist crisis for the Diem government.[34]

CITIES ACROSS VIETNAM
MID-JUNE 63

In response to the public outcry, Ngo Dinh ordered a crackdown on Buddhist protestors. He authorized the use of tear gas and truncheons, and barbed wire was stretched around pagodas. Diem and the Ngo family refused to negotiate or meet any of the Buddhists' demands. Nhu, well known for his dealing in Laotian drugs, became more and more irrational from his regular use of opium. Promises of government reform were made and broken.

The government moved four companies of armed personnel carriers with .50-caliber machine guns into Saigon from the north. Nhu ordered 1,200 ARVN Special Forces, commanded by loyalist Col. Le Quang Tung, to join the 5,800 regular troops already in place near Saigon.

Anger and fury spread from the cities to rural areas. Monks and nuns, their heads shaved, and dressed in simple robes, gathered in large groups and prayed.[35]

WASHINGTON, DC
MID-JUNE 63

To protest the behavior of the Diem government, the Vietnamese Ambassador to the United States, Tran Van Chuong—Madame Nhu's father—resigned his post. Madame Nhu's mother, the official Vietnamese observer at the United Nations, resigned her post as well. Most of the embassy staff in Washington, DC also resigned to show their disapproval of the Diem government and its treatment of the Buddhists and the people of Vietnam.

Madame Nhu said to beat the Buddhists "ten times more." She told a TV interviewer, "All the Buddhists have done for this country is to barbecue a monk."[36]

SOC TRANG
SUN
16 JUN 63

Fathers' Day. The chaplain spoke of the importance of the roles fathers play in family life and ultimately their influence on the military—thought-provoking. I thought of my father and his cavalry duty in France in World War I. The world has changed since then, and so has war. We use trucks and helicopters instead of horses, but we still use men, men who are vulnerable, men who can be maimed and killed.

I heard a report of another U.S. casualty in the Delta but didn't get the details. With the loss of the T-28 pilot, that made two American dead in the last two weeks.

A big storm had been predicted, but we had only strong winds and a little rain. The Fifty-Seventh at Tan Son Nhut suffered some wind damage to their choppers in a storm last week.

I had not heard anything from Max Schmitt. He should be at his duty station. No word from Scott either. I still hoped Frank, up in Pleiku, and I could get some R & R together in Hong Kong. Not long ago, I put in my request for October.

The PX manager told me my tape deck should be ready soon. One faulty part had to be replaced.

SOC TRANG
FRI
21 JUN 63

The medical services officer from the official inspector general's team arrived at the 134th. We were as ready as we could ever be: fresh haircuts all around, clean uniforms, and combat boots polished. The inspector, a major, was no less ready.

After closely looking over our building and equipment, the

inspector reviewed our medical records and routine reports. He showed particular interest in the accident investigations and records for military and civilian food handlers. He checked for up-to-date TB skin tests and X-rays. He didn't miss a thing.

Next, the major wanted to inspect our water supply. I accompanied him and then showed him the documents from our regular monitoring process.

Then it was on to the mess hall. Food service must be spotless and hygienic, of course. He looked at our records. Two of my duties included documentation of the temperature of the reefers where the cold food was stored and regularly recording the temperature of the water used for dishwashing. He checked to make sure foods were stored properly and looked for any insect or other vector infestations. The kitchen staff had done a class-A job. Men, equipment, and documents were flawless; no deficiencies were found.

After the inspector general's team had thoroughly inspected everything conceivable—most particularly the helicopter maintenance records—it was time to hear any gripes, complaints, or special requests from the men. With this last duty finished, the team left on a plane for Saigon to write a report about what they found and observed.

The men were glad to return to their basic routines, and the Tigers' Den and Enlisted Men's Club did a brisk business.

When I had time to read my mail, I found a letter from San Antonio. It was from a Capt. Glen Carr, the physician assigned to replace me in November when my year was up.

He would be finishing his internship at Brooke General Hospital June 30, 1963, then reporting for the Basic Medical Course. After the basic school, he would go to Ft. Rucker for the flight surgery training. He would have a brief leave, then depart CONUS for South Vietnam on October 24, 1963.

I read and re-read the letter several times. It helped, somehow, to see it in writing—to know the name of the new physician. He would arrive sooner than I expected, and I welcomed the idea. At any rate, by the end of next month, I'd probably get the "double-digit figits," the condition you developed when your tour had less than one hundred days to go.

SOC TRANG
SUN
23 JUN 63

Rain, rain, rain. Every day, the skies poured rain. There was a pattern to the weather: The mornings would be clear, but every afternoon at 1400, it rained. I planned my day around the showers. It seemed unusual to me that rain could come from any different direction on any different day. In the Midwest, the storms generally came from the west. Here, you could see dark clouds in the north, south, east, or west as they moved overhead to open up. The once-dusty brown rice paddies were now as green as the city of Oz.

I wondered if I could use my spare time to learn to play the guitar. Several guys here played pretty well. Between showers, I went into town and found a stall selling guitars. The market had a stall for everything, it seemed. The guitar seller had many instruments with varying prices. I chose one with a dark, mahogany-colored back and plain light wood top.

I held up the instrument, and the usual kind-looking, smiling man with a cigarette dangling from his mouth indicated the cost. "3,600 *p*'s." He no longer smiled or looked kindly. His dark eyes now looked beady and shrewd.

I took a breath. "1,800."

He looked offended and shook his head. "No, 3,100," he stated with firmness.

This guy was not as easy to bargain with, I thought, as the others were for my office stuff.

We finally settled on 2,900. That didn't seem unreasonable, but who knew? I counted out the money and raced to get back to the jeep before the next rain started up.

SOC TRANG
TUE
25 JUN 63

A sad day. The Ninety-Third Transportation Company would be no more; it had been re-designated the 121st Aviation Company (Air Mobile Light). Of course, everything would remain the same and in place: officers, men, equipment, and attached units. I remembered Doc Greene telling me the Ninety-Third formed at Ft. Riley, Kansas on April 1, 1954. I was a freshman in college then. What's in a name anyway? We had all those Tiger logos with the Ninety-Third painted on everything, but things change. I know I have.

SOC TRANG
SAT
29 JUN 63

The official orders were clear. Tuffy, the Soc Trang Tiger, would leave today for his next duty station in Ohio: the Toledo Zoo.

One of the men got in Tuffy's yard and undid the chain from the stake. Using the chain as a leash, they strolled together to the nearby airfield with a large crowd of about one hundred, plus assorted CBS reporters and other TV cameramen alongside. We all watched silently as Tuffy climbed the ramp and got into the waiting steel cage. With the door to the enclosure secured, the crew chief gave a wave, and the cargo ramp raised. A mighty roar of good-byes came from the crowd, and the C-147 taxied down the runway. There would be a sense of absence in Tuffy's empty yard next to headquarters, even for me.

SOC TRANG
SUN
30 JUN 63

I looked at my watch. It was 2000 as I headed toward my bunk. I planned to turn in early. *"Bac si,"* Duc, running toward me from the O-Club, yelled. "Army captain need help."

In front of the dispensary, I found a taller-than-usual Vietnamese captain carrying a small boy.

"My son, very sick," the captain said with obvious concern.

The boy, five years old, appeared toxic. I put him up on the treatment table. His temperature was 102 degrees. My examination revealed an ear infection. I injected an antibiotic and gave the father a bottle of oral antibiotics. He agreed to give the boy a full ten-day course. After giving the sick youngster an oral antipyretic to take down the fever, the father carried him out to the waiting jeep. The captain thanked me and then thanked me again before he made a U-turn and drove back toward town. I realized we had not needed a translator to communicate, as the captain had spoken such good English.

SOC TRANG
TUE
2 JUL 63

"Welcome to Soc Trang, Captain Schmitt." I greeted Max, my internship buddy, as he stepped off the Otter for an overnight visit. He had not yet been assigned a duty station.

"Long time no see, Jay." We shook hands.

Max had grown up on a farm in western Kansas, and this upbringing produced strength and sturdy good health. His light brown hair had bleached in the sun; he looked fit and ready for duty in his fatigues and combat boots.

"Good news," he said. "I'm stationed at Can Tho rather than up north."

He explained the forces in the Delta were once again reorganizing, and he might be assigned the job as a new battalion surgeon. That was extremely good news. He would not be that far away and might cover my job when and if I got some leave for R & R.

I showed him around the compound. We went to the guest room in hootch #2, and he put his gear on the bunk. I showed him my room in hootch #4. Max had heard about Tuffy. He was disappointed when we walked by the empty yard and learned the famous beast had gone stateside. Max, a gadget man and ace photographer, had brought his expensive camera and had plans to take lots of pictures.

We spent the evening in the Tigers' Den. Now complete with grill and air-conditioning, it had the reputation as one of the best O-Clubs outside of Saigon.

"Any news of Scott?" Max asked.

"Came through in March, but haven't heard anything since. He's assigned to a battalion headquarters up north." We talked about what little we knew of the others in our intern class from Harbor General.

"Can you believe it's been almost exactly one year ago we said good-bye in the hospital parking lot?" Max sighed.

"What a year!" I said.

"At least you're going home in November."

For the first time in a long time, I thought of myself as lucky. I had only four months to go and one day soon could call myself a "short-timer." Max, on the other hand, was definitely an FNG.

SOC TRANG
WED
3 JUL 63

Our brief visit went quickly. The next morning, after a hearty breakfast, Max took the milk run for Saigon, where he would have more orientation. It had been great to see him and to know he would not be far away in Can Tho.

When I arrived at the dispensary, Sgt. Tibbs said, "Doc, a Vietnamese captain brought this in for you."

He handed me a folded Viet Cong flag; divided red and blue for north and south, it had the Communist yellow star in the center. On one corner, I saw dried blood. I read the attached card, written with classic, beautiful penmanship:

> *3 Jul 1963*
> *It is a pleasure and honor for me to present you*

with an authentic Viet-Cong flag. The flag was
captured from a VC unit, lately in the vicinity of
Soc-trang by Vietnamese ground combat forces.
Please consider this flag as a token of friendship
and evidence of a common enemy.

Sincerely yours,

Wann
Captain- Arty

BAC LIEU
THUR
4 JUL 63

The L-19, wrecked and twisted, sprawled in the mud below. Our chopper eased down on a wet field, and we deplaned to try and figure out what had happened here. The pilot and an observer, who had been flying in this small fixed-wing plane when it crashed, had already been evacuated to Saigon for medical care.

We sifted through the debris to begin our preliminary investigation. I could no longer remember how many crash investigation teams I had participated in or how many official reports I had written. No matter the number, the keen sense of loss never ceased; on the contrary, I frequently recalled the tragedy of the H-21 disaster January 11 that took Sput and the six others. Often, I would think of Sgt. Patterson and the captain and crew lost at Ap Bac—all such good men—gone forever.

Each of us sorted out our area of inquiry. One of my responsibilities would be to check the safety gear to be sure it had not malfunctioned. I thought of the young flyer who had been strapped in here and how many hours of training it took for a man to become this unique individual we called pilot.

After a long, exhaustive effort, we finished and headed back to Soc Trang.

Maj. Saunders, the head of our team, said, "We'll need to go to Saigon for interviews with the crew to wrap this up."

Whether in Vietnam or the United States, we followed all FAA requirements. Our investigation would be as complete as possible.

When we arrived back at Soc Trang airfield, I remembered that it was the Fourth of July. I thought of the many celebrations back home. Soc Trang is Vietnamese territory. Since we were only guests, we didn't even fly the American flag over the airfield.

The only organized Independence Day celebration would be a reception at the MAAG house downtown for local civilian and military officials. This special day to all Americans would have little meaning in the Republic of Vietnam or to the VC, that's for sure. I put on my best khaki uniform and enjoyed the function. A dignified party, it had the feel of a diplomatic, not military, reception.

That evening, I changed into casual gear and went to the party at the Tigers' Den. It was not organized, but a Fourth of July celebration with less decorum than the party downtown ... and lots more fun.

SOC TRANG
FRI
5 JUL 63

No word yet about my request for R & R to Hong Kong in October with Frank. Since I'm all the way over here, I'd like to see at least some of the Orient. I put in another request for R & R, this time for Japan. MOM put in for the same trip, and it would be great if we got time off together. I'd not been away overnight since February. Japan would be a great place for R & R. It would not hurt to ask, and I was ready for a break.

The guitar proved to be more of a challenge than I thought it would be. I could not notice much progress. I needed to keep at it, practice more.

I would have forgotten my birthday—I turned twenty-eight— had I not received cards from my family.

SOC TRANG
SUN
7 JUL 63

The Republic of South Vietnam celebrated a national holiday today: "the double sevens." This marked the ninth anniversary of the date President Diem formed his first government. Several of us had been invited to a parade downtown at 0730. We dressed in our khaki uniforms and garrison caps for the occasion.

The morning was cool and sunny. The Vietnamese military paraded in full uniform, yellow-and-red-striped flags lined the streets, and a military band played. The Republican Youth marched by dressed in blue berets, blue shirts, and trousers. They were followed by the Women's Solidarity Movement, dressed in blue uniforms wearing stylish Aussie bush hats. These two groups, reportedly fashioned after the German Brown Shirts, had been formed by Nhu and Madame Nhu to foster loyalty to the Diem government.

The crowd seemed to me strangely subdued for a patriotic parade in a country at war.

MEKONG DELTA

To the United States, the mission seemed clear: Fight Communism to keep South Vietnam free. But America had supported the French in the past, and by propping up President Diem and his family, the Americans did not have influence in the National Revolution in South Vietnam. To many Vietnamese, the United States was on the wrong side of colonialism and stood for continued oppression and exploitation.

Many Vietnamese farmers saw the VC—like the Viet Minh before—as patriots—Vietnamese fighting for nationalistic aspirations. To them, Ho Chi Minh and homegrown Communism seemed far less onerous than Diem's regime propped up by white foreigners.[37]

SOC TRANG
1200

By the time the parade finished and we returned to the airfield, it was time for lunch. Sitting at chow in the mess hall, I was enjoying Salisbury steak and mashed potatoes with gravy when PBD came in.

"Did you hear about Southern?" he asked as he put his cap down on the table and headed for the food line.

"No. What?" I could tell by the grim look on PBD's face that it wouldn't be good news. Lt. Southern from Nevada was a great guy and a fine young pilot. Everyone liked him. He did not fly an H-21 or belong to the Ninety-Third but flew one of the HU-1B helicopters out of Saigon.

"It's bad. Really bad. He got zapped." PBD put his tray down and sat across from me. "His chopper took a round—came up through the floor. Struck him in the jaw and didn't stop until it lodged in his brain. Nothing they could do. Poor bastard." PBD shook his head. "And you know his wife had a baby since he's been over here."

"Awful," I said.

"The 114th got into a big scrape as well last week. Three crew chiefs got shot up. One may lose an arm."

"It's heating up," I said.

"For sure." PBD sighed, and took an overly large bite of steak.

SOC TRANG
WED
17 JUL 63

We flew to Saigon to complete the accident investigation. This took only a few hours, and we winged our way back to Soc Trang. A quick trip. I had hoped to see Doc Lemmon but missed him.

That afternoon, the briefing officer stood in front us near the map. "The VC hit Can Tho airfield last night. Shot a guard, and then attacked. Mortars hit the runway. They used small arms and shot out all the tower windows. Ten or so American Special Forces happened to be there. Several were wounded, but luckily none severely."

I thought of my friend Max and wondered if he had arrived there yet—quite a welcoming party.

This stunning news had an impact. We listened intently. Up to now, American installations had not been hit; up to now, they had proved safe refuges in the vast dark night of the VC-controlled Delta.

The briefing officer continued. "We have reliable intelligence Victor Charlie has changed tactics. They apparently will no longer spare facilities where the U.S. troops are garrisoned. We know they plan to hit us here in Soc Trang and also Bien Hoa. Gentlemen, be alert, be informed, be prepared.

"And be careful in town. There have been reports of Buddhist demonstrations in Soc Trang."

That sounded odd. The Buddhists monks and nuns I had met and seen all were frail, gentle, respectful, and serene with their shaved heads and simple saffron-colored robes. The whole changing picture seemed difficult to understand. According to the news services, the Buddhist crisis had escalated.

Fritz Nolting, our U.S. Ambassador to Vietnam, would be replaced by Henry Cabot Lodge. I wished him luck. The situation was a mess.

It had started to rain more. Instead of periodic heavy afternoon showers, it rained during the night as well. I wondered if this would slow down the VC. It sure hadn't seemed to. The ARVN had some recent operations that looked impressive, but when it got intense, the VC faded away.

I still did not have my Sony tape deck. The faulty part had to be ordered from Japan. If it didn't come soon, I planned to request a refund and buy another one.

In five days, I would have been here eight months—tour two-thirds over!

JULY 1963

The Buddhists hoped the pressure they put on the government

would encourage the ARVN officers to start a coup. Monks knew their actions would lead to arrests, but they were ready for conflict. They would die, if necessary, to get rid of Diem. The increasing repression from Diem directly increased the numbers of Buddhist sympathizers. New militant, intelligent, skilled Buddhist leaders offered an alternative. They were in no way dependent on Americans and offered new hope for nationalistic aspirations.

The fiery suicides made bad publicity for the government. President Diem and Nhu, ever fearful of a coup, decided to use the Combat Police—trained by the CIA to fight VC—to attack the Buddhists. Nhu drew up an assassination hit list, which included perceived disloyal ARVN officers, suspect civilians, and some untrustworthy Americans at the U.S. Embassy.[38]

SOC TRANG
THUR
18 JUL 63

At 0450, a loud blast! By reflex, I jumped out of my bunk. The explosion seemed to be right next to my quarters in hootch #4.

The OD, wearing steel pot, passed by. "It was clear over on the other side of the airstrip," he said.

It seemed much closer to me. Not convinced, I got up, dressed, and started my day early.

That afternoon, we sat on the long benches for a briefing about tomorrow's scheduled mission.

After the captain concluded, Maj. Saunders stood up and cleared his throat. I noticed he always did that before he spoke.

"Curfew in town is moved up from 2200 to 1800 hours, effective immediately," he said.

Curfew had fluctuated many times since I had been here. The CO wanted the men to get to town when they could for morale because we were so isolated, but it was always a tough balancing act. This change meant, of course, more tension ahead.

"I just want to add," the major continued in his official voice, "the Buddhist unrest is increasing. They held a big demonstration in Soc Trang on Monday. Keep your distance. They mean us no harm; they're trying to send a message to the government."

CAN THO
WED
24 JUL 63

We landed at Can Tho airfield. I had been here before, briefly, but never spent any length of time. I saw the shot-out windows in the control tower. I looked around, but the airstrip had apparently been repaired after the VC hit last week.

Max was there when our choppers set down for a brief stop.

"How did you enjoy those fireworks on the sixteenth?" I said.

"Missed 'em. Didn't come down here until the seventeenth, a week ago today," he said.

He had heard about the rumored change in VC tactics. We agreed it was not good.

"But there's good news about flight surgeons," I said. "There's one with the new helicopter company at Vinh Long. From one to three is good. We can cover for each other and hopefully get some time off. I've put in for R & R starting August nineteenth. I'll let you know when I hear for sure."

Max, always an agreeable guy, nodded his head. "I'm sure you're ready. I'm already thinking about R & R and I've only been here a week," he laughed.

"It's great knowing you're here, Max."

When I arrived back at Soc Trang, I found a welcome stack of mail. Sadly, I received a letter from my folks with the news that one of my favorite cousins had been killed in a horrific automobile accident in Illinois. Her family was injured. Death found people wherever they were. Tragic accidents, during peace or war, were always hard to accept.

SOC TRANG
SAT
27 JUL 63

Eight of us had been invited to the province chief's house for dinner. With Capt. MOM at the wheel, he drove Maj. Saunders, PBD, and me. Another jeep followed with the other four. The white stucco on the grand old villa looked faded, and the building needed some attention, but the garden had been tended with flowers and paths since I had driven by the last time. Inside, the rooms were large, spacious, and had very high ceilings.

The province chief, a man in his early forties, greeted us outfitted in an officer's dress uniform with medals. His wife, a little younger, dressed in a pale blue *au dai* and wore her hair pulled back in a bun. She was very pretty and a charming hostess. The traditional dinner in the large dining room had a colonial feel. We were served by young Vietnamese men in tailored white jackets and black pants. The delicious dinner had several courses and lasted from 2000 to 2200. A welcome diversion.

After dinner, we were driving back to the airfield, and Maj. Saunders leaned back. "Doc. How about you going to Vung Tau for some R & R next week? We got that villa lined up for short trips, and you could use a break. Maybe that new doc at Vinh Long could cover; we're doing joint missions with them now."

"That would be great," I said in understatement, trying to hide my enthusiasm. Everyone considered the modest villa the guys were renting to be the best place in all of Vietnam to get away from the war for a short respite. Nick Parsons, the young officer in charge of the gunners, and two pilots would be going as well. That guaranteed a good time.

BAC LIEU
SUN
28 JUL 63

Another day, another mission. We were going out several times a week. I lost track long ago of how many missions we had been on since I arrived. The outcome was similar: The ARVN may or may not make contact with the VC; our choppers may or may not be shot at and hit. Amazingly, none of the Ninety-Third crews had been wounded recently.

It was hard not to think about my good fortune of having time off. The new doc in Vinh Long agreed to look after the Ninety-Third.

SOC TRANG
MON
5 AUG 63

After five days in the sun at the beach in Vung Tau, I felt refreshed. It had been, as promised, fun and relaxing. Second Lt. Nick Parsons and the pilots made great company. For the first time since I arrived in Vietnam, I had felt free; for the first time, I had backup from another physician for the 134th Dispensary.

Sick call would be a rude reminder of return to work. We had an unusually busy sick call. That duty proved unpredictable—some days slow, some demanding. I finished paperwork and went to the mess hall for lunch a little late. The cooks always took good care of me, and I was grateful for their efforts.

Parsons and MOM were drinking coffee at the front table. I walked over with my tray.

"So how was R & R? Parsons here tells me you guys tore up the town," MOM said.

"Words cannot describe the beach, the women, the food, right Doc?" Nick Parsons said. "And lobster every meal. Mighty tough to come back to this," he said somewhat dishonestly, as the mess-hall food was always pretty good.

I looked at MOM's long face. "What's wrong? Surely you didn't miss us that much."

"We're trying something new tonight," MOM said dryly. "While you're living it up in the club tonight, old buddy PBD and I are taking our choppers out for a joyride."

"What for?" I said.

"The VC are flexing their muscles. Owning the night around here, right?" MOM continued.

I nodded my head in agreement.

"So the ARVN won't go out on night operations for reasons none of us understand. So we're going to take off and fly around a bit after dark to make the VC think the ARVN commanders are getting some balls. Starting night missions."

"That ought to confuse Victor Charlie some," Parsons said.

"You'll draw fire," I said.

"Sure. But at least the tracers will show us where it's coming from. Our gunners are ready." MOM stood up to leave. "I don't want to get hit, but keep the dispensary lights on, just in case." He drained the last of his coffee and bussed his tray. "I don't want to screw up our R & R in Japan next month. Doc, our request came through. We're on our way August nineteenth, come hell or high water."

"You sure?" I asked.

"Check your mail," he said and laughed and left for operations.

"Take care!" I yelled. My words echoed in the almost empty mess hall.

"You lucky SOB," Nick Parsons said, almost under his breath. "A week's R & R in Japan. What I wouldn't give for that."

TIME MAGAZINE ARTICLE
AUGUST 9, 1963

"The war is as ugly and indecisive as ever. The more bullish predictions emanate from Saigon. General Paul Harkins, commander of the U.S. forces in South Vietnam, says that the war will be over in December; statistics show that the Viet Cong launched an average of 120 attacks weekly last year, and for the first seven months this year the average was down to 74. But statistics are meaningless in South Vietnam. Despite losses of 1,000 men a month, the Reds have increased their hard-core regular troops from 18,000 to 23,000 men."[39]

SOC TRANG
SUN
11 AUG 63

The rain continued. We fought mildew in our combat boots. It was not too bad, as my mood was up thinking of R & R. MOM was right. We had orders for Japan. While I would be gone, Max would cover the 134th from Can Tho. If that didn't work out, the Eighth Field Hospital would send a physician. I had never heard anything more about going up there for a month's rotation. It would be too late now. I was sorry to miss out working in a field hospital and spending some time in Nha Trang, but the Soc Trang experience had been plenty enough.

Frank, up in Pleiku, wrote a note to tell me his tour could be extended three weeks as his replacement might be delayed. I hoped not. We wanted to go home at the same time. As far as I knew, my replacement was still scheduled to arrive here in late October. Frank already had R & R to Hong Kong, so we wouldn't take that trip together. I still wanted to go there, but Japan might be all I had time for.

My repaired Sony stereo came back and worked perfectly. I could enjoy great music in my room in hootch #4! And it would be fun to tape music as well. The eight-inch reels held a lot on one tape. The outstanding speakers were large, but still small enough to be portable. I knew this great sound system would be the only one I'd ever need for the rest of my life.

NEW YORK
THUR
15 AUG 63

In an article on the front page of the *New York Times*, David Halberstam reported on the war in the Mekong Delta. He wrote that the VC were now well-armed with captured American weapons and mounting larger attacks against the ARVN. He noted that in 1962, the VC assembled in units of 250 men; the units in 1963 were six hundred to one thousand strong.[40]

SAIGON
FRI
16 AUG 63

Another Buddhist monk burned himself to death in protest of the Deim government.[41]

SOC TRANG
SAT
17 AUG 63

We had our orders: MOM and I would spend the night at the guest bachelor officers' quarters in Saigon on August 18, take off early the next morning for Okinawa, and the following day head out for Japan. After our stay, from the twentieth to the twenty-sixth, we would return by the same route. While in Japan, we planned to get outside of Tokyo to see some of the country. MOM had been to Japan twice before, so he knew the ropes.

SAIGON
SUN
18 AUG 63

Fifteen thousand Buddhists and their sympathizers assembled at Xa Loi Pagoda for a mass rally. The combat police did not intervene.[42]

SOC TRANG
SUN
18 AUG 63

MOM and I boarded the "milk run" for Saigon. No party had assembled to see us off. Why would they? As we got on the plane, we heard the news that Soc Trang would be officially off-limits to all U.S. personnel until further notice.

SAIGON
TUE
20 AUG 63

Thirty minutes after midnight, the ARVN Special Forces—an elite group trained by the United States to fight guerrillas, and primarily Catholics commanded by loyal Catholic officers—attacked the Xa Loi Pagoda in Saigon and pagodas in several other cities. These Special Forces had disguised themselves in the uniforms of regular soldiers to put the blame on the military and not the Diem government. Monks and nuns rang their gongs, banged on pots and pans, and prayed. The attack in Saigon raged for two hours.

The results of the raids in Saigon: 1,400 monks, nuns, and lay followers arrested; thirty monks killed; seven more were unaccounted for and never seen again. In Hue: thirty Buddhist monks and students shot or clubbed to death, their great statue of Buddha destroyed.

Condemnation was swift and global. In an effort to deflect criticism, Diem directed the government-controlled Radio Saigon and the press to report these anti-Buddhist raids were led by the military, not by his government.

President Diem declared martial law. Rioting University of Saigon students were arrested. High school students joined in the protest and over one thousand of them were arrested. Diem closed the university and high schools. The prisons were full to overflowing. Many citizens, by now disenchanted with the government and now also disenchanted with the United States, became active VC converts.

In the rural areas, the VC dismantled the hated strategic hamlets. They sent the thankful peasants back to their land carrying the ripped-off tin roofs to use to rebuild their old villages. Barbed wire, taken down from the perimeters, would be cut up to be used in booby traps and as shrapnel to put in explosives aimed against the ARVN and their American advisors.[43]

SAIGON
THUR
22 AUG 63

Henry Cabot Lodge arrived in a rainy Saigon to be the new U.S. Ambassador. Immediate reports from knowledgeable sources confirmed his suspicions that the VC were gaining strength in the countryside. He soon became convinced the Ngo Dinhs were hated and incapable of pursuing the war further. Within one week, he secretly cabled JFK of the impossible situation. Lodge secretly began contacts with three ARVN Generals: the six-foot-tall, second-ranking ARVN Major General "Big Minh," Maj. General Don, and Brig. General Kim. These men knew they were losing the war to the VC, and they had become disenchanted with the blatant government corruption and graft.

U.S. Army Commander General Harkins was against any military coup, convinced the current plan was still working.[44]

SOC TRANG
FRI
23 AUG 63

Lt. Col. Wayne Phillips, CO of the Delta Aviation Battalion, and CO Maj. Saunders presented medals and saluted the men and officers who stood in ranks at attention. The Ninety-Third, now the 121st, would become the most decorated company in Vietnam. With the medals given in this ceremony, the men had earned a total of seven Bronze Stars with valor, forty-eight Distinguished Flying Crosses, 224 Air Medals, 448 Oak Leaf Clusters to the Air Medals, and fourteen Purple Hearts.

The Soc Trang Tigers had earned these awards.

SAIGON
WED
28 AUG 63

Our jet touched down at Tan Son Nhut, and immediately MOM and I returned to reality. Japan had been a great break. When I got off the plane, exotic, pungent aromas again greeted me. I loved the smells of the streets of Saigon. I knew it wouldn't take long to get desensitized to them. For our last night of freedom, we had dinner in the city. Tomorrow, we would fly back to Soc Trang.

"Look at this." I motioned to MOM as our cab threaded through the traffic. Many policeman, ARVN troops, military trucks, and even tanks crowded the teeming streets.

After a quick dinner at the floating Chinese restaurant, we returned to quarters before curfew. A captain with the Special Forces, who bunked across the hall, told us the government seemed to be falling apart, but things had settled down some for the past two days.

SOC TRANG
THUR
29 AUG 63

"Glad you're back." PBD greeted us after we checked in at headquarters. "Things are picking up. We have a mission every day this week."

I knew we were back home now, for sure. The VC had been relentless in their attacks on the outposts while MOM and I had been gone. The monsoon had been letting up, and the sun had begun to warm the rice fields.

SOMEWHERE IN THE DELTA
SAT
31 AUG 63

Trey and his co-pilot sat at the controls; the crew chief gave the thumbs-up; and our fully loaded chopper was ready for takeoff from the soccer field in a city somewhere south of Soc Trang. The two rotors began slowly turning, and the chopper shook itself awake, engines roaring, and the rotors picked up speed. We were ready to head home after another long day.

As usual, I sat on an armored vest and checked to see my earplugs were in place before I put on my prized helmet.

Our H-21 moved toward the center of the soccer field and strained to get airborne. With the nose pointed down, it gained speed and altitude.

I leaned back on the canvas sling seat and relaxed a bit for the ride home. The day had been hectic. Gunners were in their positions at the front and back cargo doors, machine guns ready. Although the soccer field was friendly territory, who knew what would be beyond in the tree lines at the edge of town?

Our chopper reached an altitude of about forty feet; it suddenly stopped in mid-air for a split second. The engines raced and labored with a grinding intensity I heard even through my earplugs and helmet. Something was terribly wrong.

My heart pounded from such a sudden rush of adrenaline that I feared it would explode. We were suspended. I knew we could not hang here long. We would have to crash. A thought flashed in my mind: Is this it? I looked toward the open cockpit; Trey and the co-pilot were a blur of activity.

Our distressed chopper surged furiously against a power greater than its own, as if caught in a web. With a huge jolt, it broke free. I held on to the sling seat so I would not be thrown to the floor. I heard a loud popping noise over the roar of the struggling engines. Sparks flew. A cable wrapped itself around the body of the chopper like a whip. We had hit dreaded high-tension electric lines—scourge of pilots the world over.

I looked out the cargo door and remembered in a flash the grave admonitions at Ft. Rucker about utility lines. Nearly invisible when airborne, they had caused many an aircraft crash. Gray wisps of smoke and a burned electrical smell filled the cabin. I sat immobilized, staring at nothing.

It took only a fraction of a second for the severed cable to wrap around the middle of the chopper. It took only another fraction for it to rebound and unwrap, falling toward the ground shooting sparks like fireworks. Trey increased power to the max. The chopper shook violently. It responded, moving forward with a jerk. Our iron bird, now escaped from the death talons of the cable, moved forward; we were freed. We were airborne. Trey glanced at the altimeter, increased the air speed, and headed northeast on a heading to Soc Trang.

I felt weak from anxiety. Our landing gear had just clipped the electric utility lines, which broke at the last possible second. Trey did not look back, but the crew chief, smiling broadly, gave two thumbs-up. I closed my eyes, took a deep breath, and silently thanked Capt. Bruce Woodford Hamilton Harrison the third for his skill in averting disaster.

If I could just survive three more months from today, I thought, I should be back in the States. But dammit, toward the end of a tour, often something awful happened.

The rest of the trip proved edgy but uneventful; we arrived at the airfield and deplaned quickly. No one attempted any jokes. Subdued by shared experience, we dispersed. Trey and his crew headed for operations and debriefing.

As for me, I went straight to hootch #4, took off my gear, and headed for the shower to wash away the smell of fear and sweat.

WASHINGTON, DC
MON
2 SEP 63

President Kennedy appeared on national TV with Walter Cronkite and made an attempt to distance the United States from the harsh and rigid Diem government. He suggested some changes in policy and personnel might help the war effort but admitted there were limits to what the United States could do. It was a guerilla war and a Vietnamese War. It would be up to the Vietnamese to win or lose the fight against the Communists.

SAIGON

Ambassador Lodge met with Nhu to pressure him into retirement from the government and to, perhaps along with Madame Nhu, accept a diplomatic post somewhere outside the country. Nhu declined and wondered how this could be done during a time of war. Ambassador Lodge suggested he announce the war was going so well that the Nhus were no longer needed and could now go into diplomatic service abroad.[45]

SOC TRANG
THUR
5 SEP 63

At 1030, after a busy sick call, the last patient was a Spec. 4 with a rash due to fungus.

"This should take care of it." I handed him a topical ointment.

Slick knocked on the door of the treatment room. "Doc, I have a special request, old buddy."

"What?" I thought the worst.

Slick stripped off his T-shirt and showed me the mole on his back. I had noted it during his flight physical.

"How about taking this sucker off? I'm going home soon and would love to get it off. It'd improve my sex appeal."

"I hate to be the one to tell you, Lieutenant Slick, but it will take a lot more than that. Besides, I can't send the tissue to a lab. There's no way I am able to get a pathology report."

"I've had it since I was born. You told me it isn't the kind that usually turns to cancer."

"True." I examined it closely. It had none of the characteristics of malignancy. "But I wouldn't want to make a mistake."

"You won't. And I promise not to sue." He laughed. "Think of it as my going-away gift."

I examined the large mole again, and it looked totally benign. I did agree it was a cosmetic problem. "I don't know why I'm doing this. But all right."

Sgt. Tibbs set up a surgical tray and left for lunch at the mess hall. I would not need an assistant for this job. Slick climbed on the treatment table and lay on his stomach to expose his back.

After a standard prep and sterile drape, the removal took quite a while. I wanted to be sure to have clear tissue below and around the growth. I placed many sutures, as it was near the left upper shoulder, in an area that had some tension with movement.

When finished, I advised him to return if he felt any changes. Otherwise, I'd plan to remove the sutures in a week.

"Thanks, Doc. I figure my firstborn will be coming along about nine months after I get home." He slipped his shirt back on over the bandage. "I'll name him after you."

I heard the phone ring; Tony Alessi called loudly from the front, "Ambulance and Doc to the flight line. Emergency!" Brooklyn scrambled out the back door for the ambulance. I'd never seen him move so fast.

"Tony, Sergeant Tibbs is in the mess hall," I yelled. "Get him over there ASAP." I grabbed the emergency kit. The medics all ran with me over to the tarmac. Slick came too.

We found Trey and a crowd watching a plane circling the field.

"What's happening?" I asked, gulping for breath from the run.

"That Mohawk 6 took a hit this morning. Must've taken out the hydraulics. The landing gear won't come down." On standby, Trey and crew left to get in the rescue chopper.

We watched, and several more observers joined us. Brooklyn and Sgt.Tibbs arrived in the ambulance. The Mohawk pilot made pass after pass over the airfield without result; the landing gear would not budge. The fire truck crews and crash and rescue team were standing by on the other side of the field. Sgt. Tibbs arrived and went directly to the ambulance. He jumped in the front seat to join Brooklyn, who had the motor running.

The operations officer came out and yelled, "He's not coming in. He's gonna eject. Fire-up rescue choppers."

The rotors on two choppers slowly started to rotate.

I grabbed an emergency bag, ran over to Trey's lead chopper, and jumped aboard.

The rotors speeded up, and we lifted off. The Mohawk turned, made one last pass, and then headed away from the airstrip. We followed.

"The canopy separated," the crew chief yelled, "there they go." He pointed to two figures ejected from the cockpit. Their parachutes opened.

The now pilot-less Mohawk made a huge loop, followed by a three-quarter roll, then headed back toward the airfield and the large crowd that by now had gathered on the tarmac. Suddenly, the plane veered steeply down and crashed on the perimeter of the airfield, just short of the POL and ammunition dumps.

"Look at that!" the crew chief yelled in awe.

On impact, the plane erupted into a large ball of orange flame; thick, black smoke rose up in a plume.

I could see the two pilots had successfully landed in a field some distance away.

"There's mines in that field," the crew chief yelled into his headset. Trey headed our chopper down for the rescue. The second chopper remained aloft, circling above, ready if needed.

Within minutes, we reached the fliers as they disengaged from the parachute harnesses. Trey hovered our chopper over the flooded field, the water whipping into a white frenzy by the rotors' wash. The crew chief and the gunner helped pull the wet American pilot and Vietnamese co-pilot aboard.

It was only a brief flight back to the airfield. The ambulance met us where we landed, and we placed the Mohawk pilots on litters. Back at the dispensary, I carefully checked them over.

The American captain sustained a back sprain when he landed in the rice field; the Vietnamese officer suffered only a superficial chest abrasion from the parachute harness.

"You are both lucky," I said. "What are you guys planning for an encore?" My attempt at levity fell flat.

WASHINGTON, DC
FRI
6 SEP 63

JFK and the National Security Council agreed to try for another special report from Saigon. General "Brute" Krulak would represent the military, and Joseph A. Mendenhall, senior foreign service officer, would represent the Department of State. They immediately left Andrews Air Force Base for Saigon.[46]

SOC TRANG
MON
9 SEP 63

We spent the day at Cam Mau just as we had the day before; like most other missions lately, frustrating and stressful. The one good thing was the weather. It felt almost like a Midwest fall, but with lots of rain off and on.

I went to bed early, promptly falling asleep. While in a restorative REM cycle about 2400, a loud, percussive explosion rudely yanked me into reality and instant wakefulness.

"Damn VCs!" I heard a voice down the hall I did not recognize. "Those are eighty-ones!."

I didn't know what size, but it had to be a big shell. Not good. Jumping into fatigues and combat boots, which I now kept at the ready by my bed, I put my steel pot on and crawled under the cot. I pulled the mattress over me for protection. The instructions had been clear. I followed them exactly.

My heart rate speeded with an adrenalin rush. Another explosion rocked the room with a concussive wave. Hard metal fragments and debris rained down on the corrugated roof of hootch #4 and rattled loudly as they rolled down the pitched roof and fell to the ground. Flares lit the sky. Through the shutters, an eerie soft glow bathed my room in a red, unnatural light.

From the west, I heard a small-arms fire fight. I assumed the

Vietnamese guards must be engaged with VC at the outer perimeter. Someone yelled a message from the next hootch, "Red alert!"

One more time, I flashed back to Camp Bullis and the live-ammunition field exercises. I still felt scared.

I needed to report to my red-alert duty station, so I left what little security my room offered. Running as low to the ground as possible, I took off for the dispensary. All lights were blacked out, and it was dark except for flares.

My men assembled in the dispensary and were fully accounted for with their issued weapons. We were ready. I stationed them as lookouts from the windows. I told them not to move from their posts or load weapons unless I personally gave the order. I feared, in the dark and chaos, we might shoot one another. I loaded my .45 handgun, though, determined to shoot any VC that might enter.

The roar of T-28 engines firing up echoed across the airfield. They scrambled to take off with only the light from the flares. Explosions continued. The T-28s made several runs and strafed the area outside the perimeter. There were no more explosions. It was silent other than the drone of the aircraft overhead. After what seemed like a long time, I breathed softly so I could hear the distant Vietnamese-speaking voices that broke the silence.

At 0300, an MP came to the door of the dispensary. "We're off alert," he said softly.

"Any casualties?" I asked.

"No, sir. You and your men can return to quarters for now."

We left in the dark silence. I fell on my bunk, fully clothed. I wanted to keep the steel pot on but couldn't; it made lying down impossible. I listened to the silence only briefly before exhaustion took over and I escaped into sleep.

SOC TRANG
TUES
10 SEP 63

After what seemed like only a moment, my alarm clock rang. I awoke in the early dawn. We had another day at Cam Mau lined up. Although I had lost count for sure, I thought this would the fifth day in a row we had been there.

When I left hootch #4, I looked for evidence of last night's attack. Things looked normal. The dirt tossed around seemed insignificant in the light of morning. The elements of surprise and cover of darkness are classic war tactics for good reason.

I ate a good portion of pancakes and bacon for breakfast. It would be a long day, and field ration lunches were getting tiresome—even the weenies and beans. PBD, fresh flight suit and fully scrubbed and shaved, came across the mess hall with his coffee cup and sat across from me. He had news. Slick and PBD always seemed to be the first to know.

"The bastards hit every province in the Delta last night. One was run over at 0215 this morning and sixty-five Civil Defense were killed. Thirty-five wounded."

The changing pattern was clear. The ARVN were on the defensive and the VC on the offensive.

We were at Cam Mau strip by 0900, and the ARVN troops, lined up on the side, were ready to take off.

Maj. Saunders, standing in the command post, motioned me over. "Want to give you a heads up. The VC hit an outpost near here early this morning. They are still in the area. Today may be our day." He added between clenched teeth, "Finally."

Our choppers ferried load after load of troops to the LZ. Five hundred paratroopers from Saigon landed in nearby fields. About midday, the H-21s returned with probably sixty or seventy ARVN wounded. Their medics were well-organized and did not really require my assistance. The stabilized wounded were transported in waiting ambulances and trucks to a military hospital. Amazingly, our choppers were not hit by sniper fire; the VC were too busy fighting the ARVN this time.

In the midst of the action, one of the T-28's flying support crashed. The two people aboard, the U.S. pilot and a VNAF observer, ejected from the aircraft. They deployed their parachutes and were uninjured. One of our choppers picked them up immediately.

The heat of the battle slowed perceptibly as the day progressed and dark shadows gathered in the dusk. We loaded up, and I rode back on Slick's chopper. It had been a long, grueling day.

By the time we got back at 2030, Soc Trang airfield looked mighty good. As I passed by the dispensary, I saw the lights were on, and it was open. I checked in.

Sgt. Tibbs was there, as well as Brooklyn and Harris. "Doc, we got word a U.S. Special Forces sergeant has been hit. They're bringing him in, along with some wounded ARVN."

Operations notified us at 2230 the H-21s would arrive in fifteen minutes. Brooklyn pulled the ambulance up to the flight line, and Sgt. Tibbs, Harris, and I stood by. I saw several ARVN ambulances lined up as well. There were many wounded ARVN aboard the two incoming choppers.

Packed in the cargo holds were fifteen wounded Vietnamese soldiers, in addition to the U.S. Special Forces sergeant. We loaded him into our ambulance, and the ARVN medics offloaded the rest to be sent by their transportation to a military hospital. It was highly unusual to be doing this at night. I wondered if they would hold the wounded ARVN at the Provincial Hospital until morning. Convoys at night were rare due to the risk of VC attack.

At the dispensary, I cut off the bulky bandage covering the sergeant's left shoulder.

"How's he doing?" Maj. Saunders came in the treatment room.

"It's a moderate wound, but pain and bleeding are under control," I said.

"It doesn't look like there is any way we can get him out until daylight. Can we wait 'til then? Is he stable enough?" he asked.

"Sure. We can watch him. It's only for a few hours."

"I'll see he gets out first thing," the major said with relief.

We fixed a cot for the sergeant, and I sent my men back to their barracks. The wounded soldier slept with the help of morphine. I stretched out on the treatment table. There was considerable action nearby, and the arms fire made me wish I had my steel helmet. I had become accustomed to having it just below my bed for reassurance. I felt exposed without it.

WASHINGTON, DC
TUES
10 SEP 63

Four days and twelve thousand miles later, General Krulak and Joseph A. Mendehall presented their official observations to JFK and the National Security Council.

General Krulak reported the war was going fine and according to schedule, particularly in the rural areas. The reported dissent was with Nhu, not President Diem, who was a good leader. All we had to do was stay the course.

Mendenhall reported the people of Vietnam were united, but unfortunately, united in opposition to Diem and the government. Civilian morale was collapsing with fear and hatred for the current regime to the point the war now almost seemed secondary.

An exasperated JFK asked, "You two did visit the same country, didn't you?"[47]

SOC TRANG
FRI
13 SEP 63

"All in favor, say 'Aye.'" The vote passed. The official officers' club business elected a new president. I had completed my stint, passing the job on to the next guy. I looked around at the club and snack bar, pleased with the improvements. Charley had done a great job as manager, and we were now serving steak and chicken dinners which included soup, salad, and French fries—a good and only alternative to the mess hall.

The city of Soc Trang had been off-limits for almost a month. I wondered how the sisters and the children at the orphanage were doing.

SOC TRANG
SUN
15 SEP 63

"So this is it." Slick looked around at the almost empty club. Billy T. and Trey had already long gone back to their hootches for the night. "I somehow had thought we'd have a bigger celebration." The loud, boisterous crowd left early, unable to celebrate properly, as there would be a mission to fly at first light tomorrow.

This was the last night for Slick, Billy T., and Trey at the Tigers' Den. They wouldn't be flying any more missions. Rather than go south to Cam Mau, they would fly north to Saigon to process out, then take off for home the next day. PBD, MOM, and I were the only ones in the club other than Duc, our faithful barman.

"Say, look at my scar," Slick said. He pulled off his T-shirt and turned to us to show his back.

I had taken the stitches out one week after the surgery, and at that time, the wound was clean, healed, and had a nice, thin scar.

"Looks good," MOM said in a mock professional voice.

I didn't think so. It had healed all right, but the scar was wide and not cosmetically pleasing. I hoped he wouldn't regret my decision to remove the lesion and told him so.

"Not to worry, Doc, ol' buddy. I'll think of you if anyone ever mentions it."

He put his shirt back on, and at this final moment, emotions were mixed. In turn, the four of us shook hands, said good-bye, and all around, we wished Slick luck. Walking back to hootch #4 with MOM, I found it hard to imagine Soc Trang without pilot Cody Williams and his talk of Little Lee Roy. I had almost forgotten Lt. Slick's real name, but I could still remember how he and Sput welcomed me my first day as a Tiger. I would miss Slick and Trey.

We were getting new pilots in all the time to replace those rotating back, but it would never be the same group. It could never be the same. I still missed Sput and the others. I wondered how Francine and Sput's mother were doing. It had been eight months. I wondered how Shirley and her three kids were dealing with only the memory of Sgt. Patterson.

Something was changing in me. I couldn't see how this mess would ever end.

Last Monday night, when mortars hit the airstrip and we went on full-alert, I had loaded my .45 for the first time since I arrived in Vietnam. I had never before thought I could shoot another person, but I now knew I would if I had to. The handgun was difficult to control at best, and I might not hit my target, but if a VC had come through the dispensary door, I would definitely have shot. An odd feeling.

Somehow, I also had the odd feeling I did not care much if I got shot or not. Weird, weird feeling. Home seemed distant and not as important as it used to be. Separated from everything familiar all my life—family, friends, groups, organizations—I felt detached from the world I had known. Risks and decisions that I would weigh carefully if I were back home seemed of little consequence. I didn't care the same way I had before. It seemed what I valued previously, I now valued less. I still valued life—mine and those of us in this together—but I realized I had changed. I could kill another person if I had to. This would not be strange to me anymore. That, in itself, seemed new and strange. More and more, the future seemed to hold less promise.

SOC TRANG
FRI
20 SEP 63
0250

Ka-bam! With this nearby explosion, all of us asleep in the hootches awoke as one.

"Shit!" I heard from an unknown voice down the hall in the darkness.

"How far away?" I recognized MOM's voice.

"I'd guess less than ten kilometers." I heard the first voice answer.

"At least. Go back to sleep," MOM yelled and let out a loud yawn.

Easier said than done. The Howitzer bombardment on some

nearby outpost continued blast after blast. Some American advisors were out in this dark night directing fire on a strategic hamlet being overrun. I lay on my bunk, exhausted, eyes closed but ears wide open. At 0345, blessed silence. How much misery had reigned down in the last fifty-five minutes? How many killed? Wounded? Maimed instantly for a lifetime? At that moment, I embraced my room in hootch #4, a safe cocoon.

When I entered the mess hall for breakfast, I joined MOM.

"Any word on what happened early this morning?" I asked.

"The VC tried to overrun an outpost about four miles from here. Thanks to firepower, they didn't succeed. The HU1-Bs took out over twenty wounded to Can Tho this morning already."

"Surprised we didn't help evacuate," I said as I felt some relief.

"We can't do it all. There's too much action now." MOM finished his coffee. Bleary-eyed, he headed for the door and said over his shoulder, "See you at the party tonight."

"See you there." This would be a big going-away party for six more veteran pilots who were rotating home and a welcoming party for several new first and second lieutenants and warrant officer pilots who were arriving as replacements.

SOC TRANG
SAT
21 SEP 63

We gathered in the Tigers' Den annex for an unusual afternoon briefing by the captain from operations with a robust physique and ruddy skin. His fresh crew cut made his ears look larger and more prominent than I remembered.

"Gentlemen," he said with authority, "field intelligence has obtained reliable reports the VC plan to attack the airfield between midnight tonight and October first."

Not good news. I looked around. Everyone was looking straight at the briefing officer.

"Be alert," the captain continued. "Do your jobs, but be aware. Don't run any unnecessary risks. None. The danger to our aircraft and maintenance capabilities are real. We can't let this interfere with our mission. This is a psychological ploy."

And it's working, I thought to myself. At least on me! I looked around again, but the attention remained focused on the captain.

"Sleep with your steel pots handy. We have plenty of sandbags and fill. We'll all need to pitch in to set up bunkers."

The meeting broke up in a somber mood. I was assigned a bunker next to hootch #4. I reported and begin filling sandbags. I thought silently as I shoveled away, I'm sure glad November is getting closer.

"Looks like Victor Charlie's going to up the ante on us," PBD drawled in a good imitation of Slick as he shoveled away vigorously, "and Little Lee Roy don't know much about filling sandbags."

"He will soon," I said.

With many willing hands, we filled what seemed like hundreds of sandbags. The shape of the bunker was clear by the time we stopped for chow. Bone-tired from the effort, I went to bed early after a shower. I checked to make sure my steel helmet was in easy reach underneath my cot.

With nightfall, tensions rose. You could sense the stress ratchet up as dusk turned to dark.

WASHINGTON, DC
MON
23 SEP 63

Secretary of Defense Robert S. McNamara and Chairman of the Joint Chiefs of Staff Gen. Maxwell Taylor left for another fact-finding mission.

Many of the highly touted strategic hamlets in the Delta had become uninhabited ghost towns.[48]

SOC TRANG
TUE
24 SEP 63

At sick call this morning, I saw an MP for follow-up for an ankle sprain.

"You're good to go back to duty," I said.

"Thanks." He stood up from the treatment table. "We are all going to need to be good for action. Tonight is some kind of VC holiday. Plus elections coming up."

"Any update about their threat to hit us?" I asked.

"Nothing specific, but the local police report they've caught lots of VC bringing mines and explosives into Soc Trang."

"Sobering news." I waved as he left the dispensary. "Stay healthy, soldier."

Exhausted, I went to my room early after chow and almost immediately fell asleep. I was startled awake by the roar of the T-28 engines taking off. They did this now almost every night to help defend some lost outpost. I was glad for our firepower, but being in the corner of the hootch #4 with the flight line only a few feet away, the aircraft made an unwanted alarm with no snooze button.

Lying on my bunk, I heard the distant, familiar fire fight of another outpost being overrun.

PBD yelled from down the hall that fireworks were starting early. I felt too tired from filling sandbags to even reply.

It was tedious, boring work—too slow for me. But it was a great motivator knowing you may need the bunker when it gets dark. Every night, you wondered if this would be the night. We were a small group of Americans inside a perimeter—a small island surrounded by a sea of guerillas.

I couldn't sleep. I thought about my replacement in the United States and what he might be thinking. He should leave the states in one month—a long time, but it was a lot less than a year. I thought about my request for R & R in Hong Kong. I'm hoping to go. Should hear soon.

SOC TRANG
THUR
26 SEP 63

Sandbag by sandbag—we spent all afternoon filling them. With so many willing workers, we made good progress building bunkers. The one I worked on and planned to head for when trouble hit was close to my room near the back door of hootch #4.

The weather was warming up, and there were now fewer rain showers and more sunny days. The monsoon was definitely winding down.

By the time the sun set, our bunkers were taking shape. We took a break for the day, and by 2030, we were well-fed and watching a movie in the Tigers' Den. I sat on a bench near the back laughing with the rest of the large crowd at the film *Don't Go Near the Water*. The comedy starred Glenn Ford and Eva Gabor—light, entertaining fare.

About one-third through, the movie broke down. Mechanical failure happened frequently with our equipment—overused reel-to-reel film and an old projector. The crowd, as usual, immediately shouted out in unmerciful hoots and jeers. A handy young officer who had an exceptionally good nature always ran the projector. Ignoring the boos from his ungrateful colleagues, as usual, he worked at getting the entertainment restarted. Wild clapping and cheers, as usual, greeted his efforts when the film started to roll again. I admired our volunteer projectionist and his coolness under fire. A noble person, he did not appear to be bothered by the behavior of his fellows, and the movies—ancient or not—were one of our best and most popular diversions.

After only a few minutes, Maj. Saunders entered the room. He stood in front of the movie screen. Colors and images covered his face and body, his silhouette black on the screen. The noisy machine was turned off, and the club lights were turned back on. There was no booing or hissing, and the laughing crowd suddenly became silent.

"Report to your hootches. Get in battle gear, and prepare to stand by. A patrol spotted some Victor Charlies at the west end of the perimeter."

The terse instructions had immediate impact. The moments-before jolly group left silently and rapidly. Never before had I seen the club empty so fast.

In my room, I quickly donned my gear, including flak vest. With a fleeting thought of our grousing at Camp Bullis, I now felt thankful again for the training.

Someone yelled, "Black out!" The darkness was complete. I reported to my bunker and wished now we had worked harder and finished the job. We still needed several more rounds of sandbags for it to be full height.

I looked up at the moon. Almost full, it provided a lot of light. Good for us, but good for the VC too, I thought. We were all silent in the bunker, listening.

"I hope those fuckers just do it. I'm tired of waiting for them." I recognized MOM's whisper.

"Be careful what you wish for, MOM. Haven't you heard that before?" PBD whispered back.

"I just wish you guys would shut up," I heard my own whispered voice say.

I wanted to be invisible. I was scared. My heartbeat felt so loud, I was certain it could be heard several feet away. I am a wimp doctor, I thought, after all. Finally, I whispered, almost to prove to myself I could talk, "Guys, let's finish this bunker tomorrow, for sure."

"For sure," PBD echoed softly.

Thirty minutes can drag, and drag slowly it did. From across the airfield, sounds of a lone L-19 engine reverberated. It took off in darkness. From the distance, I heard the echo of a small-arms-fire fight and mortars exploding. Then nothing more. Twenty minutes later, "All clear" passed from bunker to bunker.

On the way back to my hootch, I saw the XO.

"What happened out there?" I asked.

"For once, the ARVN performed. They killed ten gooks. The rest of the VC high-tailed it back to where they came from."

Things weren't good. The VC were testing our resolve.

In the safety of my room, I took off my sweaty uniform, layer by layer. I looked at my watch. It was 2400. I felt exhausted, but adrenalin still flushed my system. I crawled into the bunk and took out my diary to make an entry. How could anyone sleep? I had received some bad news earlier in the day; my request for R & R in Hong Kong had been turned down. Disappointed, I immediately submitted a new request for a later trip.

Mortar rounds, at some distance from the airfield, seemed comforting, like distant thunder, because they were so far away.

SOC TRANG
SUN
29 SEP 63
0310

"Doc," I faintly heard in a distant dream. "Doc, wake up." This was accompanied by a light touch to my left shoulder.

I opened my eyes, and in the dim darkness, I saw the XO at the side of my bunk.

"Doc, I hate to wake you, but we've got a young PFC from maintenance in the orderly room. He's really upset. Could you come over and see if you can help him out?" Urgent concern reflected in the request.

I threw on a pair of shorts and slipped into flip-flops. We headed down the dark, dusty company street in silence.

When we entered the orderly room, I saw a stocky youth standing in the harsh light of the naked light bulb. I had never seen this PFC before.

The XO said in a soft voice, "Chandler here came over about half an hour ago. Said he was looking for the CO. When they went to get the OD, Chandler left and took off for the major's hootch. He went into the wrong end of the hootch and walked in where the air force Hawker pilots sleep. He woke them up saying something like, 'Jesus tells me the VC are going to attack again tonight.' A Hawker turned on a light. Chandler said, 'Praise Jesus for the light.' That's about it."

The XO continued, "The OD and Major Saunders brought him back over here and sent me to get you."

PFC Chandler stood by without saying a word, listening to the XO's report; he looked fatigued, disheveled, and dazed.

"Chandler, I'm Doctor Hoyland. Let's go over to the dispensary. We can sort this out better over there."

"Yes, sir," he mumbled.

The XO walked us across the street, and I opened up the dispensary and turned on all the lights.

Chandler told me he had been all right and in his usual mental state before going to bed the night before. He had not been drinking. Unable to sleep after the alert, he tossed and turned on his bunk in the dark but suddenly felt possessed and agitated, as if he'd had an electric shock. He clearly heard the voice of Jesus telling him of an impending second attack by the VC and urging him to deliver this communication immediately to the commanding officer. If he didn't, the whole airfield and all personnel would be blown up and lost. He jumped out of his bunk and tried to alert the CO as quickly as he could.

I gave him a mild oral tranquilizer, and in the harsh light of the infirmary, he was less certain about the message. He readily agreed to spend the rest of the night in the dispensary, having successfully passed on the message. I pulled up a nearby chair and told him I would sit there close by. He fell almost immediately to sleep. I tried hard not to, but so did I.

The next thing I knew, I heard the dispensary door open. A little early, as was his custom, Sgt. Tibbs arrived for duty. The gray morning sky filtered through the shutters at the window and gave the dispensary a plain, hard look.

"What's going on? he asked, surprised to find all the lights on and the two of us asleep.

I explained the situation. PFC Chandler still slept peacefully. We awakened him gently. He was disoriented at first, and then shocked to find himself in the dispensary. He had no recollection of the precipitating events, talking to the Hawkers or to Maj. Saunders.

"Oh, my God," was all he could say over and over.

I assured him he was not in any trouble, and I gave him an

off-duty slip for the day and told him to rest and take it easy. He reluctantly agreed to come in for the next sick call, or sooner if he noticed anything out of the ordinary. Sgt. Tibbs walked him over to the chow hall for some breakfast.

"Anyone make trouble for him?" I asked when Sgt. Tibbs returned.

"No. They ribbed him a little, but they all knew it could have been any one of them. He's anxious to get back on duty, but he decided filling some sandbags might be better than working in the shop today."

"The troops are restless," I joked, "and so am I."

"Well, the VC have only two more nights if they are going to attack before October first. Everyone is on edge, sleeping with one eye open."

"Hold the fort," I said. "I'm going to go over and get cleaned up and get some breakfast. And thanks, Sarge."

"Just doing my job, *bac si*," Sgt. Tibbs said with a smile.

SOC TRANG
TUE
1 OCT 63

Late afternoon faded the rice paddies brown and the distant lines of palm trees into black silhouettes. Across the dusty company street, I saw MOM sprinting toward operations.

"Mohawk's landing gear failed," he called over his shoulder.

A crowd gathered at the side of the airfield as Brooklyn pulled the ambulance up to the early-ready position. The fire trucks and firefighters quickly lined up. I crossed over the tarmac to the ambulance.

"This is getting old, Doc," Brooklyn said characteristically out of the corner of his mouth as he got out from behind the steering wheel to better tuck in his shirt and adjust his belt. "We just went through this drill a month ago! It's like déjà vu."

The distressed plane took a low pass over the airstrip.

"Gear looks down to me," Brooklyn said.

I agreed and headed back over to operations. MOM stood outside assessing the plane as it did another flyover.

"It's down, but the indicator light reads it's not locked in place. He's going to come in."

A fire truck moved down the line with flashing red lights and sirens blaring. It headed toward us, but then left the airfield headed toward the company area. It stopped outside the mess hall.

"What the hell?" MOM looked across to see smoke coming from the kitchen.

"I'll find out," I yelled.

By the time I got to the kitchen, the expert firemen had put out a grease fire. The cooks were embarrassed and unhappy but pleased by the quick response.

I ran back to the tarmac. MOM had heard about the kitchen fire, and he was reassured to see the fire truck and personnel had returned and were ready to take care of the Mohawk crisis as it unfolded.

The disabled aircraft descended and touched down. We held our breath. The wheels turned on contact. The gear held for a picture-perfect landing. Cheers went up from the large crowd. I thought of my old friend Sput and could almost hear him say, "It's been a good day."

Walking back toward the Tigers' Den with a visibly relieved MOM, I said, "Just got word my second request for Hong Kong was approved. A doc from Saigon will come down and cover for me."

"Lucky stiff," he muttered.

"I turned my name in for booking. A four-day trip. Wish you were coming along."

WASHINGTON, DC
WED
2 OCT 63

JFK received the McNamara-Taylor report of continued progress in the war and the suggestion that some one thousand U.S. troops could be withdrawn by Christmas. The White House announced the U.S. role might be completed by

the end of 1965, although some troops could still be needed for training. The CIA advised JFK the Diem government was deteriorating.

In spite of the press releases, JFK knew circumstances were not good and the war was going downhill. He thought there would be time to deal with the Vietnam situation in 1964, as he felt more and more confident he would be re-elected for another term.[49]

SAIGON
SAT
5 OCT 63

Vietnamese Generals Minh, Tran Van Don, and Tran Van Kim, convinced the war was being lost, resumed planning for a coup d'etat as the only hope to improve the government. JFK asked Ambassador Lodge for a guarantee of success if there should be a coup. Ambassador Lodge responded that he could not guarantee success, and if it did not work, we would just have to pick up the pieces.[50]

WASHINGTON, DC
SUN
6 OCT 63

JFK cabled to Ambassador Lodge that although the United States did not want to stimulate a coup, it would not thwart one.[51]

TAN SON NHUT
MON
7 OCT 63

At twelve noon, the jet speeded down the runway, and we were thrust into the air, headed for Hong Kong—only about six hours' flight time from Saigon. I didn't know anyone on the plane when we took off, but by the time we landed, all of us had plans.

SOC TRANG
THUR
11 OCT 63

"Doc," Sgt. Tibbs said thoughtfully, "welcome back. We got along fine, but we missed you."

"Sarge, I'll be honest; I didn't miss being here. Hong Kong was worth the wait. But you had some good practice being without me. This Doc is going home the end of the month."

"You sure know how to hurt a guy." Sgt. Tibbs feigned pain.

I opened my mail, and my heart sank. "Sarge, looks like I'll be here a little longer than I thought." Amended orders for my replacement moved the date from October 24, 1963 to November 8, 1963.

SOC TRANG
SUN
20 OCT 63

There were now many joint missions with the two other helicopter companies in the Delta. We had to have an aid station for every mission, as American pilots and crews could get shot up at any turn. With Max stationed at Can Tho and the new flight surgeon at Vinh Long, we now rotated the duty—a huge relief for me not to go on every one. Yesterday, Max was at the Cam Mau strip. Two Americans were wounded and had to be evacuated by Dust Off. Seven other crewmen had minor wounds. Max had been properly initiated.

Today, it was my turn, and we were back at Cam Mau. The ARVN reported no contact, and there were no hits on our choppers. When we were released to go home, black clouds banked in the sky. By the time we took off, the rain started; it poured so hard, it took us twice as long as normal to get back to Soc Trang. It seemed to me we'd had more rain here at the end of the monsoon than we did at the beginning. I was ready for dry weather, but it could be I was just ready for change.

SOC TRANG
FRI
24 OCT 63

Sgt. Tibbs maneuvered the jeep into a good position to unload the provisions at the front of the orphanage: cases of detergent, dried milk, and soap. Sister Mary Cecil saw us and came out. She bowed in greeting, her hands hidden in her black habit. I again wondered how old she was; how many years had she been here, and when she died, would she be buried in Soc Trang, so very far away from France? Two other Vietnamese Sisters, both dressed in white habits, followed closely behind, smiled broadly, and bowed.

The three of them showed us a lean-to in the back. It was the new laundry room. The white washing machine looked too stark, too white, and too modern in this primitive setting. It was not running. The French nun managed to explain the electricity was off. The city electric supply was not reliable and frequently shut down for hours at a time. Not a worry to them, she somehow communicated with her beatific smile. It would come on later.

They showed us the crib room. The screens controlled the flies. The bedding was cleaner, and babies were crying with robust, lusty cries. Two young girls in black pajamas were washing babies. Sgt. Tibbs could not resist playing peek-a-boo with a laughing child. Several older children stood in their cribs, soliciting attention. The improvements were real, and I would write the women's club to let them know.

I tried to tell the Sisters a final *au revoir* to explain I would not be back, and that I would be leaving for *les Etats-Unis*. Did they understand? I wanted them to know I admired them for their dedication and work and to encourage them despite my misgivings that they faced such awful odds.

Sgt. Tibbs skillfully turned the jeep around, and we headed back to the airfield. I was lost in thought. What had we accomplished? What future did these children face? We had helped them in the short run, but maybe they would have been better off without our help. For these children, if they survived into childhood and adolescence, what would Vietnam be like?

"Sergeant Tibbs, you'll keep checking on them?" I asked.

"You don't need to ask. Too many of us care about these little guys to let them down."

"I'm thinking we might pick up an extra generator somewhere. Then they could use the washer whenever they want to."

"I'm way ahead of you. I know a guy who knows a guy who knows where a surplus one is. It needs a little work. We'll get him to bring it over and get it going real soon." Sgt. Tibbs let out a deep, warm laugh but kept his eyes on the road and chaotic traffic. "And they could use a dryer."

"I should have known; you're way ahead of me. Thanks."

At the main gate to the airfield, I returned the MP's salute and thought of Doc Greene for the first time in many months. I knew now what he must have felt before I arrived last year. What would he be up to now? Probably getting out of the army and going into a civilian practice or residency training.

We pulled up at hootch #4, and I got out. Sgt. Tibbs smiled and his face beamed. "Now don't forget, before you leave for good, I get to buy you a beer at the Enlisted Men's Club."

"I'd be honored."

SOC TRANG
SAT
26 OCT 63

Duc told me this was a Vietnamese national holiday, an independence day of sorts, to commemorate the day in 1955 when Emperor Bao Dai was deposed and Diem took over the government. Last year, according to Duc, there were parades and celebrations. What a difference. This year, it seemed, they didn't like him so much.

SOC TRANG
SUN
27 OCT 63

Doc Lemmon called to let me know he would leave Saigon the

next morning. His replacement had taken over. I would miss the good Doctor Lemmon. My replacement would hopefully come down to Soc Trang by November 10, but I hadn't heard anything for certain. Surely, he would be here by the fifteenth. It was getting harder to wait now.

SAIGON
SOMETIME IN OCTOBER, 1963

President Diem and Nhu learned of the coup being plotted by Generals Minh, Don, and Kim. In response, Nhu devised a fanciful false counter-coup which involved two loyal senior military officers: General Dinh, who had saved them from the paratroopers' coup in 1960; and Colonel Tung, Commander of Nhu's Special Forces.

These two were instructed to act as if they were a part of the real coup. But in the chaos, their mission would be to kill the mutinous generals, any rebellious troops, and several "disloyal" Americans at the U.S. Embassy. Diem's government would then claim they had smashed a "neutralist plot" driven by the misguided generals bent on kicking out the Americans. Diem could then declare martial law, reclaim control, and hopefully regain the esteem of a grateful America.[52]

SOC TRANG
TUE
29 OCT 63

PBD sat at the bar in the Tigers' Den drinking a soft drink. He looked up as I entered.

"Hey, Doc," he said. "We've got our work cut out for us tomorrow."

"What's up?"

"An ARVN patrol was ambushed and shot to hell. Three American advisors are out there with them: a captain, a first lieutenant, and a sergeant medic. Tonight, choppers from Can Tho are dropping in troops."

"A night operation?"

"Yeah. We're taking off first light tomorrow for that beauty spot, Cam Mau. We're doing a gigantic operation to try and reach them."

"Doesn't sound good."

"Those advisors are in some deep shit. Those ARVN are scrappy fighters. I admire them. It's the leadership—those up the chain of command—that are the problem."

I went back to my bunk. As I took a warm shower and got ready for bed, I thought of those guys out in the middle of the Delta. Here I was, warm, clean, and safe. Those three men—somebody's brothers, husbands, and fathers—were in a terrible place at this moment. Their families back home, going about their lives, could not know. It was a good thing they didn't. I went to sleep hoping our help would be enough.

SAIGON
WED
30 OCT 63

General Harkins, MACV commander, discovered Ambassador Lodge and Washington, DC had been in constant contact about a coup. He had been totally left out of the loop. In an attempt to find out what had been transpiring behind his back, he met at some length with both General Tran Van Don and General Minh. The generals denied any knowledge of a coup. They misled General Harkins out of fear that he would inform Diem and Nhu if he knew of the plan.[53]

SOC TRANG
WED
30 OCT 63

Dawn broke over the enormous Mekong Delta. I looked from our chopper and saw only a misty, flat land covered with rivers, canals, and rice paddies crisscrossed by endless tree lines. Smoke, fog, and haze combined to give the landscape the impressionistic beauty of a Chinese watercolor.

I thought of the many peasants, uncaring about politics or Communism, struggling to make a life, caring about their rice crops, families, water buffalo, and whether the palm thatch would keep their hootches dry in the monsoon season.

I thought again of the American advisors and the ARVN troops who spent the last night in some dark jungle hell, hoping for reinforcements. Knowing the dark belongs to the enemy, I knew if they survived, they would welcome this dawn.

I looked over at Sgt. Tibbs, who was sitting across the hold from me. He seemed lost in thought, staring out through the cargo door at the passing scenery. If we needed to stabilize our men, we could do it. Dust Off, with their med-evac Hueys, would be at the ready. Glad when we finally started the descent, I wanted to go to work.

We landed at the familiar strip. Sgt. Tibbs and I unloaded our gear.

"It's at least a fair day," I commented as the sun began to break through the early morning clouds. "Do you suppose there's any hope for those advisors? The troops?"

"There's always hope," he said. "I learned that a long time ago."

The rotor wash from the long line of H-21s stirred up huge dust clouds. The small knots of soldiers with battle gear clambered aboard, and lift after lift of troops disappeared in the distance.

The day became hot and oppressive. Word filtered down the line that again there was no contact with any VC. They had melted away. At noon, intelligence reported two of the Americans had been killed outright when the unit had been ambushed. The third had been severely wounded and died a short time later. Their bodies had been recovered and already taken back to Saigon. The only consolation was that they wouldn't be tortured and held in some unlivable jungle prison. I thought again of the families in the United States, who now would soon know the fates of these three men.

When we landed at Soc Trang at 2000 hours, Sgt. Tibbs and I unloaded our gear and took it to the dispensary. We had done no work today. Neither of us talked. I knew we shared the same heavy feeling and sadness; we felt powerless, and this business seemed so futile.

"Goodnight, Doc." We parted on the dark company street.

"See you in the morning." I headed toward hootch #4. The end of a long day.

I turned back to my own thoughts. I knew now I wanted to go home. I could leave my buddies, but I was afraid. Gnawing at the edges of awareness, I knew too many who got zapped just as tours were ending. Give it up, I thought. You're no hero, but you've come too far to give into fear. You may not be as brave as you want to be, but you've got to do this job until the day you leave.

SAIGON
THUR
31 OCT 63

Ambassador Lodge and the CIA notified Washington a coup was set for early afternoon the next day. Harkins, still unaware, prepared a cable to send to Washington stating he doubted a coup was imminent. A few hours later, MACV asked that General Harkin's cable not be sent.[54]

SOC TRANG
FRI
1 NOV 63

A strange sound awoke me from a deep sleep. It was the sound of flags flapping in the brisk wind. I got up and saw many yellow-and-red-striped flags of the Republic of Vietnam lining the airstrip.

PBD was leaving as I approached the shower room.

"What's happening?" I asked.

"A UN team due today or tomorrow. Looking into Buddhist repression. Heads may roll."

After a busy sick call, I found MOM and Hartley Davis eating lunch in the mess hall.

"Big news, Doctor," MOM said. "It looks like some changes

ahead. Diem's soldiers are finally fighting, but rather than going after the VC, they're going after him and his brother."

I stopped by the O-Club after lunch. "What's happening, Duc?" Our hardworking man behind the bar looked grim.

"Don't know, *bac si.*" He wiped the already clean bar. "Radio Saigon off the air. This afternoon. Trouble. For sure."

Headquarters called for a briefing at 1600.

Capt. Joe Andrews looked serious. "We don't know for sure what's going on. We are under condition 'gray.' The only news has been from the teletype messages we've managed to get from being hooked up to one of the news bureaus out of Saigon. He read:

> *"Reports of fighting reached other Far Eastern*
> *capitals from Saigon. In Seoul, informed sources*
> *said the South Korean embassy in Saigon reported*
> *government forces were battling paratroopers.*
> *(There was no indication of the strength of the*
> *insurgent forces.)*
> *The position of Diem's armed forces commander,*
> *Major En Tran Van Dong, was unclear. The*
> *general refused to see newsmen and say whether he*
> *opposed the coup.*
> *The insurgent force was believed to have seized*
> *control of the government radio station.*
> *Diem's crackdown on the Buddhists last spring*
> *and summer caused widespread disaffection with*
> *his regime, but the war against the Communists*
> *continued, and U.S. officials in Vietnam said only*
> *this week that the Buddhist dispute had had no*
> *apparent effect on troop morale.*
> *A United Nations observer team was in South*
> *Vietnam to investigate charges of repression*
> *against the Buddhists.*
> *The TIMES of VIETNAM, a pro-Diem English-*
> *language newspaper in Saigon, charged September*
> *2 that the Central Intelligence Agency had*
> *planned a coup against the regime August 28 but*

*'postponed the plot' because the 'Vietnamese knew
and were prepared to fight to the end.'"*

I left the briefing with PBD and Hartley Davis. We headed over
to the Tigers' Den.

"Look at the sky," I said. Huge, threatening thunderheads, dark
and pierced with lightning bolts, filled the western half of the Delta
sky. A beautiful full moon lit the eastern half, flawlessly clear and
indigo. "Tonight, the sky is as divided as the country."

We sat down at a vacant table and ordered beers. Maj. Cutter,
the MAAG advisor who lived in the downtown compound, came
in and headed our way.

"News?" PBD asked.

"Don't ask me, but we're under yellow alert now. No one in town
knows anything, but it looks serious. With no radio, we're as much
in the dark as the civilians. Even the province chief doesn't know,
and he's tight with Diem and Nhu."

"A change of administration without an election," I said, "never
would happen in the good old U.S."

"It's totally weird," PBD said.

Seated at the bar, a tall civilian with a square jaw and short, dark
hair overheard us. "I'm a United Nations observer, and I can tell
you the Buddhists have had it with Diem. I'm not at all surprised to
hear a coup is underway." He took a final drink from his glass and
stood to leave. "I wouldn't be surprised at anything that happens
here. It's a damned dramatic place."

**SAIGON
FRI
1 NOV 63
1330**

**A battalion of Vietnamese Marines overran the Saigon
National Police Headquarters, and the military coup Diem had
been dreading since 1960 was underway. Soon, Diem and Nhu
learned General Dinh, their most trusted officer, had joined
the coup. The only other supporter the brothers had in Saigon,**

Colonel Tung, could not help; he had been shot by the generals as a traitor. There would be no false counter-coup. The last remaining government loyalist, General Cao, was far south of Saigon in Can Tho.

Rapidly, the entire city fell to the rebelling troops except for Gia Long Palace, protected by Nhu's palace guards—funded by the CIA—the only loyal unit left.

With a phone call to the palace, Gen. Minh and his fellow generals offered Diem and Nhu safe conduct out of Vietnam if they would surrender and Diem resign from the government.

Diem and Nhu declined. At 4:30 p.m., Diem placed a call to Ambassador Lodge to determine if the United States was involved. By 8:00 p.m., the Ngo brothers knew it was hopeless. They escaped from the palace through a secret tunnel and went to the house of a Chinese supporter in the area south of Saigon known as Cholon. The presidential guards could no longer hold out; the palace barracks fell.

SAIGON
SAT
2 NOV 63

In the early morning hours, Diem, implying he and Nhu were still at the Gia Long Palace, telephoned Gen. Minh and agreed to resign. Minh went to the palace to escort the surrendering brothers, but he and the palace guards were stunned to discover Diem and Nhu had not been there all night. The Ngo brothers, discovered in the Cholon Chinese Catholic Church attending Mass, were taken into custody. With their hands secured behind their backs in handcuffs, they were herded into an armored personnel carrier. Instead of transport to the victorious generals—by now fed up with the treachery—both Diem and Nhu were shot in the head. Nhu's body was bayoneted.

Crowds in the city cheered both the demise of the Ngo brothers and news of the success of the military coup.

LOS ANGELES, CALIFORNIA
SAT
2 NOV 63

While in the United States trying unsuccessfully to raise popular support for the Ngo family, Madame Nhu and her eighteen-year-old daughter Le Thuy were staying at the Beverly Wilshire Hotel. In her hotel room, Madame Nhu received a telephone call from Ambassador Lodge with the news of the coup. She said, "The blood will flow to Washington."

Arrangements were made to fly her and Le Thuy to Rome, where the remaining three Nhu children would join them. One of Diem's brothers, Archbishop Thuc, was already living at the Vatican. Diem's younger brother Can, an unpopular administrator for Central Vietnam, would not be so lucky. From Hue, he was flown to Saigon and shot by a firing squad. Thus ended the Ngo family reign in the Republic of South Vietnam.[55]

SOC TRANG
SAT
2 NOV 63

I happened across a current copy of the *Stars and Stripes*. A headline quoted General Harkins: "Viet Victory Near."

Here we go again. He must have known something we didn't know down here in the Delta—or vice versa.

We soon learned President Diem's government had fallen. His army generals and troops deposed him. Both President Diem and his brother, Nhu, had been assassinated. Rumors were everywhere. Some said the CIA was behind the coup. This seemed hard to believe. I saw that Vietnamese flags still lined our runway to welcome the UN team, but I wondered if there would be anything left for them to investigate. And how about our Soc Trang province chief and his wife? Nice people, but they were close to Diem and Madame Nhu. I remembered meeting her once when she flew in to visit them.

The turmoil would make it harder to sort out this mess. Personally, I would be glad to leave and read about it in the newspapers from now on. Most of the Vietnamese civilians I knew seemed glad the government had been overthrown. Many of them felt certain the VC were behind the coup. We did not have facts, and they would emerge only later with time.

SOC TRANG
TUE
5 NOV 63

"Hey, Doc Hoyland." Capt. Hartley Davis came to the dispensary carrying a teletype message. His gray eyes looked somber. "I don't know how to break this to you, so here. Read it yourself."

I took the message:

> FM US ARMY SUPPORT VIET NAM
> TO 134 MED DET
> BT
> CAPT JAY HOYLAND SR NR
> HIS DUTY AT SOC TRANG HAS BEEN
> EXTENDED 30DAYS
> DO TO EMERGGENCIES IN THE FAMILY OF
> HIS REPLACEMENT

I read and re-read it.

"What bum luck," Hartley Davis said. "I'm sorry." He then burst out laughing. He could not contain himself.

"What's so funny?" I said, somewhat unkindly.

"The look on your face. I can't stand it," he laughed. "It's a joke."

I re-read the message slowly and noted the misspelled word and lack of military jargon. I'd been had. It was a joke. A good one. In my anxiety, I had swallowed it hook, line, sinker, and fishing pole! Completely duped!

"You son of a gun," I said. "Wait till we get to Huachuca. I'll get even. You'll see."

Capt. Davis threw back his head and laughed with gusto. We both would be stationed there after our tours in Vietnam.

"Still friends?" he said, wiping tears of laughter from his eyes.

"Still friends," I answered the sheepish way people do when they've been taken in and still can't quite believe it.

We shook hands, mine still a little sweaty from the thirty-day extension. I was glad this good friend and I, along with another young pilot I liked and admired in his unit, would be reunited in Arizona.

I was getting more and more spooked. Every night, the explosions seemed closer. Aircraft took off on bombing runs, and flares lit up the sky bright as day. In the morning, smoke hung in the distance from some burned-out hamlet. My attitude about going out on flights had changed. It was sad to think of putting in a year here and then not getting to go home. I didn't want to give in to this, but I seemed to be losing courage. Maybe I never had any. Maybe I just conned myself enough to get through this. I needed to redouble my efforts. How many more missions could there be before I left, anyway?

MEKONG DELTA
FRI
8 NOV 63

Newly formed VC battalions of the National Liberation Front began violent, relentless attacks in the Delta. They called this "The Second Phase of the Ap Bac Emulation Drive." Outposts were overrun and burned. Most of the highly touted strategic hamlets no longer existed. VC snipers and ambushes threatened daytime roads with shifting road blocks. Emboldened by success, they started daytime attacks on outposts. With the collapse of the government war effort in rural areas, the VC commanders no longer wanted or needed Soviet small arms or ammunition from North Vietnam. They preferred the simpler supply of American arms and ammunition. (By July 1, 1964,

the VC would have captured approximately two hundred thousand U.S. arms, enough for every guerrilla combatant in South Vietnam.)[56]

SOC TRANG
SAT
9 NOV 63

My final diary entry: great news! My replacement arrived!

I heard from Frank that his replacement had also arrived up north. We would go home on the same flight after all—booked to leave Tan Son Nhut November 15, 1963, date certain.

SAIGON

U.S. military personnel numbered seventeen thousand in South Vietnam. To-date, 120 Americans had been killed and about 250 injured. It was becoming more of an American war.[57]

SOC TRANG
WED
13 NOV 63

I took my installation clearance record around the airfield. Each stop had to be signed off to allow for my departure. Each stop filled me with memories: I turned in my thankfully unused .45-caliber sidearm; at unit supply, I turned in my prized helmet; at the PX, I turned in my card; the tool room signed me out, as did Mr. Tong, who made sure I had no laundry left behind. On to the 134th Medical Detachment (I signed this one myself), the officers' mess, and the Tigers' Den. I finished signing out except the officers' register at headquarters; my first act when I arrived last November would be my last official act before departure.

After walking all over the base, I went back to the dispensary for one last time, for one last look.

Sgt. Tibbs, waiting for me, smiled his great, generous smile.

"Come by the EM Club tonight about eight for that beer I promised you, Doc."

"You're on. See you there."

I had never been in an enlisted men's club. Army custom dictates that officers don't go to enlisted men's clubs, and enlisted men don't go to officers' clubs. Both inviolate spaces are social safety valves where peers unwind from twenty-four-hour-a-day duties, places to blow-off steam from twenty-four-hour-a-day confined environmental stress.

I arrived on time. The EM Club, housed in the barracks-style building like the O-Club, was lit with a festive permanent display of Christmas lights. It was noisy and crowded, and the men were singing along to a popular Patsy Cline record. Everyone seemed to be having a good time. I knew most of these men by sight and many by name. A part of my family, too, they smiled and waved as casually as if I were a regular patron.

Sgt. Tibbs brought me a beer from the long bar, and we sat around table with Brooklyn, Tony, Harris, and the rest of our crew. They still had a month or so to go. I looked at these young, familiar faces and knew we would never see one another again, yet we had been through a life-changing experience none of us would ever forget. They had done such a job. I felt humble, proud, and strangely lonely. I would tonight leave forever this family, forged by fate.

We recalled some of the experiences we had together; we talked a lot. I drank my beer with the team. We had done our part; this team was going home and did not need beers to be happy or maudlin.

I stood to leave. We shook hands all around, except for Sgt. Tibbs, who walked outside with me. In the dark Delta night, I said, "Sgt. Tibbs, stay safe. You get home to your family. You're the best sergeant anyone could ever ask for. Best of luck." I shook his hand. He had a strong grip.

"Thank you, sir. And the best of luck. Be sure and look me up if you ever get down Louisiana way. We'll have some gumbo you'll never forget."

I slowly walked back to the Tigers' Den and looked at the star-filled sky. I hoped the new doc would be blessed with a crew of medics as dedicated as mine. I was glad Sgt. Tibbs would be there to help out for a while. The mission of the 134th and the Vietnam War would go right on without me.

TAN SON NHUT
FRI
15 NOV 63

Frank and I departed for CONUS in a chartered commercial jet: Good-bye Saigon; hello San Francisco.

LOS ANGELES

Madame Nhu and Le Thuy checked out of the Beverly Wilshire Hotel and went directly to LAX. Before their plane departed for Rome, Madame Nhu said, "Judas has sold the Christ for thirty pieces of silver. The Ngo brothers have been sold for a few dollars."[58]

TAN SON NHUT
THUR
21 NOV 63

Ambassador Lodge left for Washington, DC to attend a meeting with high-level U.S. officials, including Robert McNamara and Gen. Max Taylor. Ambassador Lodge was prepared to insist JFK be fully informed that the situation was going from bad to worse, and there could be no real certainty any government could be workable in South Vietnam at this point.[59]

SAIGON
FRI
22 NOV 63

The VC increased weekly offensives to the highest total recorded: 1,021 incidents. The ARVN sustained the highest weekly casualties of the war, including eighty-nine out of a company of 130 ambushed in a Delta swamp near Soc Trang. The VC initiated daring daylight raids.

With few strategic hamlets left in existence, the government had little control in the countryside other than district centers and provincial capitols.

Gen. Harkins attended a Honolulu meeting and insisted the war was not going badly. He still planned to withdraw at least several hundred U.S. military men, as announced, in December. He also reported that 1964 would be decisive.[60]

COLUMBIA, MISSOURI
FRI
22 NOV 63

Back home, safe with my family in Missouri, I reveled in civilian life—my still almost-new reclaimed convertible, civilian clothes, the freedom to roam. One of my first stops was the venerable old Missouri Book Store in Columbia. A bookstore had been one of the luxuries (necessities) I missed most during my year's duty at Soc Trang. While I was totally absorbed in the luxury of browsing overloaded shelves, the store intercom interrupted my pleasure with a terse, rude announcement. It stunned the crowd and world into absolute silence: "President Kennedy has been shot."

My mind could not comprehend what I heard. I raced to the nearest TV set. Numb, I watched and recalled my words just three weeks before when the Vietnamese government changed hands without an election: "That could never happen in the United States." I was wrong.

LAGUNA BEACH, CALIFORNIA
WED
21 NOV 2007

It took me over forty years to want to record recollections of Soc Trang, and six years to write them—many events and details, of course, have been distorted with time. Time, however, could never diminish my memory of those young, daring adventurers who chose the U.S. Army helicopter training and life, pilots and their crews, without exception, who were bright, energetic, and blessed with great humor. They understood teamwork and possessed positive outlooks in impossible situations.

I clearly remembered the day the new aviation medical officer arrived at Soc Trang. The Otter rolled up and came to a stop, and a young, fresh-faced army doctor emerged. "Captain Carr," I said and tried unsuccessfully to hide my enthusiasm, "welcome to Soc Trang."

I flashed back to Doc Greene, who had welcomed me on this same spot almost exactly one year before. He and I—and now Doc Carr—were parts of a huge human machine; a cog wears out, becomes ground-down, and a new cog could be inserted. The 134th Dispensary would keep humming.

With my replacement's arrival, I felt elated; now it would be my turn to leave. But from the moment his foot touched the tarmac, I knew I was no longer the officer in charge. My men would be passed off to someone else, and so would the medical responsibility for Soc Trang airfield. Simultaneously, I experienced loss and relief, feelings mixed and confused. This was the best and the worst; I would never see the mighty Soc Trang Tigers again.

Duties blurred as I showed him the ropes. We went through the same rituals Doc Greene and I had completed the year before. With steady Sgt. Tibbs, we counted, inventoried, and ordered. I introduced the new flight surgeon to everyone.

The last hours sped. I gathered my gear to board the plane, and the pilots of the 121st, with whom I shared a lifetime in one year of turmoil, gathered to say good-bye and present me with a gift to remember them—the Rolex I had coveted in the PX. This was the most unexpected and appreciated gift I ever received before or since.

Aloft on the Otter headed north toward Tan Son Nhut for the last time, I looked back. Soc Trang airfield no longer looked like a medium-security prison; it looked like my home—the concertina wire no longer menacing, but instead a protection from the vast empty rice paddies and lurking VC. My vision blurred, not from the sun shimmering on the water below, but from stinging tears of separation, forever, from the Tigers of Soc Trang.

No longer a young physician just out of an internship, I was also no God-almighty doctor, no wannabe miracle worker, no great physician. I was only a wiser man who now knew what great limitations life and living imposed. I may have possessed some skills and training, but I had no special powers to change the course of events. Nothing could ever bring back sergeants or captains or doomed pilots and crews or lost soldiers.

Four years in medical school and my friends in the class of 1961 now seemed far away; my year at Harbor General Hospital and fellow interns seemed distant, although undeniably indelible for my lifetime. The Soc Trang experience was a different order of experience; I had been practicing out here all alone and isolated. Thank God for Dust Off and the med-evac system. I could not have survived without them.

But I realized two things I missed most and I felt hungriest for ... colleagues with whom to "talk medicine" and books. Vietnam had been the opposite of immersion-rich medical-training programs. I felt behind on my reading. I had perused the medical journals but not digested them, having no complex cases to research. I felt lesser for it and afraid I'd be behind, not just for now but forever. This was a formative year, the first out of internship.

But I had an overriding feeling: I didn't care if I would be behind or not—I had the privilege of learning something of even greater value, something training programs could never provide. I learned I could make it on my own if I had to. I would never choose to, but I knew I could—a good feeling. I would now be content to move on to Ft. Huachuca as ordered; a medical doctor and now veteran flight surgeon. That would be enough for now. My future beyond that would take care of itself.

Frank and I arrived at Travis Air Force Base, California on November 16, 1963, back where we had started our journey. The air seemed somehow brighter, the smell sweeter, and the world familiar and safe. After we deplaned, I joined many others and knelt down to kiss the ground.

I knew the main lasting benefit from my war experience would be the memory of the group of diverse soldiers called Tigers, brought together in the prime of life in a far-off place, melded together into a unit with a common mission. This crucible forged life-affirming bonds. Helicopter pilots and the men who supported them became my heroes. These warriors had courage; my constitution was made of lesser stuff. Nonetheless, during my tour of duty, I tried not to let my fears show and to unconditionally support these men and their mission.

For even a few hours, I would love to be back with the crowd in the Tigers' Den. Life there, basic and raw, seemed honest and stripped of pretense. I would savor being together as we were back then. That could never be, of course. With time, we've become old and gray, but in my memory, we all persist as we were—forever young and vigorous—facing life head on.

I miss the Tigers of the Ninety-Third. I miss Tuffy, even though I had considerable ambivalence about his presence at the Soc Trang airfield. I loved the pride he gave our unit, but this was always tempered by my fear of potential disaster. Thankfully, he never demonstrated his power destructively.

As I read my diary and letters, I could see the closer my rotation home approached, the more I developed an intense desire for self-protection. Too many friends had been killed just as their tours were almost over. I'd heard too many unfortunate stories about the calamities which often finished-up tours. More and more, I dreaded night flights. I found myself sitting on several flak jackets for emotional protection. I gave up my façade of bravery. It probably hadn't been very effective, anyway. I wanted to go home, to pick up my life and resume the search for meaning and career.

I wanted to feel free to roam wherever I wanted after all this time confined to a small space. I knew, of course, I would have no personal decisions to make for the next year until I completed my active-duty obligation. I would then be discharged to reserve status. A citizen soldier.

When I received my official discharge from active duty on August 1, 1964, I would be back where I started in 1962. After discharge, my future would be up to me; decisions would be my responsibility. There would be no promotion lists, no regular-asclockwork paychecks, and no army brothers. I could do without promotion lists and checks, but I could never replace my Soc Trang brothers. Because of them, the real world, the "outside," the civilian world, had become, in this short time, less important. With no small amount of surprise, I realize I loved the military and the life of a medical officer in this well-organized system. The military culture—demanding as it is to fulfill the mission—proved exciting, dangerous, and yet comfortable and satisfying. It suited me.

LAGUNA BEACH, CALIFORNIA
SAT
1 MAR 2008

Time is relative. If it "flies when you're having fun," it's a "slow stroll" when you're under stress and have serious responsibility. It has now been forty-five years since my tour in Vietnam, but November 1962 to November 1963 has remained the longest year of my life. I knew, when I first got home, if even a good friend said, "It's sure been a quick year; doesn't seem you've been gone that long", I'd likely have popped him one without apology or explanation or regret.

And what of Thomas (Mac) McCloud, whose letter and e-mail in July 2001 started this process? I never heard from him again. I hoped this meant he resolved his problems with the V.A. Sadly, author Richard Tregaskis—that great friend of GIs everywhere—drowned August 15, 1973 while swimming in the ocean near his home in Hawaii. Tuffy, our great mascot, lived a contented life at the Toledo Zoo, where he fathered several cubs. I regret I never went there to see him before he was euthanized for kidney failure June 13, 1980. And as for me, I decided it was time to stand up and be counted; today, I put on my old Tiger cap with Father Hoa's swallow pin and marched with other Vietnam vets in our town's Patriots' Day Parade.

My prized Rolex is still on my wrist every day, enduring as the memory of those steadfast Tigers of the Ninety-Third and my extraordinary Soc Trang journey.

THE END

AFTERWORD

Men disagree on what they believe. Never will we all believe in the same thing. We do not want to; perhaps it is not in our nature. But if destruction is the only recourse of those who believe differently, war is as inevitable as death.

In the early years of our involvement in that small, beautiful country of Vietnam, problems of perceptions and rationalizations misled the U.S. military, civilian leaders, and ultimately, the commander in chief. This well-meaning but humanly flawed chain of leadership decided my fate and the fates of legions of others—indeed, a whole generation. I admired the many courageous Vietnamese civilians and soldiers who fought and bled for their country, but the leadership from the Diem government and Nhu family—whom the CIA selected and backed to the end—proved disastrous.

To a large extent, I believe the final, unhappy outcome of the war had already been determined by the time I returned home in November 1963. Would the outcome have been different if JFK had not been killed? We will never know, but are left to speculate for eternity.

War, an evil Midas, transforms lives with just a touch and alters the natural course of societies and the history of peoples. Heartless, war indiscriminately squanders the irreplaceable resource of young lives and plunders the souls of nations. A passionate tyrant, war is uncompromising and demands its will by force. Truth and reason get lost along the way. The compass cannot find north. Lies and propaganda become tools; truths—natural allies of peace—regularly fall mortally wounded as surely as combatants in the field.

War reduces life to basic functions and defies the basic tenets of civilization. Its wake leaves wounds which cannot heal incised into memory; survivors are left to grieve; threads of generations and relationships are broken forever; entire lineages are extinguished.

I believe in human goodness. I know it exists in this world in great abundance. But evil exists, too. The idealist always sees hope for peace, while the pragmatist sees wrongs that cannot be righted without force. I want to believe in idealism, much as I want to believe in the scientific method; a rational world built on order, facts, and civilization's past successes. However, gritty reality drags me by the throat to the conclusion that there will be no peace in my lifetime.

We can achieve peace only when all tribes respect pluralism. When all men respect and live the one universal belief in all religions: "I will not profit from another man's misfortune." Treating others as we wish to be treated is our only hope for humankind to live apart and yet together.

In the final analysis, I ask: "Have I been lucky or unlucky to have had this Vietnam experience in this lottery we call life?" My response: "Lucky." I am forever enriched by the opportunity to see this remarkable life experience through the eyes of a tiger.

JH
Laguna Beach, California

GLOSSARY

ARVN: Army of the Republic of Vietnam

Bac Si: Vietnamese word for *doctor*

Civil Guards: Provincial (territorial) troops similar to a state National Guard. Usually under control of province chief. Better-prepared of two territorial forces.

CO: Commanding officer

CONUS: Continental United States

CWO: Chief warrant officer

DEFCON 2: Defense readiness condition: Level 5, normal peacetime; Level 1, imminent attack.

DEROS: Date of return from overseas

FNG: Fucking new guy; slang for new arrivals in-country.

LZ: Landing zone; area where ARVN troops would be dropped off for operations.

MAAG: U.S. Military Assistance and Advisory Group; subordinate command for training and equipment.

MACV: U.S. Military Assistance Command, Vietnam; created by JFK February 1962.

NCO: Non-commissioned officer. Senior enlisted.

OD: Officer of the day

OIC: Officer in charge

Piastres: Vietnamese currency

POL: Petroleum, oil, lubricants

Province chief: Civil governor of province, which is roughly similar to a state. Appointed by and responsible directly to President Diem. Usually from a loyalist Catholic family. There were ten provinces in the Mekong Delta.

SDC: Self Defense (territorial) Corps. Operated as district or town militia. Most numerous and least-equipped of the three Vietnamese forces.

VC: Vietnamese Communists: 1) Regulars, organized in elite battalions (equivalent to the ARVN); 2) Regionals, provincial troops (equivalent to Vietnamese Civil Guards); and 3) Guerrilla Popular troops, farmers during day, part-time troops at night (equivalent to Vietnamese Self Defense Corps). Collectively called themselves the National Liberation Army.

VNAF: Vietnamese Air Force

WO: Warrant officer

XO: Executive officer

ENDNOTES

1. Millet, *Terror in Vietnam*, 39.
2. Fall, *The Two Viet-Nams*, 286–287. Sheehan, *A Bright Shining Lie*, 218. Halberstam, *The Best and Brightest*, 201.
3. Sheehan, *A Bright Shining Lie*, 118.
4. Sheehan, *A Bright Shining Lie*, 123–124; 184–185; 289. Karnow, *Vietnam, A History*, 255–258; 323. Halberstam, *The Best and Brightest*, 182, 209.
5. Halberstam, *The Best and Brightest*, 200–201. Fall, *The Two Viet-Nams*, 376.
6. Sheehan, *A Bright Shining Lie*, 100–101; 124–125.
7. Sheehan, *A Bright Shining Lie*, 90–91; 124–125.
8. Fall, *The Two Viet-Nams*, 287.
9. Sheehan, *A Bright Shining Lie*, 77, 94, 198.
10. Sheehan, *A Bright Shining Lie*, 37.
11. Sheehan, *A Bright Shining Lie*, 203.
12. Fall, *The Two Viet-Nams*, 287, 381. Karnow, *Vietnam, A History*, 260–262. Sheehan, *A Bright Shining Lie*, 204–265. Tregaskis, *Vietnam Diary*, 388–389.
13. Sheehan, *A Bright Shining Lie*, 262–264.
14. Halberstam, *The Best and Brightest*, 202–203.
15. Sheehan, *A Bright Shining Lie*, 263–264.
16. Tregaskis, *Vietnam Diary*, 391–392.
17. Sheehan, *A Bright Shining Lie*, 308.
18. Sheehan, *A Bright Shining Lie*, 291.
19. Sheehan, *A Bright Shining Lie*, 292, 298, 303.
20. Fall, *The Two Viet-Nams*, 333.
21. Halberstam, *The Best and Brightest*, 208–209. Fall, *The Two Viet-Nams*, 333.
22. Halberstam, *The Best and Brightest*, 276.

23. Sheehan, *A Bright Shining Line*, 328–329. Halberstam, *The Best and Brightest*, 201.
24. McArthur, *History of Viet Conflict*, 5.
25. Sheehan, *A Bright Shining Lie*, 329.
26. Sheehan, *A Bright Shining Lie*, 311–312.
27. Halberstam, *The Best and Brightest*, 276.
28. Fall, *The Two Viet-Nams*, 331, 373.
29. Halberstam, *The Best and Brightest*, 213.
30. Sheehan, *A Bright Shining Lie*, 334. Halberstam, *The Best and Brightest*, 250.
31. Halberstam, *The Best and Brightest*, 276.
32. Karnow, *Vietnam: the edge of chaos*, 34. Halberstam, *The Best and Brightest*, 276.
33. Halberstam, *The Best and Brightest*, 253.
34. Sheehan, *A Bright Shining Lie*, 334, 356–357.
35. Halberstam, *The Best and Brightest*, 252, 288.
36. Karnow, *The Crisis in Vietnam*, 31–36. Sheehan, *A Bright Shining Lie*, 357.
37. Sheehan, *A Bright Shining Lie*, 49, 144, 179–180, 353.
38. Sheehan, *A Bright Shining Lie*, 351–353.
39. Mohr, *South Vietnam*, 25.
40. Sheehan, *A Bright Shining Lie*, 345–346.
41. Halberstam, *The Best and Brightest*, 261.
42. Sheehan, *A Bright Shining Lie*, 354.
43. Karnow, *Vietnam: A History*, 324. Halberstam, *The Best and Brightest*, 261. Sheehan, *A Bright Shining Lie*, 345, 354–356.
44. Sheehan, *A Bright Shining Lie*, 358.
45. Halberstam, *The Best and Brightest*, 272.
46. Halberstam, *The Best and Brightest*, 275. Sheehan, *A Bright Shining Lie*, 365.
47. Halberstam, *The Best and Brightest*, 277. Sheehan, *A Bright Shining Lie*, 365.
48. Halberstam, *The Best and the Brightest*, 283. Sheehan, *A Bright Shining Lie*, 365.
49. Clurman, *Mac Finds What's Gone Wrong*, 323–329. Karnow, *Vietnam: A History*, 268. McArthur, *History of Viet Conflict*, 5. Halberstam, *The Best and Brightest*, 284–286.
50. Halberstam, *The Best and Brightest*, 287.
51. Haalberstam, *The Best and Brightest*, 288. Sheehan, *A Bright Shining Lie*, 367.
52. Sheehan, *A Bright Shining Lie*, 367–370.
53. Halberstam, *The Best and Brightest*, 289, 363.
54. Halberstam, *The Best and Brightest*, 289–290.
55. Sheehan, *A Bright Shining Lie*, 285, 368–371.
56. Sheehan, *A Bright Shining Lie*, 372–374.
57. Sheehan, *A Bright Shining Lie*, 374–375.

58. *South Vietnam. The War is Waiting*, 27.
59. Halberstam, *The Best and Brightest*, 298. *South Vietnam. The War is Waiting*, 26.
60. Sheehan, *A Bright Shining Lie*, 372–374. *South Vietnam. The War is Waiting*, 26.

REFERENCES

Clurman, Richard. 1963. "Mac Finds What's Gone Wrong." *Life.* Vol.55, No. 15: 25–29.

Fall, Bernard. *The Two Viet-Nams.* New York: Frederick A. Praeger, 1963.

Halberstam, David. *The Best and Brightest.* New York: Random House, 1969.

Karnow, Stanley. September 28, 1963. "Vietnam: The edge of chaos." *The Saturday Evening Post* 27–37.

Karnow, Stanley. *Vietnam:A History.* New York: Viking Press, 1983.

McArthur, George. "History of Viet Conflict: Murky Start, Uncertain End." *Los Angeles Times,* Jan. 24, 1973.

Millet, Stanley. "Terror in Vietnam: An American's Ordeal at the Hands of Our 'Friends.'" September 1962. *Harper's Magazine* Vol. 225, No. 1348: 31–39.

Sheehan, Neil. *A Bright Shining Lie.* New York: Vintage Books, 1988.

Mohr, Charles. "South Vietnam: The Queen Bee." 1963. *Time Magazine* Vol. 82, No. 6: 21–25.

"South Vietnam: The War is Waiting." 1963. *Time Magazine* Vol. 82, No. 21: 26–27.

Tregaskis, Richard. *Vietnam Diary.* New York: Holt, Rinehart, and Winston, 1963.

Unit History, 1963.

CPSIA information can be obtained
at www.ICGtesting.com
Printed in the USA
LVOW12*0023050418
572392LV00001B/5/P

32 95